MW01052526

ARISTOTLE ON HAPPINESS, VIRTUE, AND WISDOM

Aristotle thinks that happiness is an activity – it consists in doing something – rather than a feeling. It is the best activity of which humans are capable and is spread out over the course of a life. But what kind of activity is it? Some of his remarks indicate that it is a single best kind of activity, intellectual contemplation. Other evidence suggests that it is an overarching activity that has various virtuous activities, ethical and intellectual, as parts. Numerous interpreters have sharply disagreed about Aristotle's answers to such questions. In this book, Bryan C. Reece offers a fundamentally new approach to determining what kind of activity Aristotle thinks happiness is, one that challenges widespread assumptions that have until now prevented a dialectically satisfactory interpretation. His approach displays the boldness and systematicity of Aristotle's practical philosophy.

BRYAN C. REECE is Assistant Professor of Philosophy at the University of Arkansas. He has published various articles on ancient Greek ethics, metaphysics, and philosophy of action.

ARISTOTLE ON HAPPINESS, VIRTUE, AND WISDOM

BRYAN C. REECE

University of Arkansas

CAMBRIDGE
UNIVERSITY PRESS

CAMBRIDGE
UNIVERSITY PRESS

University Printing House, Cambridge CB2 8BS, United Kingdom

One Liberty Plaza, 20th Floor, New York, NY 10006, USA

477 Williamstown Road, Port Melbourne, VIC 3207, Australia

314–321, 3rd Floor, Plot 3, Splendor Forum, Jasola District Centre,
New Delhi – 110025, India

103 Penang Road, #05–06/07, Visioncrest Commercial, Singapore 238467

Cambridge University Press is part of the University of Cambridge.

It furthers the University's mission by disseminating knowledge in the pursuit of
education, learning, and research at the highest international levels of excellence.

www.cambridge.org
Information on this title: www.cambridge.org/9781108486736
DOI: 10.1017/9781108762403

© Bryan C. Reece 2023

First published 2023

A catalogue record for this publication is available from the British Library.

Library of Congress Cataloging-in-Publication Data
NAMES: Reece, Bryan, 1985– author.
TITLE: Aristotle on happiness, virtue, and wisdom / Bryan C. Reece,
University of Arkansas.
DESCRIPTION: Cambridge, United Kingdom ; New York, NY, USA : Cambridge
University Press, 2022. | Includes bibliographical references and index.
IDENTIFIERS: LCCN 2022020676 | ISBN 9781108486736 (hardback) |
ISBN 9781108762403 (ebook)
SUBJECTS: LCSH: Aristotle – Influence. | Conduct of life. | Happiness. |
Virtue. | Wisdom. | BISAC: PHILOSOPHY / History & Surveys /
Ancient & Classical
CLASSIFICATION: LCC B485 .R375 2022 | DDC 185–dc23/eng/20220701
LC record available at https://lccn.loc.gov/2022020676

ISBN 978-1-108-48673-6 Hardback

For my parents and grandparents

Contents

Preface

There are various kinds of starting-point (*archê*), as Aristotle tells us in *Metaphysics* 5.1. One starting-point of this book was my first exposure to the problem of happiness in the *Nicomachean Ethics* in an engaging and formative Oxford tutorial with David Charles. My systematic dissatisfaction with existing answers motivated a sustained inquiry, which continues even now to be inspired by David's merits as a teacher and scholar. Another starting-point was the realization, which occurred during breakfast in my cousin's kitchen, that a key idea that I had developed in my PhD thesis on Aristotle's theory of actions and causes offered a solution to the problem of happiness. A third starting-point was Hilary Gaskin from Cambridge University Press, who reached out to me proactively before I knew that I had a book in mind to tell me that she predicted that I had. We talked at a meeting of the American Philosophical Association in 2018 and my thoughts about happiness then began taking shape as a book. I am grateful to her. A fourth starting-point was the observation that those who see and appreciate the most fundamental truths about reality are the very same people as those who act best toward others. Those who do these things have long seemed to me to be closest to wisdom, something that I want very much to have. Perhaps I should say that they are the starting-points, or at least, echoing Aristotle, that they have the correct starting-points (*Nicomachean Ethics* 1.4, 1095^{b}4–13).

The previous paragraph began with Aristotle's *Metaphysics* and ended with his *Nicomachean Ethics*. Other paragraphs in this book do so, too. There are questions about the extent to which it is appropriate to clarify Aristotle's practical science by referencing his theoretical science. Polansky (2017) and Roche (1988b), for example, give sustained and spirited arguments that the former is an autonomous science and should not rely on theoretical principles. Irwin (1980), Whiting (1988), and Henry and Nielsen (2015), as well as several contributors to their volume, especially

Shields (2015b), are among those who disagree. Scott (2015) thinks that while for Aristotle practical science borrows from various theoretical sciences, familiarity with the former does not require mastery of the latter. While I do sometimes appeal to works outside of Aristotle's treatises on practical philosophy, the way in which I do so does not require taking a firm position in this dispute. My most extended excursion beyond the precincts of his practical works occurs in Chapter 5, where I appeal to a distinction that Aristotle draws in the *Organon*, his set of treatises that lay out the logical toolkit for scientific inquiry in general. Even Polansky (2017, 280) agrees that Aristotle's practical science can make free use of this logical toolkit. Chapter 4 involves extensive discussion of *Metaphysics* 12, among other texts from Aristotle's theoretical philosophy. I address these theoretical texts in order to respond to a theoretical problem that is raised in the secondary literature on the *Nicomachean Ethics* about whether divine beings contemplate in the same way that we do, thus threatening Aristotle's claim in the *NE* that contemplation is peculiar to us. Aristotle does not raise divine contemplation as a problem for his view; recent interpreters have done that. To respond fully, we must investigate what Aristotle thinks that divine contemplation is. This is his subject in *Metaphysics* 12.7–9. So, in addressing that text, I do not commit to any particular view about the extent to which Aristotle's practical philosophy as he understands it depends on his theoretical philosophy. In Chapters 2 and 5, I appeal to some of Aristotle's psychological claims, such as that contemplation is voluntary, in order to explain why he might have been attracted to certain positions that he states in the *NE* but does not clearly defend. Those who, like Polansky (2017) and Roche (1988b), believe that what Aristotle tells his audience in the *NE* needs no further assistance from theoretical premises can consider my remarks about his psychological claims to be offered to someone who, however unreasonably in their estimation, feels a need for further explanation than Aristotle gives in his practical works.

There are also scholarly disputes about the extent to which it is appropriate to look for guidance from Aristotle's practical works other than the *NE* when interpreting that treatise. This book does not indiscriminately combine Aristotle's ideas from multiple practical works. Rather, I enlist claims from practical works other than the *NE* if those claims do not contradict his claims about relevantly similar subjects in the *NE* and they better illuminate Aristotle's view in the *NE* than other interpretations do. The reason that someone might cite for not drawing on other practical works is that Aristotle is taken to have developed in his thought over time. But the reason for taking him to have developed is the view that some of his doctrines are incompatible with others. Since my project is that of vindicating Aristotle's coherence in the *NE*, I think that it is legitimate to draw on views of his that reveal coherence and do not produce incoherence. In addition to this blanket policy statement, I will also sometimes offer local reasons for thinking it legitimate to appeal to particular claims in other practical works in light of some special relevance that they have to the context.

At some points I had thought of comprehensively addressing Aristotle's remarks about happiness not only in the *Nicomachean Ethics*, but also in the less-studied *Eudemian Ethics*. That became too complicated a task, though. I do sometimes discuss the *Eudemian Ethics*, but the systematic treatment of it that I have in mind must wait.

Unless otherwise noted, Greek texts cited and translated are from those listed in the *Thesaurus Linguae Graecae Canon of Greek Authors and Works (TLG)* (Berkowitz and Squitier, 1990). For Plato and Aristotle these are usually those from the *Oxford Classical Texts* series. Translations are my own unless otherwise noted. For the books common to the *Eudemian Ethics* and *Nicomachean Ethics*, I use the *NE*'s book numbers for brevity's sake. I transliterate single Greek words, or occasionally a combination of two orthographically uncomplicated Greek words, if they do not occur in close proximity to untransliterated Greek. For passages for which comparison between the translation and original is especially likely to be helpful, I set the two in parallel columns with standard reference numbers (Immanuel Bekker's line numbers for Aristotle) in the margin.

I offer a new approach to a problem, or set of problems, that has long troubled scholars of Aristotle. I aim not only to present a new interpretation of Aristotle's theory of happiness, but also to focus attention in new ways. To this end, I devote less attention than is standard in discussions of happiness in the *NE* to topics like self-sufficiency and finality/perfection/completeness as properties of happiness and the question of whether Aristotle is an egoist. I touch on those issues, with the exception of egoism, though I focus more than usual on less familiar aspects of them. My main subject throughout is the nature of human happiness.

The first chapter argues that Aristotle's theory of happiness faces an even more difficult problem than the one that has produced mountains of literature on the subject. I call this more difficult problem "the Conjunctive Problem of Happiness." No existing interpretation solves it. There are three commonly accepted theses that thwart solving the Conjunctive Problem. Most interpreters accept at least two of them. Many accept all three. I address one each in Chapters 2–4. Chapter 5 synthesizes the insights gained in arguing against these theses, offering a solution to the Conjunctive Problem of Happiness.

I have many thanks to render. David Charles, Gabriel Richardson Lear, and Anthony Price provided valuable comments on the manuscript as a whole. The following people gave helpful feedback on at least one chapter or an ancestor of it: Joachim Aufderheide, Neera Badhwar, Rachel Barney, Eric Brown, Jean Clifford, Caleb Cohoe, Brian Embry, Lloyd Gerson, Mary Louise Gill, Marta Heckel, Brad Inwood, Jakub Jirsa, Rusty Jones, Richard Martin, Jozef Müller, Konstantine Panegyres, Wayne Riggs, Mark Schiefsky, Mor Segev, Ravi Sharma, Christopher Shields, Harald Thorsrud, and Stephen White. Rusty Jones, my cousin aforementioned, has read numerous drafts of mine on this and other topics and has given comments at various stages of this project, including at one of its starting-points.

I want to thank the following people for helpful conversations about the contents of this book: Elizabeth Asmis, Samuel Baker, Sarale Ben Asher, Brian Bitar, Matthew Boyle, Stephen Brock, Arnold Brooks, Matthew Evans, Daniel Ferguson, Eric Funkhouser, Jessica Gelber, Paula Gottlieb, Jerry Green, Sukaina Hirji, Doug Hutchinson, Dhananjay Jagannathan, Aryeh Kosman, Emily Kress, Gavin Lawrence, Harvey Lederman, Jongsuh James Lee, Susan Sauvé Meyer, Daniel Moerner, Allison Murphy, Stephen Ogden, Gary Osmundsen, Antoine Pageau-St-Hilaire, Christian Pfeiffer, Evan Rodriguez, Malcolm Schofield, David Sedley, Rachel Singpurwalla, Nicholas D. Smith, Frans Svensson, Josh Trubowitz, Anubav Vasudevan, Candace Vogler, Matthew Walker, Mark Wheeler, and Joel Yurdin.

Ancestors or parts of chapters were presented in the following venues: the American Philosophical Association Central Division meeting in 2018, the American Philosophical Association Pacific Division meeting in 2018, Bryn Mawr College, the Center for Hellenic Studies, Providence College, San Diego State University, the University of Arkansas, the University of Chicago, the University of Hawai'i, the University of Toronto, and the University of Victoria. I thank the members of the audience on each occasion for their helpful feedback.

Chapters 3 and 4 substantially overlap with two articles that I have previously published (Reece, 2020a,[1] 2020b). I wish to thank the anonymous referees and the editorial staff for *Classical Philology* and *Ergo*.

[1] © 2020 by The University of Chicago.

My research has frequently been aided by the *Diogenes* open-source software application developed by P. J. Heslin, as well as by the Perseus Digital Library. Typesetting and bibliographic compilation for this book were made much easier by a custom software application designed by my father, Wyatt Reece.

I am grateful to Cambridge University Press, and in particular to Hilary Gaskin, for making this book possible. I have benefited from the feedback of the anonymous referees and wish to thank them for their careful attention and suggestions that have improved the book. I also appreciate the assistance of David Tranah of Cambridge University Press in optimizing LaTeX options.

Work on this book was generously supported through two fellowships: a Fellowship in Hellenic Studies at Harvard University's Center for Hellenic Studies in 2018–2019, and the John and Daria Barry Postdoctoral Fellowship at the University of Chicago's Department of Philosophy in 2019–2020. Among those at the CHS I want in particular to thank Gregory Nagy, Mark Schiefsky, Zoie Lafis, and Richard Martin. I am grateful, too, for the kind assistance of the CHS library staff: Erika Bainbridge, Sophie Boisseau, Lanah Koelle, Michael Strickland, and Temple Wright. At the University of Chicago I received helpful guidance and mentorship from Candace Vogler, whose kindness made my year there a very special and productive time. I am grateful to her, to Michael Kremer, and to the John and Daria Barry Foundation for making the fellowship possible.

Thanks are due to my wife, Sharon, who has been with me throughout the writing process. I also wish to thank all of those who in their words and deeds have pointed me toward happiness, virtue, and wisdom. These include my parents and grandparents, to whom this book is dedicated.

Abbreviations

APo	*Analytica Posteriora* (*Posterior Analytics*)
Cat.	*Categoriae* (*Categories*)
DA	*De anima* (*On the Soul*)
DC	*De caelo* (*On the Heavens*)
EE	*Ethica Eudemia* (*Eudemian Ethics*)
GA	*De generatione animalium* (*On the Generation of Animals*)
GC	*De generatione et corruptione* (*On Generation and Corruption*)
HA	*Historia animalium* (*On the History of Animals*)
MA	*De motu animalium* (*On the Movement of Animals*)
Metaph.	*Metaphysica* (*Metaphysics*)
Meteor.	*Meteorologica* (*Meteorology*)
MM	*Magna Moralia* (*Great Ethics*)
NE	*Ethica Nicomachea* (*Nicomachean Ethics*)
PA	*De partibus animalium* (*On the Parts of Animals*)
Phys.	*Physica* (*Physics*)
Pol.	*Politica* (*Politics*)
Protr.	*Protrepticus* (*Exhortation to Philosophy*)
Rhet.	*Rhetorica* (*Rhetoric*)
Top.	*Topica* (*Topics*)

CHAPTER I

From the Dilemmatic Problem to the Conjunctive Problem of Happiness

1.1 Introduction

How should we live? Aristotle's answer is, in broadest outline, that we do not have to choose between what is best, noblest, and most pleasant to do (*EE* 1.1, 1214^{a}7–8, *NE* 1.8, 1099^{a}24–25). We need not worry that in eschewing the pastimes of the voluptuary, for example, we are missing out on anything genuinely worthwhile. Plato had offered similar reassurance, but in contrast to him Aristotle argues, for reasons that will become clear, that if what is best, what is noblest, and what is most pleasant for humans are to coincide, they must converge on a characteristic *activity* of human beings. Such an activity, he thinks, is what is designated by the word 'happiness' ('*eudaimonia*').[1] But Aristotle's theory of happiness, particularly as it is developed in the *Nicomachean Ethics*, faces a well-known problem: It is not obvious how his remarks at different points in the treatise about how to understand that theory are supposed to fit together. Interpreters have proposed various types of solutions to this problem. But in this chapter I will argue that we should distinguish between two versions of the problem. I will begin by describing the traditional Dilemmatic Problem of Happiness and how existing views address it. Next, I will argue that the main strategies for addressing the Dilemmatic Problem feature mutually incompatible central commitments about the kind of activity that happiness is, and for this reason these strategies have remained dialectically resilient, their proponents steadfastly unpersuaded by the others' arguments. A dialectically satisfactory interpretation of Aristotle's theory

---

[1] Today we can ask: What kind of thing is happiness? Is it a feeling, a condition, something we do...? Ancient Greek philosophers raised such questions about *eudaimonia* and gave a variety of answers. Similar questions can be asked about well-being, flourishing, or other terms that one might employ as translations of '*eudaimonia*.'

of happiness must accommodate these central commitments despite their apparent incompatibility. This is, in outline, the Conjunctive Problem of Happiness. No existing interpretation solves it, or even attempts to solve it. This is not to say, preposterously, that no existing interpretation is aimed at persuading another interpretation's proponents, but rather that none attempts to take the position on the kind of activity that happiness is that a solution to the Conjunctive Problem would require. In fact, I will argue in Chapters 2–4 that three commitments common among proponents of each of the main strategies for responding to the Dilemmatic Problem make it impossible for them to solve the Conjunctive Problem. Those commitments, though, unlike the ones that figure in the Conjunctive Problem, are ones that they can, and should, give up.

1.2   The Dilemmatic Problem of Happiness

Aristotle advertises from the outset of the *Nicomachean Ethics* that the work will concern the nature of happiness. The fact that most of the work discusses such things as courage, temperance, justice, generosity, magnanimity, and friendship, and *NE* 6 treats of intellectual virtues and their relationship to ethical virtues,[2] encourages the idea that happiness consists in ethically and intellectually virtuous activities, which make a far more central contribution than do such prepossessing candidates as wealth, honor, favorable circumstances, or bodily pleasure (see, e.g., 10.6, 1176^{a}35 – ^{b}9, 1177^{a}9–11). But readers tend to be surprised upon being informed that happiness is contemplation (*theôria*), the manifestation of theoretical wisdom (*sophia*) in active reflection on a systematic grasp that one already has of the first principles of reality, such as the divine prime mover (10.7, 1177^{a}12 – ^{b}26).[3] We are liable to feel bewildered: In pursuit of what end(s) are we to live? What activities are we to choose? In the terms that have characterized much of the literature for roughly the past half-century, does Aristotle think that the happy life features an inclusive end or a dominant end?[4]

---

[2] I use 'ethical virtue' and 'practical virtue' synonymously.

[3] I will discuss the nature of contemplation later in this chapter and even more extensively in subsequent ones.

[4] Hardie (1965, 279) is the one who puts this last question squarely on the agenda, but his formulation of it, and therefore the agenda, grows out of Austin's (1979) responses in the late 1930s and 1940s to Prichard (1935) about the distinction between analysis and specification of 'happiness' in the *NE*, as pointed out by Irwin (2012, 496 n. 4). Inwood (2014, 10) thinks that some of Aristotle's key ideas in his ethical works, including about happiness, exhibit "indeterminacy" and "basic tension" that allow subsequent ancient writers space to explore innovative and divergent ways of interpreting him.

Ackrill (1974, 339) gives a succinct and influential statement of the problem:

> Most of the *Ethics* implies that good action is – or is a major element in – man's best life, but eventually, in book x, purely contemplative activity is said to be perfect *eudaimonia*; and Aristotle does not tell us how to combine or relate these two ideas.

Numerous scholars, especially Hardie (1965), Ackrill (1974), Cooper (1975), and others of their generation and the following one, have maintained that two genuinely incompatible theories of happiness are presented in the *NE*: one in most of the work and the other in 10.7–8.[5] Most subsequent interpreters, though, have taken the position that while the two theories are genuinely incompatible, Aristotle merely *seems* to offer evidence for both in the *NE*.[6] In fact, they maintain, he subscribes to one or the other of the two incompatible theories and our interpretive problem is that of determining which one he favors and explaining away the apparent evidence that he holds the other. This is the Dilemmatic Problem.[7]

Dilemmatic Problem of Happiness

We must determine which of the following incompatible propositions about happiness Aristotle believes and explain away the apparent evidence that he believes the other:

A) Happiness (the activity) is virtuous activity, a composite that includes not only contemplative activity, but also ethically virtuous activities as parts.[8]

---

[5] Bostock (2000, 200–203) and Wilkes (1978, 566) think that Aristotle's account of happiness is outright incoherent. Nagel (1972, 252), more gently, says that Aristotle "exhibits indecision between two accounts." Moline (1983) regards the account of happiness as contemplation in *NE* 10.7–8 as so un-Aristotelian that it must be an expression of Anaxagoras's view meant as a joke at the latter's expense. Annas (1993, 216 n. 9), Barnes (1997, 58–59), and Nussbaum (2001, 375–377) contend that the text of the *NE* as we now have it contains two inconsistent theories, but they were never intended to coexist in one treatise by one author. Their allegation of textual disunity has been met with substantial counterevidence presented by, for example, Aufderheide (2020, 164), Natali (1989, 282), Roche (1988a, 193 n. 38), and Whiting (1986, 89). Such counterevidence includes various back-references from *NE* 10.7–8 to the other *NE* books and forward-references from other books to those chapters.

[6] This is the position of Kraut (1989, 4), for example: "Of course, if Aristotle says in one place that happiness consists in contemplation alone, and says elsewhere that it consists in other goods as well, then he has contradicted himself. One of my main concerns will be to argue that the *NE* does not contain this internal conflict."

[7] I am grateful to David Charles, Gabriel Richardson Lear, and a referee for Cambridge University Press for especially helpful suggestions about how best to formulate the Dilemmatic Problem and the problem that I introduce later, the Conjunctive Problem.

[8] Ackrill (1974, 343) cites the relation between putting and golfing as an instance of the relevant relation between part and whole where the part and whole are both activities and to be engaged in the part is to be engaged in the whole, though there is more to the whole than that part.

B) Happiness (the activity) is contemplative activity, which does not include ethically virtuous activities as parts.

Various ways of addressing this problem have been explored. These are helpfully divided into the following groups, though other systems of categorization could be implemented:

Monism

Happiness (the activity) *is* contemplation. A life made happy in virtue of it is derivatively devoted to ethically virtuous activities insofar as they are for the sake of contemplation.[9]

Pluralism

Ethically virtuous activities and contemplation are parts of the composite essence of happiness (the activity). A life made happy in virtue of such happiness is devoted most of all to contemplation in the sense that special attention should be given to contemplation when reasonable.[10]

Relativism

Perfect happiness (the activity) is contemplation and the happiest life is devoted to that. Ethically virtuous activities are parts of another kind of happiness and another, inferior kind of happy life is devoted to that. Neither kind of happiness sets the standard for the kind of life characterized by the other kind of happiness, so there is no split devotion in any happy life.[11]

---

[9] Monists differ primarily over the nature of the *for-the-sake-of* relation that holds between ethically virtuous activity and contemplation and grounds the inclusion of ethically virtuous activities in happy lives. Proposals include, for example: instrumentality/causality (Cleemput, 2006), (Jirsa, 2017), (Kraut, 1989), (Reeve, 1992); centralizing relations, for example, approximation (Lear, 2004, 2014, 2015) or focality (Tuozzo, 1995); and being regulated/governed by (Aufderheide, 2015), (Cooper, 2004), (Meyer, 2011). Some monists are principally concerned to argue that Aristotle endorses pluralism in the *Eudemian Ethics* and/or in at least some parts of the *NE*, but endorses monism as the *NE*'s final and official view (Cooper, 1975), (Hardie, 1965), (Kenny, 1978, 1992). Others focus more on the startling nature of a monist account of happiness (Adkins, 1978), (Lear, 1988, 309–320), (Nagel, 1972).

[10] Pluralist interpreters have often derived inspiration from Ackrill (1974), who, though like Hardie (1965) and others believes that Aristotle offers us genuinely inconsistent evidence, finds the pluralist conception more plausible in its own right and argues forcefully for a pluralist interpretation of *NE* 1–9. Pluralist interpreters include Broadie (1991), Cooper (1987), Crisp (1994), Dahl (2011), Herzberg (2016), Irwin (1978, 1980, 1985, 1991, 2012) and (1988, 608 n. 40 and 616–617 n. 24), Keyt (1983), Natali (1989), Pakaluk (2005), Price (1980, 2011, 2014), Roche (1988a, 2014a,b, 2019), Urmson (1988), Walker (2011, 2018), White (1986, 1988), and Whiting (1986, 1988). For my purposes it will be unnecessary to distinguish between versions of pluralism according to which goods other than ethically and intellectually virtuous activities (e.g., honor, money, good looks) count directly as parts of happiness and those according to which they do not.

[11] Relativists include Bush (2008), Cooper (2013, ch. 3), Curzer (1990, 1991, 2012), Devereux (1981, 2014), Heinaman (1988), Lawrence (1993, 2005), Long (2011), Scott (1999), and Thorsrud (2015). The view of Charles (1999, 2014) resists categorization as monist, pluralist, or relativist as I have

Debates rage on about whether the passages relied upon by each group have been correctly interpreted. Monists think that the happy life is devoted most of all to contemplation in a straightforward way: The activities that figure in the happy person's life are devoted to contemplation because they are performed for its sake. Other goods are not directly included in the activity of happiness, but are choice-worthy within a happy life because they are for the sake of happiness, contemplation. These other goods, including ethically virtuous activities, are choice-worthy as parts of the happy life only to the extent that they are related to contemplation as being for its sake, even if they are choice-worthy in their own right. This way of including ethically virtuous activities makes pluralists suspect it of reflecting too dimly Aristotle's enthusiasm about ethically virtuous activities.[12]

Pluralists, who think that ethically and intellectually virtuous activities are parts of a composite activity, happiness, say that the happy life is devoted to such activities because they are parts of what makes such a life happy. They can add that among the virtuous activities that happiness comprises, the one to which special attention, for example, celebration (Broadie, 1991, 413–414), should be given, when reasonable,

described those positions, but I think that this taxonomy is still useful for revealing points at which I and others differ from Charles. His account resembles the monism of Lear (2004, 2014, 2015) insofar as it appeals to a centralizing relation between contemplation and other virtuous activities. Whereas in Lear's case this is the relation of approximation, in Charles's it is analogy. But Charles's appeal to a centralizing relation does different work from what Lear's does. Charles thinks that virtuous activity is made a case of happy activity by instantiating fineness in the particular way that it does, and that fineness is paradigmatically instantiated in contemplation, to which paradigmatic instantiation the fineness of other virtuous activities is analogically related. He would thus affirm only a weakened version of (B), according to which happiness is *paradigmatically* contemplation. As later arguments will indicate, I think that this would be too weak to do justice to the evidence for (B). Charles differs from pluralists in denying that virtuous activities are parts of happiness and from relativists in denying that virtuous activities are parts of any separately available kind of happiness. I am grateful to him for clarification about the relationship of his view to others. Baker (2021), who distinguishes between the human good and *eudaimonia* for beings more generally, gives an account of the latter that is similar in certain respects to Charles's account of the former. Baker thinks that divine *eudaimonia* is the paradigm case of *eudaimonia* and other cases of it, such as human contemplation or general justice, are gradably related to the paradigm case. When it comes to the human good specifically, Baker favors monism. I thank him for helpful conversations about his account.

[12] For such expressions of pluralists' suspicions, see, for example, Irwin (1991, 385), Keyt (1983, 364–366), Natali (1989, 281), and Whiting (1986, 92 n. 48), who argue that if ethical activities are for the sake of contemplation, then they will not satisfy the criteria for fully virtuous activity as expounded in *NE* 2.4 or the description of fine activity (*eupraxia*) in 6.5. Whiting argues, more specifically, that even if ethical activities are performed for their own sake as well as for the sake of contemplation, they will fail to conform to the stricture in 2.4 that fully virtuous activities be performed reliably.

is contemplation, though monists will accuse them of attenuating the devotion to contemplation on which Aristotle insists.[13]

The third type of interpretation, relativism, has arisen as a reaction to pluralists' and monists' attempts to address the Dilemmatic Problem. Relativists claim that the apparently discrepant bits of textual evidence that correspond to (A) and (B) apply to two different kinds of happiness that are separately achievable, depending on one's circumstances or endowments. Happiness consisting in contemplation is open to those who are especially well-situated, while happiness consisting in ethically virtuous activity is the best achievable by those who are less fortunate. Relativists typically think that it is possible to be happy without ethically virtuous activity or without contemplation, but not if one lacks both. This possibility would be denied by monists and pluralists. Relativist interpretations aim to accommodate the textual evidence that has seemed problematic for monists, on the one hand, and pluralists, on the other, by sorting it into two boxes: Aristotle's two incompatible theories of happiness are not both meant to be true of any one agent; rather, one theory, that encapsulated by (B), is about the kind of happiness that is possible for agents with certain circumstances or endowments, the other, that encapsulated by (A), about another.

Several features of the dialectic between these groups of interpreters are important to mention at this point. The first is that pluralists and monists have been persistently dissatisfied with relativism for good reasons. Relativists think that the two sets of textual evidence (viz., that for happiness comprising virtuous activities generally and that for happiness consisting in contemplation) apply to two different kinds of happiness that are separately achievable, depending on one's circumstances or endowments. This of course requires that Aristotle countenance two kinds of happiness to which the two sets of evidence corresponding to (A) and (B) can be relativized *and* that he relativizes precisely one of them to each kind. There are several reasons why this claim does not gain dialectical traction. First, pluralists think that the best kind of happiness that an agent can enjoy must consist in intellectually and ethically virtuous activities. Relativists, though, must deny precisely this if they are to pursue the strategy of relativizing the evidence corresponding to (B) to the best kind of happiness, which in

---

[13] For criticisms of pluralists along these lines, see, for example, Charles (1999, 209–211) and Lear (2004, 25–46). Urmson (1988, 125), a pluralist, certainly invites such responses: "There is surely no solution to all these difficulties. We must agree that Aristotle has let his enthusiasm get the better of him in his discussion of the theoretical life and replace his extreme claims with the more moderate view that the life of the scholar is the most choiceworthy, only in the sense that it is the best career to choose, not as the sole constituent in the good life."

turn they must do on pain of their view being immediately unacceptable to monists. In short, pluralists have no more reason to accept relativism than they do to accept monism, so from their point of view relativism offers no dialectical advantage.[14] In the absence of any new hope offered by relativism for convincing pluralist opponents, monists in their turn see no reason to retreat to relativism.

Second, pluralists and monists, unlike relativists, maintain that Aristotle gives several reasons to suggest that his claims are true of one and the same kind of happiness: Prior to *NE* 10.8, and indeed after 10.8 and even in the *Politics*, Aristotle offers no hint that there are two kinds of happiness. His introduction to the inquiry in book 1 strongly suggests that there should be a unique answer to the question of what happiness is. After all, his stated objective is to discover *the highest* good for human beings achievable in action (1.2, 1094[a]18–26, 1.4, 1095[a]14–17), and it is this highest good that he takes himself to have given "in outline" in the *ergon* (function) argument of 1.7 (1098[a]20–21). The first line of 10.7, as well as back-references at 10.5, 1176[a]3–4 and 10.6, 1176[a]30–32, indicate that he intends his remarks on happiness in book 10 as a resumption of the outline account of happiness from 1.7, a resumption that he foreshadowed in 1.7.[15] The immediately ensuing lines of 10.7 argue that happiness, as he here twice explicitly says he described it before and as he now describes it, is highest, most continuous, most pleasant, most self-sufficient, most perfect, and most leisurely. Pluralists and monists find it scarcely credible that there could be more than one kind of happiness with these properties, most of which were announced in book 1 as properties that the correct theory of happiness must show to belong to happiness.[16]

---

[14] Charles (1999, 209) offers a series of arguments that relativism fails to avoid problems typically associated with monism. He also contends that relativism's key distinction is ungrounded in the text.

[15] Various forward and backward references linking books 1 and 10 are enumerated by Aufderheide (2020, 164), Bostock (2000, 190–191), Natali (1989, 282), Roche (1988a, 193 n. 38), and Whiting (1986, 89).

[16] Irwin (2012, 519–520) thinks that 6.12, 1144[a]29–36 gives evidence against two kinds of happiness, though his specific reasons for thinking so are contested by monists. Pakaluk (2005, 322) and Whiting (1986, 93–94 n. 50) argue that if there are the two possibilities for happiness upon which relativists insist, then at least one of them will not meet Aristotle's stated criteria for anything that could count as happiness: perfection and self-sufficiency. Lear (2004, 195) alleges that relativism encounters an obstacle at 10.8, 1178[b]20–32: "One might suggest that we read Aristotle as saying here that contemplation is responsible for the happiness of only the philosophical life. But this cannot be correct either. The utter failure of the beasts to participate in contemplation in any way is supposed to explain why they cannot be happy. If the presence of contemplation is just one way to grasp happiness, his claim that the beasts do not participate in contemplation would be insufficient to rule out the possibility of their happiness."

It is no accident that upon first exposure to the *NE* many have reacted with bewildered astonishment to the suggestion that the life in accordance with theoretical intellect is happiest and "the life in accord with the other kind of virtue ⟨i.e., the kind concerned with action⟩ ⟨is happiest⟩ in a secondary way" (10.8, 1178ª9, Irwin 2019 trans.). This is the passage that relativists claim as evidence that Aristotle delivers two kinds of happiness to readers who had been led by the entirety of what had preceded to expect only one. Irwin's translation makes clear that '⟨is happiest⟩' is a proposal for an elided predicate. The Greek indicates only that the practical life is secondary in some respect, but does not specify the respect.[17] Irwin proposes 'happiest' merely because it occurs in the previous line. But, as I will argue in Chapter 3,[18] understanding the elided predicate as 'proper to a human being'[19] from the line preceding the one to which Irwin looks makes better sense of Aristotle's argument in the immediate context. Doing so also exhibits him following up on a related claim with which he ended 10.5 (with very similar wording) rather than committing him to an unanticipated announcement in 10.8 that there are two kinds of happiness. This proposal also renders intelligible the fact that he resumes speaking, for the rest of the *NE* and throughout its sequel, the *Politics*, as if there is only one kind of happiness. Indeed, Aristotle says on the next Bekker page (10.8, 1179ª29–30) that the person who manifests theoretical wisdom (*sophia*), the one who relativists think enjoys the superior kind of happiness, is most of all (*malista*) such as to act rightly (*orthôs*) and nobly (*kalôs*). But one who is most of all such as to act rightly and nobly is, according to relativists, the one who exemplifies the secondary kind of happiness. So, this passage gives us reason to doubt that Aristotle is, as relativists allege, relativizing the two sets of evidence to two kinds of happiness. There is, then, plenty of standardly recognized textual evidence against relativism, and even the one line alleged to support it is most conservatively interpreted as doing no such thing. But even if there were good evidence that Aristotle countenances two kinds of happiness (the activity), we could not safely say that the two sets of evidence, those corresponding to (A) and (B) of the Dilemmatic Problem, are true of precisely one kind of happiness each. While relativists have made important contributions to understanding Aristotle's theory of happiness, often sharpening the terms of the debate or offering

---

17 Δευτέρως δ' ὁ κατὰ τὴν ἄλλην ἀρετήν
18 This argument has its origin in Reece (2020a). Aufderheide (2020, 194–198) offers additional commentary on how the argument that follows 1178ª9 should be viewed in light of that proposal.
19 ⟨οἰκεῖος⟩ τῷ ἀνθρώπῳ

formidable arguments with which all parties must contend, relativism is not a strategy for addressing Aristotle's claims in a way that can satisfy pluralists or monists. Neither does it feature any textually motivated fundamental commitment that pluralists or monists should feel any dialectical pressure to accept. If a way of accounting for the evidence were to emerge that respected the fundamental commitments of pluralists and monists alike, relativists should be prepared to accept it.

The second feature of the dialectical landscape that we should observe is that pluralists and monists are most charitably interpreted as having a genuine disagreement with each other, that is to say, disagreeing about the same thing rather than talking past each other. This is why I have formulated the Dilemmatic Problem not in terms of the happy *life*, but rather of happiness, which Aristotle thinks is an activity.[20] (From now on when I use 'happiness' unmodified I refer to the activity unless otherwise specified and I use 'happy life' to refer to the life made happy by happiness.) On his view, happiness is what makes a life a happy one. If pluralists thought that ethically virtuous activities were parts of the happy life, but not of happiness, then they would not continue to raise the objections to monists that they in fact raise. Put another way, a real disagreement between pluralists and monists requires that they be pluralists or monists *about the same thing*. Both groups tend to be pluralists about the happy *life*, so a real disagreement between them cannot be about what that consists in.

Reeve (1992, 158–159) is a prominent early adopter of the distinction between happiness and the happy life who leverages it in an effort to soften the blow of monism for pluralists. Many others have subsequently appealed to the distinction. However, pluralists hold their view not because Aristotle lists ethically virtuous activities as parts of the happy *life* (along with external goods, etc.), but because they think that he discusses ethically virtuous activities for much of the *NE* as an elaboration of the conclusion of the *ergon* argument in *NE* 1.7.[21] Pluralists and monists tend to agree that the conclusion of the *ergon* argument is about happiness rather than the happy life. That is because the argument explicitly excludes as candidates for the human *ergon* (work, function, characteristic activity) elements that the life includes, such as perception and nutrition. Put another way, whatever the *ergon* argument identifies as the human *ergon*, even

---

[20] Thanks to David Charles for discussion about the relationship between the happy life and the activities that it includes.

[21] Ackrill (1974, 353–354) cites 1.9, 1100^{a}4–5 and 1.13, 1102^{a}5–6 as evidence for this, and Irwin (2012, 519) adds 2.6, 1106^{a}15–24.

merely in outline, it excludes elements that pluralists and monists would agree are included in the happy life. The *ergon* argument is not meant to identify the components of the happy human life, but rather to identify, at least in outline, what happiness is.

Another indication that the conclusion of the *ergon* argument is about happiness rather than the happy life is that Aristotle intends his statement of the human *ergon* to be an answer to the same question to which he ruled out virtue (the state) as an answer. He ruled out virtue (the state) for the reason that a state is not an activity. One might retort that a happy life is an activity. The problem then would be that we would have eliminated much of the motivation for distinguishing between the happy life and happiness (the activity).

Further evidence that the conclusion of the *ergon* argument is about happiness rather than the happy life is that otherwise his way of situating that conclusion among the reputable opinions in *NE* 1.8 would make little sense. For one thing, happiness is a good of the soul, comprising action(s) rather than external goods. Since external goods are part of a happy life, this restriction would be unmotivated if Aristotle means to be saying that the conclusion of the *ergon* argument was about a happy life. For another, why take the trouble of stressing at this stage that happiness, as it has just been specified, is not a virtuous state, but rather a virtuous activity? Also, why add 'in a complete life' (1.7, 1098ª18) if the excellent performance of our *ergon* is already a life?

The persistent disagreement between pluralists and monists is best interpreted as a genuine disagreement. They genuinely disagree about that in which happiness (the activity) consists, but need not disagree about what the happy life includes. So, I have stated the Dilemmatic Problem in terms of happiness rather than of the happy life.

The third feature of the dialectical situation will motivate the rest of the present chapter: Pluralists and monists have been persistently dissatisfied with each other's approach, but each has strong, principled reasons to resist the other's attempts to explain away the apparent evidence for (A) or (B). That is what has prevented solving the Dilemmatic Problem in a dialectically satisfactory way.

1.3   The Conjunctive Problem of Happiness

I will begin this section by identifying the factors that explain the dialectical resilience of pluralism and monism. Pluralists are reluctant to accept the monist account for several reasons. I will focus on the ones that I think are the strongest. For now, I merely list these; I will later explain them in detail. Not every pluralist would offer all of these reasons, but each is prevalent in the literature in some form or other. First, pluralists tend to interpret Aristotle as saying explicitly that happiness is an activity with intellectually *and* ethically virtuous activities as parts, whereas monists deny this. Second, they tend to believe that without affirming that happiness has such parts, one cannot show how contemplation brings ethically virtuous activities into the frame of happiness in a way that differs from how it brings in external goods (e.g., health, wealth). Third, pluralists tend to think that since monists deny that happiness has such parts, they face the immoralist objection. This objection is that if happiness is simply one activity, contemplation, then happiness could come at the expense of ethically virtuous activity. Such a result, in addition to being disturbing, would seem at odds with Aristotle's emphasis on the importance of ethically virtuous activity throughout his ethical works. These objections that pluralists have long maintained against monists support viewing (A) of the Dilemmatic Problem as a fundamental and non-negotiable constraint on a way of accounting for the textual evidence:

Pluralist Constraint
   Happiness (the activity) is virtuous activity, a composite that includes not only contemplative activity, but also ethically virtuous activities as parts.

Monists are unsatisfied with pluralist accounts primarily because they think that without affirming that happiness is a single activity, contemplative activity, one cannot give a plausible explanation of Aristotle's argument in *NE* 10.7–8, which monists interpret as saying that various features that belong uniquely to happiness belong uniquely to contemplation. It is in the course of this argument, monists standardly think, that Aristotle explicitly claims that happiness is contemplation. This compelling monist objection to pluralism supports viewing (B) of the Dilemmatic Problem as a fundamental and non-negotiable constraint on a way of accounting for the textual evidence:

Monist Constraint
   Happiness (the activity) is contemplative activity, which does not include ethically virtuous activities as parts.

It is standardly believed that a theory that meets the Pluralist Constraint would violate the Monist Constraint and vice versa: If, as the Monist Constraint says, happiness is contemplative activity and this does not include ethically virtuous activities as parts, then happiness is not a composite that includes contemplative and ethically virtuous activities as parts, contrary to the Pluralist Constraint, and conversely. In other words, as I have already said, Aristotle is standardly regarded as providing a confusing body of evidence that might be taken to support either of two genuinely incompatible theories. The Dilemmatic Problem of Happiness is that of determining whether Aristotle's theory of happiness affirms (A) or instead (B) and explaining away the apparent evidence that his theory affirms the other.

Discussions of Aristotle's theory of happiness typically proceed in this way. Interpreters muster evidence in favor of monism or pluralism and then explain why the evidence that has been taken to favor the other interpretation does not favor it as strongly as has been supposed or should be downplayed. This way of proceeding has generated many valuable insights about the structure and content of the *NE*. However, we must take the present dialectical situation very seriously: Each party has given compelling reasons in favor of a fundamental constraint on an acceptable explanation that the other party has been unable to meet. Pluralists are persistently dissatisfied with putative solutions to the Dilemmatic Problem that do not affirm (A), monists with those that do not affirm (B). We should gather from this that an interpretation of Aristotle's remarks about happiness that would satisfy both groups must meet both the Pluralist Constraint and the Monist Constraint. That is to say, it must affirm (A) *and* (B). Furthermore, it must affirm them of the same kind of happiness (the activity). Otherwise, pluralists, monists, or both will think that their constraint has not been met. Nobody has successfully attempted this. Doing so is what I call "the Conjunctive Problem":

Conjunctive Problem of Happiness
We must explain how Aristotle can consistently believe both of the following propositions about the same kind of happiness:

Pluralist Constraint
Happiness (the activity) is virtuous activity, a composite that includes not only contemplative activity, but also ethically virtuous activities as parts.

Monist Constraint
Happiness (the activity) is contemplative activity, which does not include ethically virtuous activities as parts.

I regard solving the Conjunctive Problem as important because I believe that pluralists and monists have stood their ground for good textual and theoretical reasons. Their most fundamental concerns need to be accommodated by a satisfactory interpretation. I will now spell out in detail what I regard as the strongest considerations that pluralists and monists, respectively, have tended to adduce in favor of the claims that the Pluralist Constraint and Monist Constraint, respectively, underpin. I will sometimes devote more systematic attention to a point than existing literature does when I believe that it has been merely stated in the literature and not sufficiently elaborated, and less when it has been thoroughly discussed. The aim of this section is not to rehearse all of the considerations that pluralists and monists offer in support of their interpretations. Rather, the aim is to lend conviction to the thesis that pluralists and monists will not and should not be satisfied by any interpretation that stops short of saying that Aristotle has precisely one theory of happiness and it is one that satisfies the Pluralist Constraint and Monist Constraint for the same kind of happiness.

It will be noticed that in what follows I refrain from addressing how the *ergon* argument of *NE* 1.7 should be understood in light of Aristotle's claim that happiness is something perfect (*teleion*) and self-sufficient (*autarches*) (*NE* 1.7, 1097^{b}20–21). I will have more to say about other aspects of the *ergon* argument in subsequent chapters, especially the fourth.

Aristotle says this about happiness's perfection and self-sufficiency:[22]

> [We call] perfect (*teleion*) without qualification that which is always desirable (*haireton*) in its own right and never because of something else. Happiness seems most of all to be like this. (1.7, 1097^{a}33–34)[23]

> We posit that the self-sufficient (*autarches*) is that which on its own renders life desirable (*haireton*) and lacking in nothing. We think that happiness is like this. (1.7, 1097^{b}14–16)

---

[22] There is of course more that can be said and more context that can be given, but nearly anything else about perfection and self-sufficiency would be laden with controversy. I say only enough here to provide a very basic orientation to the denotation of these terms and to direct attention to relevant passages.

[23] Translations are mine unless otherwise noted. I translate '*teleion*' as 'perfect,' the comparative '*teleioteron*' as 'more perfect,' and the superlative '*teleiotatēn*' as 'most perfect.' Other common translations of the superlative are 'most complete' or 'most final.' 'Most complete' is more commonly preferred by pluralists, 'most final' by monists. None of my points hangs on this translation. Charles (2015, 68–69) argues, on the basis of *Metaph.* 5.16, for understanding '*teleiotatēn*' as 'most perfect.'

The conclusion of the *ergon* argument in *NE* 1.7 and its recapitulation in 1.8 are as follows:

> [I]f all of this is so, then the human good turns out to be activity of the soul in accordance with virtue, and if there are multiple virtues, then in accordance with the best (*aristên*) and most perfect (*teleiotatên*). (1.7, 1098ᵃ16–18)

> For all of these [being most noble, most desirable, and most pleasant] belong to the best activities, and these activities, or one of them (the best), we say to be happiness. (1.8, 1099ᵃ29–31)

Pluralists think that Aristotle must mean that the various virtuous activities are parts of a best and most perfect activity, the *ergon* of a good human (hereafter abbreviated as 'human *ergon*'). Monists, by contrast, think that he takes there to be one particular kind of virtuous activity, which we later discover is contemplation, to be the best and most perfect, and therefore the human *ergon*. Their disagreement, I think, is fundamentally about whether the human *ergon*, and therefore happiness, has multiple kinds of virtuous activities as parts. Each group maintains that only its preferred interpretation of the conclusion of the *ergon* argument respects Aristotle's claim that happiness is something perfect (*teleion*) and self-sufficient (*autarches*), as these features are understood by each. Though pluralists and monists frequently use their preferred interpretations of perfection and self-sufficiency to score points for their chosen account of Aristotle's theory of happiness, I do not view these as arguments that disproportionately favor either the Pluralist Constraint or the Monist Constraint. Rather, these are part of the contested territory that the arguments that I will discuss are used to seize.[24]

1.3.1 Motivating the Pluralist Constraint

Pluralists' typical reasons for dissatisfaction with monists' responses to the Dilemmatic Problem indicate that pluralists view (A) as a constraint on an acceptable interpretation. Pluralists tend to interpret Aristotle as saying explicitly that happiness (the activity) has parts and as making points about happiness that require it specifically to have ethically virtuous activities as parts.

---

[24] Charles (2015) and Baker (2019) argue that from one point of view (namely, that of meaning rather than of reference for Charles and of speaker's reference rather than semantic reference for Baker) the claims are neutral. Charles is a neutralist about the formulations of perfection and self-sufficiency, Baker about the conclusion of the *ergon* argument. For a current discussion of the *ergon* argument with an extensive bibliography, see Baker (2021).

The Claim That Happiness Has Parts

Aristotle speaks of happiness as including virtues or virtuous activities as parts in *Eudemian Ethics* (combining 1.2, 1214^{b}26–7, 1.5, 1216^{a}39 – ^{b}2, 2.1, 1219^{a}29–39, ^{b}11–13, 1220^{a}2–4) and *Protrepticus* (ap. Iamblichus, *Protrepticus* ch. 7, 43.12–14). So does whoever wrote *Magna Moralia* (1.1, 1184^{a}14–28). Even in *Rhetoric* (1.5, 1360^{b}4–30), where such a claim more closely reflects reputable opinions (*endoxa*) about happiness, it is clear that the idea of happiness (the activity) having ethically virtuous activities as parts is one that is intelligible to Aristotle and his original audience. What is of most acute interest to pluralists, though, is that Aristotle speaks directly of happiness's parts in the *NE*:[25]

5.1, 1129^{b}17–19

So, in one way the things that we call "just" are those that produce and preserve happiness and its parts for the political community.

ὥστε ἕνα μὲν τρόπον δίκαια λέγομεν τὰ ποιητικὰ καὶ φυλακτικὰ εὐδαιμονίας καὶ τῶν μορίων αὐτῆς τῇ πολιτικῇ κοινωνίᾳ.

---

[25] Thanks to Gabriel Richardson Lear, Anthony Price, and Christopher Shields for discussion of these various passages. Monists might argue for the immediate dismissal of the *NE* 5.1 passage since it comes from one of the books common to the *Eudemian* and *Nicomachean Ethics*. Pluralists would be unmoved by such an argument for at least the following reasons. First, and most simply, monists readily draw on passages from the common books in motivating their interpretations of Aristotle's theory of happiness as articulated in *NE* 1 and 10. It is, after all, difficult to describe what contemplation is without adverting to the virtue of which it is a manifestation, theoretical wisdom, which is discussed in detail only in *NE* 6. Monists also look to *NE* 6, especially chapter 13, for guidance in spelling out the kind of *for-the-sake-of* relation that they think holds between theoretical and practical wisdom. They also appeal to Aristotle's remarks on justice in *NE* 5 and on political wisdom in 6 to fill out their account of the practical or political life in 10. Second, if one's objection to considering passages from the common books is based on the thought that Aristotle's theory of happiness changed between the writing of the *Eudemian* and *Nicomachean Ethics*, that simply pushes the problem of coherence encapsulated by the Dilemmatic Problem back a step: What alleged discrepancies between the two works motivate this thought, are they the discrepancies that we find in this passage, and are they in the end genuinely discrepant? Irwin (2012, 520) argues that pushing the problem back in this way is a mistake, on the grounds that since either Aristotle included the common books among the *NE* books or an early editor did, we should not discount the authority of this ancient person's opinion that they presented no problem of consistency for Aristotle's theory of happiness. Even pluralists who think that the editorial history of the common books is sufficiently complicated to damage Irwin's argument might be persuaded by Frede's (2019) contention that any passage that presupposes a distinction between general and particular justice (which this one does) is more Nicomachean than Eudemian. Third, pluralists are likely to believe that unless we interpret Aristotle as saying in the *NE* that happiness has no parts, which is simply the monist position, we would have no good reason to think that his view on the subject of whether happiness has parts differs between the *EE* and the *NE*. But without such a reason, according to pluralists, dismissing a claim in the common books about parts of happiness as being purportedly un-Nicomachean is question-begging.

Aristotle's primary contention in *NE* 5.1–2 is that things might be called "just" in two ways, namely in accordance with general justice or with particular justice. General justice comprises every virtue insofar as each of these virtues relates to other people. Particular justice is one among the ethical virtues and has to do with proportional distribution or retribution. In this passage that speaks of parts of happiness, Aristotle is referring to general justice rather than particular justice. That is the intended contrast marked by 'in one way.'[26] The claim is that the things that general justice (rather than particular justice) comprises, namely all of the virtues or virtuous activities as related to other people, produce and preserve happiness and its parts for the political community.[27, 28]

---

[26] Burnet (1900, 207) and Stewart (1892, vol. 1, 391) argue that '*men*' in this line corresponds to '*de*' in 5.2, 1130ᵃ14, which introduces particular justice.

[27] *NE* 1.2, 1094ᵇ7–8 and *Pol.* 7.1, 1323ᵇ21–36 indicate that happiness for the individual and for the political community have the same structure.

[28] Those who have a monistic interpretation of the entire *NE* are remarkably silent about this passage. Among recent commentators who do address it, all but two identify the parts of happiness mentioned in this passage as virtues and virtuous activities, which Aristotle proceeds to list in the immediately succeeding lines. This majority view is held by Austin (1979, 15–16), Bostock (2000, 22), Broadie (2002, 337), Engberg-Pedersen (1983, 54–55), Gauthier and Jolif (1970, vol. 2.1, 340), Kenny (1978, 59, 66), Lee (2014, 109–113), Nussbaum (2001, 375), Stewart (1892, vol. 1, 392) and Urmson (1988, 13). Every early commentary and scholium on this passage of which I am aware agrees that happiness has ethically virtuous activities as parts: Anonymous (*In EN* 209.13–18), Michael of Ephesus (*In EN* 6.33–7.1), Georgios Pachymeres (*In EN* 182.11–12), a scholium in the hand of the anonymous twelfth-century copyist of cod. Parisiensis 1854 f. 71r, who Rose (1871) argues transmits an interpretive tradition independent from that of Anonymous and Michael of Ephesus, possibly that of Aspasius, who is presumed to have made comments, now lost, on *NE* 5, and a remark *supra lineam* in cod. Laurentianus 81.18 f. 35r, which has been re-dated to the twelfth century by Brockmann (1993, 46), partially collated by Vuillemin-Diem and Rashed (1997), and fully collated by Panegyres (2020). (I am grateful to Konstantine Panegyres for assistance in deciphering this last scribe's difficult hand.) Aspasius (*In EN* 8.17–30, 19.7–8, 21.33 – 22.1, 22.14–34, 24.3–5) and Alexander of Aphrodisias (*Eth. Prob.* 150.10–12) attribute to Aristotle the view that ethically virtuous activities are parts of happiness, whereas external goods have some non-parthood relation to happiness, on the basis of passages in *NE* 1 and 2. Doxography C (ap. Stobaeus, *Anth.* 2.7.17.1 – 2.7.18.86), commonly (though not uncontroversially – see Inwood 2014, 78 and 129 n. 25) dated to the first century BC, identifies this as the view of Aristotle and other Peripatetics without reference to particular passages. These ancient commentators, doxographers, and scholiasts think that "What are the parts of happiness?" is a sensible, controversial, and interesting question. They would not regard it as such a question if it were merely about the ingredients of the happy life. Aspasius (*In EN* 24.3–5), for example, would not see any difficulty in claiming that external goods are parts of the happy *life*, though he rejects the notion that external goods are parts of happiness. I know of two alternatives to the majority interpretation of the *NE* 5.1 passage. Reeve (2014, 261 n. 341) suggests that Aristotle means these parts of happiness to be external goods. This is presumably a specification of his (1992, 122) claim, made in defense of his overall monistic account of happiness, that the passage does not foreclose the possibility that the parts of happiness are the sorts of things that happiness limits and measures. External goods, according to Reeve, fit this bill. I regard the suggestion that the parts of happiness in this passage are external goods as implausible since, aside from the fact that the idea is not derivable from the context, it is unlikely that Aristotle

What does it mean for virtues or virtuous activities to produce and pre-serve happiness and its parts? In general, manifestations of virtues, namely virtuous activities, produce and preserve those virtues, which continue to be manifested in virtuous activities.[29] In other words, virtue is productive and preservative in the sense that virtuous activities are self-reinforcing in the way just mentioned. The whole of virtue, which in its other-regarding aspect is general justice, has parts: virtues. According to pluralists, the parts of the whole of virtue, virtues, produce happiness in the sense that their self-reinforcing actualizations, virtuous activities, are the parts of happiness.

The Difference between Parts of Happiness and External Goods
Another motivation for the Pluralist Constraint has been a tendency to believe that without affirming that happiness has parts, a solution to the Dilemmatic Problem cannot respect the fact that Aristotle sees a difference between how ethically virtuous activities and external goods are related to happiness. Put another way, making them all for the sake of contempla-tion, as monists do, rather than making ethically virtuous activities parts of happiness along with contemplation, prevents us from being able plausi-bly to say in what that difference consists. The evidence that Aristotle sees such a difference, according to pluralists, is as follows.

One kind of evidence is that the relevance of external goods to happi-ness depends asymmetrically on the relation of ethically virtuous activities to happiness. External goods are related to happiness *to the extent that* ethi-cally virtuous activities are related to happiness and require, or are enabled

would want to *contrast* general justice with particular justice in respect of producing and preserving external goods. Burger (2008, 93–94, 167) thinks that the parts of happiness are individual citizens' happiness, on the supposition that this passage is anticipating *Politics* 2.5, 1264^{b}15–25, where Aristo-tle says, objecting to Plato, that the happiness of the state depends on the happiness of individuals from all classes (not only the lawmakers). The first problem with this suggestion is that, as I have already mentioned, Aristotle thinks that happiness for individuals and for the political community have the same structure. See Jagannathan (2019) on this point. Relatedly, if indeed Aristotle is here anticipating *Pol.* 2.5, we need to ask what Aristotle thinks makes individuals from all classes happy. His view throughout the *Politics* is that happiness includes ethically virtuous activities (see especially 7.1, 1323^{b}21–36). So, if Burger's interpretation of parts of happiness in *NE* 5.1 is correct, we would need an account of *how* general justice, the whole of virtue as it relates to others, produces and pre-serves virtuous activities, and thereby happiness, for individuals. The explanation given on behalf of pluralists in what follows in the main text does precisely this. So, even if Burger's interpretation is correct, it presupposes the availability of an explanation like the one that pluralists would give for the truth of the more typical interpretation of this passage, the interpretation that the parts of happiness are virtuous activities. Since Burger's interpretation presupposes this, but goes beyond it, the interpretation that nearly all other commentators advocate is preferable.

[29] *NE* 2.1, 1103^{a}26 – ^{b}8; 2.2, 1104^{a}11 – ^{b}3; 2.4, 1105^{b}5–12; 3.5, 1114^{a}9–10; 6.5, 1140^{b}11–20; 7.8, 1151^{a}15–20.

by, such goods (*NE* 1.8, 1099^{a}31–33, 1.10, 1100^{b}8–11).[30] Pluralists think that if this is true, then external goods and ethically virtuous activities cannot have the same kind of relation to happiness. They think that Aristotle has a distinction between being needed as a sort of auxiliary or enabler dispensable in principle, and being constitutively determinative of the thing in question, and that such a distinction holds between external goods and ethically virtuous activities with respect to happiness.[31]

A second kind of evidence is that ethically virtuous activities share certain properties with happiness that external goods do not share. For example, virtuous activities, as well as happiness, are more strictly goods than external goods are (Broadie, 1993, 53). This is because whereas external goods can be used well or badly, this is not true of happiness, or of virtuous activities.

Another property that happiness shares with virtuous activities, but not with external goods, is being a good of the soul. Aristotle says that it is because virtuous activities are goods of the soul that we can infer that happiness is a good of the soul, as it should be if certain popular opinions about it are to be vindicated, whereas external goods are not goods of the soul (*NE* 1.8, 1098^{b}12–20, *EE* 2.1, 1218^{b}32 – 1219^{a}39). We can infer that happiness has a particular property, namely being a good of the soul, from the fact that virtuous activities are goods of the soul. We cannot draw any such inference about this property of happiness from facts about external goods since they lack the property. Pluralists can say that this situation is easily explicable if virtuous activities are the parts of happiness and external goods are related to those activities in some other way, perhaps as instruments or preconditions (*NE* 1.9, 1099^{b}25–28), but difficult to explain otherwise. In addition to this, it is natural to think that the difference between ethically virtuous activities and external goods with respect to happiness is that the former, but not the latter, are *parts* of happiness because Aristotle's standard contrast class for instruments and preconditions is parts.[32]

---

[30] See Brown (2006), Crisp (1994, 122), and Roche (1988a, 189 n. 27). See also Curzer (2012, 417), who, though I categorize him as a relativist rather than a pluralist, offers this as an argument against monism. Whiting (1986, 91–93) gives a related, but slightly different, argument based on *NE* 10.8.

[31] Indeed, one might suppose, though the point does not depend on this, that such a distinction is in view in his mysterious pronouncement in *Pol.* 7.13, 1332^{a}7–10 that in the "ethical works" he has said that happiness "is complete/perfect/final (*teleian*) activity and use of virtue, and this not from a hypothesis, but unqualifiedly" (ἐνέργειαν εἶναι καὶ χρῆσιν ἀρετῆς τελείαν, οὐκ ἐξ ὑποθέσεως ἀλλ' ἁπλῶς).

[32] *Pol.* 7.8, 1328^{a}21 – ^{b}4, 7.9, 1329^{a}34–39, *EE* 2.1, 1214^{b}24–27. Keyt (1983, 368) mentions this.

The Immoralist Objection

According to pluralists, unless ethically virtuous activities are partially constitutive of happiness, then happiness could come at the expense of ethically virtuous activities, a result that pluralists deem un-Aristotelian and unpalatable in its own right. This is the immoralist objection to monism.[33] Another way of formulating the objection is this: If, as monists think, happiness is contemplation and ethically virtuous activities are for the sake of contemplation, then for any case in which contemplation is available, it is possible that the agent has sufficient reason to choose it over any other course of action. After all, why choose an activity that is merely instrumental for, or an approximation of, happiness if happiness is directly available?[34]

Pluralists' reason for thinking that immoralism is un-Aristotelian is that, according to them, Aristotle thinks that happiness and ethically virtuous activities covary in such a way that the happiest person will be the most ethically virtuous: The more one has every virtue (courage is the star example in the context), the more one's life will be worthwhile and happy (*NE* 3.9, 1117^{b}7–13).[35] The happiest person is the one who is most of all (*malista*) such as to act rightly (*orthôs*) and nobly (*kalôs*) (10.8, 1179^{a}29–32). This is why Aristotle can say that happiness is in accordance both with theoretical wisdom and with practical wisdom (1.8, 1098^{b}22–25).[36] If happiness and

---

[33] See, for example, Ackrill (1974, 358), Bostock (2000, 203), Keyt (1983, 368–371), Pakaluk (2005, 322), Roche (1988a, 176), and Whiting (1986, 94). There is also an immoralist objection to relativism, a point noticed by, for example, Charles (1999, 209). Relativists think that one kind of happiness, the best kind, is contemplation and this activity does not include ethically virtuous activities (though on at least some relativist views the happy *life* does). On their view, then, the best kind of happiness comes at the expense of ethically virtuous activities, which, again, pluralists will see as un-Aristotelian and unpalatable.

[34] Some monists, such as Adkins (1978, 313), Cooper (1975, 164), Kenny (1978, 214), and Lear (1988, 314–316), admit that on their interpretation of the *NE* Aristotle is an immoralist. Whiting (1986, 94) argues that at least some monists – her paper specifically targets Cooper (1975) – make Aristotle a particularly strong immoralist, one who thinks that we are *required* in every case to maximize contemplation at the expense of ethically virtuous activities. Kraut (1989) thinks that although "the more [contemplation] one engages in, the better off one is" (9), it will usually turn out that pursuing further opportunities for contemplation will not conflict with justice, but cases of unjust pursuit of contemplation *can* occur (181). Kraut, then, contends that his monistic view does not commit Aristotle to such a strong immoralism, but a pluralist might argue that he still makes him an immoralist of a weaker sort, one who thinks that one is *permitted* to maximize contemplation at the expense of ethically virtuous activities, and that even this weaker immoralism is not in keeping with Aristotle's view that happiness and ethically virtuous activities covary, which view I discuss in the main text below.

[35] Whiting (1986, 73) cites this passage to make this point.

[36] Saying that happiness is activity in accordance with theoretical and practical wisdom is his way of partially accommodating two *endoxa*: one that happiness is theoretical wisdom and another that it is practical wisdom. Thanks to Anthony Price for urging clarity about this.

ethically virtuous activities indeed covary in this way, then we see again that ethically virtuous activities cannot have the same relation to happiness that external goods have, for Aristotle indicates that external goods lack this covariation with happiness: Past a rather low limit, additional external goods are not needed for happiness (10.8, 1178^{b}33 – 1179^{a}17) and indeed can become impediments to contemplation (10.8, 1178^{b}3–5). Instead, pluralists think, ethically virtuous activities must be parts of happiness.

1.3.2   Motivating the Monist Constraint

Monists likewise have compelling reasons for dissatisfaction with pluralists' responses to the Dilemmatic Problem and thus for regarding (B) as a constraint on an acceptable interpretation. Monists tend to interpret Aristotle as saying explicitly that happiness is a single activity, contemplation, and as making points about happiness that require it specifically to be such an activity.

Contemplation's Superlative Features
Monists think that without affirming that happiness is a single activity, contemplation, an interpretation cannot account for Aristotle's argument in *NE* 10.7–8, which they interpret as saying that various features that belong uniquely to happiness belong uniquely to contemplation.[37] Aristotle begins the argument as follows:

> But if happiness is activity in accordance with virtue, it is reasonable that it should be in accordance with the highest (*kratistên*) one, and this will be the virtue of the best (*aristou*) part. Whether, then, this part is intellect (*nous*) or something else that seems naturally to rule, lead, and understand what is noble and divine, whether by being itself something divine or by being the most divine part in us – this part's activity in accordance with its proper (*oikeian*) virtue will be perfect (*teleia*) happiness. We have already said that it is contemplative (*theôrêtikê*) activity. (10.7, 1177^{a}12–18)

---

[37] See, for example, Kenny's (1992, 88) memorable simile: "In book 1 and book 10 of the *NE* Aristotle behaves like the director of a marriage bureau, trying to match his client's description of his ideal partner. In the first book he lists the properties which people believe to be essential to happiness, and in the tenth book he seeks to show that philosophical contemplation, and it alone, possesses to the full these essential qualities." Bostock (2000, 192) states forcefully that "Chapter 7 [of book 10] can only be understood, it seems to me, as offering arguments for the claim that *eudaimonia* is to be *identified* with the activity of the highest of the virtues, namely contemplation" (emphasis in original). He then proceeds to rehearse these arguments for contemplation's superlative features.

Monists interpret this passage as saying that happiness is the activity of our highest, most divine virtue, which is the virtue of our highest and most divine part. They standardly believe the following: According to Aristotle our highest and most divine part is theoretical intellect, the virtue of it is theoretical wisdom, and its manifestation is the activity of contemplation. This is why he says that happiness is contemplative activity. Contemplative activity does not have ethically virtuous activities as parts. Neither does theoretical wisdom have ethical virtues as parts, nor theoretical intellect any other parts of the soul. In short, happiness is a single, contemplative activity. This is precisely what we should expect since happiness is the single highest and most divine activity of our single highest and most divine part.

According to monists, Aristotle then offers a series of arguments in 10.7–8 meant to show that the conclusion that happiness is a single activity, contemplation, is "in agreement both with what was said before and with the truth" (10.7, 1177ᵃ18–19).[38] The purport of each argument is that contemplation, and only contemplation, has the features that happiness is supposed to have. Such arguments, monists think, rule out the pluralist claim that happiness has ethically virtuous activities as parts. According to monists, Aristotle believes that happiness is contemplation because it alone among activities has the features that happiness (the activity) must have: It is the activity that is highest (1177ᵃ19–21), most continuous (ᵃ21–22), most pleasant (ᵃ22–27), most self-sufficient (ᵃ27 – ᵇ1), most perfect (ᵇ1–4), most leisurely (ᵇ4–15), in accordance with what is a human being most of all (1178ᵃ2–8), and most divine (10.8, 1178ᵇ7–32). Aristotle takes particular care to argue that ethically virtuous activities lack these properties. Monists infer from this that happiness is contemplation and not ethically virtuous activities.[39]

According to monists, Aristotle has indirectly prepared the way for such a conclusion in *NE* 10.6, where he argues that happiness should be sought among virtuous activities rather than among amusements:

> But the happy life seems to be in accordance with virtue, and this is one that involves seriousness (*spoudēs*) and does not consist in amusement. And we say that serious things are better than comical ones and those that involve amusement, and that in every case the activity of what is better, whether

---

[38] For a recent detailed analysis of these arguments, see Aufderheide (2020).
[39] Cleemput (2006, 155) thinks that even in *NE* 1 Aristotle is committed to the idea that while happiness is divine, no composite activity, such as a composite of ethically virtuous activities, could be divine.

of a part or of a human being, is more serious. But the activity of what is better is higher and for this reason is more characteristic of happiness (*eudaimonikôtera*). (1177ᵃ1–6)[40]

Amusement cannot be happiness because happiness is the best activity and amusement is not, for virtuous activities are better than it is. That is at least in part because virtuous activities are activities of that which is better in a human being, and activities in accordance with what is better in a human being are themselves better, and therefore better candidates for happiness. This latter, general principle is what Aristotle applies in 10.7–8 to arrive at the conclusion that among virtuous activities one stands out as best: contemplation. Just as happiness could not be amusement because amusement is not the best activity, happiness could not be ethically virtuous activities because these are not best. Rather, happiness is the best activity: contemplation.[41]

Various ways of resisting such an interpretation of Aristotle's argument in *NE* 10.7–8 have been suggested. These are most relevant to the last two of the arguments in the series of arguments in 10.7–8 that Aristotle gives. Monists think that in the first of these, T1, Aristotle argues that since theoretical intellect is what is a human being most of all, and happiness is activity in accordance with what is a human being most of all, happiness must be activity in accordance with theoretical intellect:

T1 (10.7, 1178ᵃ2–8)

Each ⟨human being⟩ would in fact seem to be ⟨intellect⟩, since it is the determinative and better ⟨part⟩. So, it would be bizarre if one did not choose a life characteristic of oneself, but rather a life characteristic of something else. What was said previously applies now, too. For what is proper by nature to each thing is best and most pleasant to each thing. Indeed, life in accordance

δόξειε δ᾿ ἂν καὶ εἶναι ἕκαστος ᵃ2 τοῦτο, εἴπερ τὸ κύριον καὶ ἄμει- νον. ἄτοπον οὖν γίνοιτ᾿ ἄν, εἰ μὴ τὸν αὑτοῦ βίον αἱροῖτο ἀλλά τινος ἄλλου. τὸ λεχθέν τε πρό- τερον ἁρμόσει καὶ νῦν· τὸ γὰρ 5 οἰκεῖον ἑκάστῳ τῇ φύσει κράτι- στον καὶ ἥδιστόν ἐστιν ἑκάστῳ· καὶ τῷ ἀνθρώπῳ δὴ ὁ κατὰ τὸν

---

[40] I translate '*eudaimonikôtera*' as 'more characteristic of happiness,' following Irwin's (2019) 'has more the character of happiness.' Some other possibilities include 'more of the nature of happiness,' 'more conducive to happiness,' or 'more productive of happiness.' None seems ideal to me, but none of my points depends on the translation. Thanks to Christopher Shields for discussion of this issue.

[41] Note that I am not saying that Aristotle's argument that happiness is not to be sought in amusement has, in its own right, any direct bearing on whether one virtuous activity stands out as best. Rather, a general principle implicit in that argument is used to address that question in 10.7–8. Thanks to Anthony Price for urging clarity on this point.

with intellect is proper to a human being, since ⟨intellect⟩ is a human being most of all. So, this ⟨life⟩ also is happiest.

νοῦν βίος, εἴπερ τοῦτο μάλιστα ἄνθρωπος. οὗτος ἄρα καὶ εὐδαιμονέστατος.   8

According to monists, the second of the two passages, T2, argues that happiness is contemplation because contemplation is the most divine activity:

T2 (10.8, 1178^b7–32)

It would appear from the following considerations, too, that perfect happiness is a contemplative sort of activity. We suppose the gods most of all to be blessed and happy. But what kind of actions ought to be ascribed to them? Actions that are just? Or will they not appear ridiculous entering into contracts, returning deposits, and all such things? Courageous actions, enduring fearful things and facing danger because doing so is noble? Or generous actions? To whom will they give? It would be odd for them to have money or anything of that sort. And what would their temperate actions be? Or would not such praise be cheap since they do not have base appetites? If we were to go through all of the things concerned with such actions, it would appear that they are trivial and unworthy of gods. But all suppose them to be alive and therefore active, for surely they cannot suppose them to be sleeping like Endymion. So then, if acting (and still more, producing) is removed from living, what is left besides contemplation? The result would be that the activity of the god, exceeding in blessedness, is contemplative. And indeed, among human activities the one that is most akin to this is the most characteristic of happiness.[42] An indica-

ἡ δὲ τελεία εὐδαιμονία ὅτι θεω- ^b7
ρητική τις ἐστιν ἐνέργεια, καὶ ἐν-
τεῦθεν ἂν φανείη. τοὺς θεοὺς γὰρ
μάλιστα ὑπειλήφαμεν μακαρίους
καὶ εὐδαίμονας εἶναι· πράξεις δὲ
ποίας ἀπονεῖμαι χρεὼν αὐτοῖς;   10
πότερα τὰς δικαίας; ἢ γελοῖοι φα-
νοῦνται συναλλάττοντες καὶ πα-
ρακαταθήκας ἀποδιδόντες καὶ ὅ-
σα τοιαῦτα; ἀλλὰ τὰς ἀνδρείους
* * ὑπομένοντας τὰ φοβερὰ καὶ
κινδυνεύοντας ὅτι καλόν; ἢ τὰς
ἐλευθερίους; τίνι δὲ δώσουσιν;
ἄτοπον δ' εἰ καὶ ἔσται αὐτοῖς νόμισμα ἤ τι τοιοῦτον. αἱ δὲ σώφρο-   15
νες τί ἂν εἶεν; ἢ φορτικὸς ὁ ἔπαινος, ὅτι οὐκ ἔχουσι φαύλας ἐπιθυμίας; διεξιοῦσι δὲ πάντα φαίνοιτ' ἂν τὰ περὶ τὰς πράξεις μικρὰ καὶ ἀνάξια θεῶν. ἀλλὰ μὴν
ζῆν γε πάντες ὑπειλήφασιν αὐτοὺς καὶ ἐνεργεῖν ἄρα· οὐ γὰρ
δὴ καθεύδειν ὥσπερ τὸν Ἐνδυμίωνα. τῷ δὴ ζῶντι τοῦ πράττειν   20
ἀφαιρουμένου, ἔτι δὲ μᾶλλον τοῦ
ποιεῖν, τί λείπεται πλὴν θεωρία;
ὥστε ἡ τοῦ θεοῦ ἐνέργεια, μακαριότητι διαφέρουσα, θεωρητικὴ
ἂν εἴη· καὶ τῶν ἀνθρωπίνων δὴ ἡ
ταύτῃ συγγενεστάτη εὐδαιμονι-

---

[42] See my p. 22 n. 40 on the translation of '*eudaimonikōtera*,' the comparative form of the adjective that here appears in superlative form.

tion of this is that the other animals do not share in happiness, being completely deprived of this sort of activity. For in the case of the gods the whole of life is blessed, whereas in the case of human beings this is so only so far as there is some semblance of this sort of activity. But among the other animals none is happy since none shares in contemplation in any way. Indeed, happiness extends as far as contemplation does, and to those to whom it more belongs to contemplate, it more belongs also to be happy, not accidentally, but rather in accordance with the contemplation, for this is valuable in itself. The result would be that happiness is a type of contemplation.

κωτάτη. σημεῖον δὲ καὶ τὸ μὴ μετέχειν τὰ λοιπὰ ζῷα εὐδαιμονίας,
τῆς τοιαύτης ἐνεργείας ἐστερη-   25
μένα τελείως. τοῖς μὲν γὰρ θεοῖς
ἅπας ὁ βίος μακάριος, τοῖς δ᾽ ἀνθρώποις, ἐφ᾽ ὅσον ὁμοίωμά τι τῆς
τοιαύτης ἐνεργείας ὑπάρχει· τῶν
δ᾽ ἄλλων ζῴων οὐδὲν εὐδαιμονεῖ,
ἐπειδὴ οὐδαμῇ κοινωνεῖ θεωρίας.
ἐφ᾽ ὅσον δὴ διατείνει ἡ θεωρία,
καὶ ἡ εὐδαιμονία, καὶ οἷς μᾶλλον
ὑπάρχει τὸ θεωρεῖν, καὶ εὐδαιμο-   30
νεῖν, οὐ κατὰ συμβεβηκὸς ἀλλὰ
κατὰ τὴν θεωρίαν· αὕτη γὰρ καθ᾽
αὑτὴν τιμία. ὥστ᾽ εἴη ἂν ἡ εὐδαιμονία θεωρία τις.

A standard monist interpretation of Aristotle's argument in T1 is as follows:[43] In its beginning and penultimate sentences, Aristotle affirms that human beings are their theoretical intellect most of all (*malista*), which is to say that a human being is more appropriately identified with theoretical intellect than with anything else. The final sentence of T1 tells us that the happiest life for a human being will be that of theoretical intellect. When the argument of T1 is understood in light of the other arguments for contemplation's superlative properties throughout 10.7–8, including the arguments that contemplation is best (10.7, 1177[a]19–21) and most pleasant ([a]22–27), to which the final sentence of T1 refers, we can see that such a life will be happiest because the activity of happiness is theoretical intellect's virtuous activity: contemplation. In short, according to monists, the happy life is a theoretical one because human happiness is contemplation, and human happiness is contemplation because human beings are theoretical intellect most of all.

Monists typically understand T2 as adding to Aristotle's previous arguments that contemplation is the activity that is highest (10.7, 1177[a]19–21) and most pleasant ([a]22–27) the further argument that it is the activity that is most divine. According to [b]23 of T2, happiness must be that activity which is most akin to what divine beings do. In our case, the activity

---

[43] I discuss this passage further in Chapters 4–5.

that is most akin to the divine is contemplation. One reason for thinking so is furnished by his previous argument that contemplation is the
most self-sufficient of our activities (10.7, 1177^{a}27 – ^{b}1). For humans, contemplation is most self-sufficient because it requires less involvement with
other people than, say, just, courageous, or generous actions require.[44]
For a divine being, T2 tells us, those kinds of acts are not even possible
in the first place, so such a being's contemplation is obviously his most
self-sufficient activity. The superlative self-sufficiency of an activity, Aristotle thinks, is a mark of its divinity. Having thus added 'most divine'
to the list of superlative properties that uniquely qualify contemplation
as happiness, in ^{b}28–32 of T2 Aristotle gives a restatement of the overall
claim that he has made in various forms throughout 10.7–8 that happiness
is contemplation. The inference in ^{b}28–32 from the non-accidental coex-
tension of happiness and contemplation to the claim that happiness is a
type of contemplation explicitly depends on Aristotle's invocation, at the
end of the sentence, of the conclusion of a previous argument that contemplation, like happiness, is preeminently loved for its own sake (10.7,
1177^{b}1–4). This passage, monists think, is a keystone for the stacks of arguments that Aristotle has given in 10.7–8 for contemplation's claim to be
happiness.

But, as I have said, various ways of resisting these interpretations of
T1 and T2 have been proposed. One strategy is to claim that Aristotle is
not expressing his own view in these passages. Moline (1983), for example, thinks that the account of happiness as contemplation in *NE* 10.7–8
is so discordant with the rest of the *NE* that it must be an expression of
Anaxagoras's view meant as a joke at the latter's expense. Whiting (1986,
86–87), highlighting the fact that Aristotle's claims in the beginning and
penultimate sentences of T1 are grammatically conditionals, argues that it
is possible to avoid imputing to Aristotle the acceptance of the antecedents
of these conditionals, and thus also to avoid committing him to the conclusion that contemplation is the activity of what is most of all a human
being. Rather, according to Whiting (1988, 37–38), we should think that
theoretical intellect is only one part of a composite human essence, and
thus is not most of all what a human being is.

---

[44] Brown (2014) describes this as "solitary self-sufficiency," which he thinks differs from the "political
self-sufficiency" described in book 1. Bostock (2000, 24 n. 42) and Kenny (1992, 36) also think
that the meaning of 'self-sufficiency' shifts between books 1 and 10. Gasser-Wingate (2020) offers a
response, arguing instead that self-sufficiency in books 1 and 10 should be understood as a certain
sort of "independence from external contributors to our activity."

I think that the general suspicion about the arguments in *NE* 10.7–8 that Moline expresses, stripped of his proposal about Anaxagoras, is at bottom an insistence on the Pluralist Constraint, a constraint that Moline thinks cannot possibly be met by monistic interpretations of these chapters. But what about Whiting's composite essence proposal? Charles raises a problem for it in his (2017a, 107) and (2017b, 96), a problem that is partially anticipated by Nagel (1972, 259): The view that humans have a composite essence gives no principled way of including theoretical intellect in the composite essence, and therefore contemplation as part of the excellent performance of the composite *ergon* of such an essence, without also including the perceptive part of our soul in our essence and perceptual activity in our *ergon*. Interpreters ought to have a principled explanation for such an exclusion, though, since Aristotle decisively excludes perception from our *ergon* (*NE* 1.7, 1098ᵃ1–3). A proponent of the composite essence view might respond that the human essence is restricted to the rational soul and excludes perceptual capacities for that reason, but monists would presumably regard such a response as unprincipled and as complicated by Aristotle's discussion of practical intellect in perceptual terms in *NE* 6.8 and 6.11.

One who attempts to avoid monism by arguing that Aristotle disbelieves the conclusion of T1 faces pressure to say that he also disbelieves the conclusion of T2, the claim that "happiness would be a type of contemplation." Such an interpreter might take the first part of ᵇ32 of T2, 'the result would be,' to indicate that such a claim *would* follow if, counterfactually, the argument that precedes it were correct. But monists see the mere possibility of this as no principled reason to think that the argument of T2 is meant as anything other than Aristotle's genuine statement of what he takes to be the fact of the matter, for it is at least as plausible that this construction is used to flag a claim as a conclusion of a series of premises that Aristotle accepts,[45] or simply as an optative of politeness.[46]

Another strategy for resisting monistic interpretations of T1 and T2 is to suppose that Aristotle's conclusions in these passages are relativized to

---

[45] See, for example, *DA* 2.2, 414ᵃ13–14, *NE* 1.2, 1094ᵇ6–7, 5.4, 1136ᵇ1–3, 6.5, 1140ᵃ30–31, 6.7, 1141ᵃ18–19.

[46] For a similar use of the optative, see *Metaph.* 12.7, 1072ᵃ20–21 (λύοιτ' ἂν ταῦτα), where Aristotle means to say that the difficulties that he had been addressing in the previous chapter have indeed been resolved. Laks (2000, 211) identifies the optative in *Metaph.* 12.7 as an optative of politeness. Natali (2010, 315), comments as follows about an optative construction in the *ergon* argument in *NE* 1.7, which presumably no pluralist would want to view as counterfactual: "The conclusion, formulated in a slightly dubitative form (οὕτω δόξειεν ἂν), but only as a rhetorical device, can be found at lines 1097ᵇ27–28: 'so it would seem for the human being'."

one kind of happiness rather than another. But, as I have already mentioned, the case for relativism is not strong and has not persuaded monists or pluralists.

Yet another strategy for resisting the standard monist interpretation of these passages is to claim that Aristotle here employs a notion of 'contemplation' so capacious that it includes the activities that pluralists view as parts of happiness. Curzer (2012, 401) takes "the objects of contemplation to be primarily the matters of ordinary human life." He reports that Aristotle uses 'contemplation' in multiple ways, one of which does refer to practical affairs. The problem is that, however he uses 'contemplation' elsewhere, in these passages Aristotle clearly means contemplation to be the manifestation of theoretical wisdom, and Aristotle explicitly denies that theoretical wisdom is concerned with human things (*NE* 6.7, 1141ª16 – ᵇ14). Curzer, realizing this, says that such passages have been overemphasized by medieval philosophers with religious interests and should therefore perhaps be "backgrounded" (397). Monists presumably have not experienced any strong temptation to background such passages in accordance with Curzer's suggestion.

Guthrie (1981, 396–398), Jirsa (2017), Roochnik (2009), and Walker (2017) take a different type of liberal view of contemplation according to which it can sometimes be virtuous *inquiry*. I doubt that this could be what Aristotle has in mind in *NE* 10.7–8. Expanding on the evidence of 10.7, 1177ª26–27, which appears to deny that contemplation could be inquiry, two main arguments are given for interpreting Aristotle as having a more restrictive view of what contemplation is:[47] First, an inquiry takes time to develop toward completion, but since contemplation is an *energeia* (activity) and an *energeia* is fully complete at all times, contemplation could not be an inquiry. Second, contemplation is supposed to be "for its own sake alone" (10.7, 1177ᵇ1–4), but since an inquiry is valuable at least for the sake of that for which it is conducted, an inquiry is not valuable in the same way, so contemplation could not be an inquiry.[48] I will add another argument to these: Given the way in which Aristotle opens *NE* 10.7, contemplation ought to be the manifestation of a virtue, but inquiry is not the manifestation of any virtue recognized by Aristotle. At most, it would be

---

[47] These are given by Aufderheide (2020, 124 and 172), Bostock (2000, 198), Gauthier and Jolif (1970, 855–856), Kenny (1992, 103), Kraut (1989, 68 n. 48), Lawrence (2005, 135), Nightingale (2004, 208–209), and Urmson (1988, 121).

[48] The point here does not depend on whether "αὐτὴ μόνη δι' αὐτὴν" is translated as "for its own sake alone" or "alone for its own sake." Either way, contemplation will be valued differently from how inquiry is valued. Thanks to Anthony Price for discussion of this point.

part of *developing* a virtue, perhaps theoretical wisdom. But Aristotle says that pleasures do not arise when we are acquiring some capacity, but when we are manifesting it (7.12, 1153^{a}10–11). Yet the sort of contemplation at issue in *NE* 10.7–8 is supposed to be "most pleasant" (10.7, 1177^{a}22–27). This point about pleasure would explain *why* Aristotle would deny, as he appears to do (^{a}26–27), that the sort of contemplation that he is discussing could be inquiry, making it more difficult for commentators to downplay the relevance of that remark.

Broadie (1991, 415) suggests yet another liberal view of contemplation that avoids at least the first and the third of the arguments that I have just listed against the view that contemplation can be an inquiry. She proposes, with some hesitation, that contemplation (*theôria*) is not the manifestation of theoretical wisdom, but rather of a nameless ethical virtue, love of *theôria*, and the activity amounts to practical wisdom celebrating itself. Monists think that it is far more likely that Aristotle intends contemplation to be the manifestation of theoretical wisdom than of a nameless ethical virtue. This is evidenced by the way in which Aristotle sums up the discussion at 10.8, 1179^{a}31–32: "In this way, too, the result would be that the *theoretically* wise person most of all is happy."[49]

Lear (2004, 194–196), though she is a monist, offers another possibility for assigning an expansive meaning to 'contemplation' in ^{b}32 of T2. She thinks that in the context of T2 '*theôria*' unmodified by '*tis*' refers to the manifestation of theoretical wisdom, Aristotle's technical use, but in ^{b}32 '*tis*' makes a difference: A manifestation of *practical* wisdom is *theôria tis*, "contemplation of a sort." She cites three passages (*NE* 6.1, 1139^{a}6–8, 6.4, 1140^{a}10–14, and 6.7, 1141^{a}25–26) supporting the idea that there is a use of 'contemplation' according to which the kind of thinking involved in practical deliberation about variable particulars or the kind involved in the manufacture of products of art would count.[50] But, as she recognizes, these passages are unrelated to Aristotle's account of happiness. Most monists think that here, at the culmination of his account of happiness, Aristotle is unlikely to mean 'contemplation' in any but his technical sense, namely as the manifestation of *sophia*, theoretical wisdom, as evidenced by the way in which he sums up the discussion at 10.8, 1179^{a}31–32, a passage that I have already mentioned, and by the similarity of ^{b}32 and ^{b}7–8 of T2, which indicates that the argument to follow is another way of showing what he

---

[49] ὥστε κἂν οὕτως εἴη ὁ σοφὸς μάλιστ' εὐδαίμων.

[50] Price (2011, 77 n. 67) cites additional passages, but concedes that "it is true that generally, in that chapter [10.7], ['*theôria*'] specifically connotes 'the activity of *sophia*' (1177a24)."

has already shown, namely that contemplation has a higher status than ethically virtuous activities have.[51] Lear (2004, 194) insists that manifestations of practical wisdom *should* be accommodated by Aristotle's claim in ^{b}32 of T2 since he has already said that the practically wise person is happy. But this is better seen as a way of stating that it would be desirable to reconcile the Pluralist Constraint and Monist Constraint than as a principled reason for drawing any particular conclusion about the significance of '*tis*.'

It is more probable that '*tis*' is used in ^{b}32 of T2 in a classificatory sense, encoding in this case a contrast between the type of contemplation of which humans are capable and the types, whatever they are, that might be possible for other beings.[52] Aristotle has just been arguing that there is a divine type of contemplation that is the highest divine activity and that there is no type of contemplation of which animals are capable. Wherever we see contemplation (of whatever type), we see happiness of the corresponding type. It is, then, informative to say that human happiness is a type of contemplation: the type proper to humans.

Most monists think that in T1 and T2 Aristotle genuinely means to say that happiness is theoretical contemplation: He is not distancing himself from this conclusion, suggesting its limited applicability, or signaling a use of 'contemplation' other than his technical notion of theoretical contemplation. In short, monists standardly think that Aristotle's various arguments throughout *NE* 10.7–8, including T1 and T2, for the superlative properties of contemplation place what I have called "the Monist Constraint" on any acceptable interpretation. An acceptable interpretation

[51] Greenwood (1909, 76–78) systematically presents evidence that Aristotle uses 'contemplation' in *NE* 10.6–8 to denote the manifestation of theoretical wisdom. Frede (2020, 973) adds another reason for doubting Lear's proposal: The inference to ^{b}32 of T2 runs through ^{b}22–23 and ^{b}25–27, which require that the activity in which human happiness consists be one that bears some semblance, indeed the greatest semblance, to the divine activity, but the preceding sentences argue that no ethically virtuous activity is characteristic of the divine.

[52] See *Phys.* 4.11, 219^{b}5 for a clear example of classificatory '*tis*.' Aufderheide (2020, 212) offers reasons in favor of a "determinate" (as opposed to indeterminate) reading of '*tis*' in ^{b}32 of T2 according to which it marks an implicit classification of kinds, but he does not consider my specific version of a determinate/classificatory reading. Something similar is true of Zingano (2014, 152 n. 31), who sees as options "contemplation of divine as opposed to human things" or "scientific as opposed to other forms of contemplation, such as theatrical contemplation" and prefers the second. Lear (2004, 195–196 n. 43) briefly considers translating '*theôria tis*' as "a kind of contemplation," but her way of parsing this and her reasons for finding it misleading are specific to the possibility that the relevant kinds implicitly distinguished would be theoretical contemplation and practical contemplation. I am proposing instead that the kinds implicitly distinguished are human contemplation and divine contemplation. Herzberg (2013, 115) thinks that '*tis*' here marks a difference in degree between divine and human contemplation. I argue in Chapter 4, as in Reece (2020b), that for Aristotle the difference between divine and human contemplation must be a difference not merely in degree, but in type.

must square with what they view as Aristotle's insistence that happiness is a single activity, contemplation. This constraint is the Monist Constraint.

1.4   Conclusion

The Conjunctive Problem reveals why a dialectically satisfying solution to the Dilemmatic Problem has proven elusive. Both the Pluralist Constraint and Monist Constraint rest on firm textual foundations and important philosophical intuitions. Pluralists have good reasons for their constraint, the claim that happiness is a composite that includes not only contemplative activity, but also ethically virtuous activities as parts, monists for theirs, the claim that it is contemplative activity, which does not include ethically virtuous activities as parts. Both groups have held their ground and have given compelling arguments for doing so. The best explanation for this stalemate is that Aristotle really is committed to the Pluralist Constraint *and* the Monist Constraint. The Conjunctive Problem, rather than the Dilemmatic Problem, is the one that interpreters need to be trying to solve. As I have said, it is standardly believed that an interpretation of Aristotle's remarks about happiness cannot simultaneously meet the Pluralist Constraint and the Monist Constraint. I think that it is possible to do so, but not if one labors under the crippling weight of certain false assumptions. In the next three chapters I will argue that three theses thwart the project of solving the Conjunctive Problem. These are the Divergence Thesis, the Duality Thesis, and the Divinity Thesis. Most interpreters hold at least two of these. Some hold all three. I argue that all three are false. The considerations that emerge in the course of discussing these three theses will come together in the final chapter in a solution to the Conjunctive Problem.

CHAPTER 2

Theoretical and Practical Wisdom

2.1 The Divergence Thesis

In the previous chapter I introduced the Conjunctive Problem of Happiness, that of saying how Aristotle could coherently maintain that the same kind of happiness (the activity, not the life) is virtuous activity, a composite that includes not only contemplative activity, but also ethically virtuous activities as parts, and that happiness (the activity, not the life) is contemplative activity, which does not include ethically virtuous activities as parts. This problem has not been solved. In this chapter and the two following it, I will identify three popular commitments, any of which makes it impossible to solve the Conjunctive Problem. Most interpreters hold at least two of these commitments, and many hold all three. The commitment that I will discuss in this chapter is as follows.

Divergence Thesis

Aristotle thinks that it is possible to possess theoretical wisdom and reliably manifest it in contemplation without possessing practical wisdom and reliably manifesting it in ethically virtuous activities.[1]

This thesis is motivated by a passage in *NE* 6.7 that appears to suggest that some people, namely Anaxagoras and Thales, possess theoretical wisdom without practical wisdom.[2] Part of the current chapter will feature an analysis of this passage. The Divergence Thesis, common among

---

[1] Hereafter I typically abbreviate 'possess and reliably manifest' to 'possess' or 'reliably manifest' since for Aristotle manifesting a virtue (acting virtuously) requires possessing the virtue and possessing the virtue requires reliably manifesting it insofar as one acts within the domain covered by that virtue. One could possess a virtue and not manifest it because one is asleep or otherwise inactive, but one could not possess a virtue and reliably act contrary to its characteristic manifestation. The relevant notion of reliability is not a matter of absolute frequency, but rather of correct fit with what is called for in the circumstances and consistent appropriateness. (Compare the claim that I have a reliable attorney if she intervenes helpfully when needed, but she is needed infrequently and irregularly.)

[2] The Divergence Thesis is attributed to Aristotle by Albertus Magnus (*Ethica* 6.2.22.439[b]), Aquinas (*Quaestio Disputata de Virtutibus Cardinalibus* 2 ad 8), Bostock (2000, 205–206), Broadie and Rowe

monists, pluralists, and relativists, makes it impossible to solve the Conjunctive Problem. That is because if one affirms Divergence then one must either deny that happiness is contemplation (the manifestation of theoretical wisdom) in any straightforward sense (the Monist Constraint), or deny that happiness has ethically virtuous activities as parts (the Pluralist Constraint). Here is why. Suppose that the Divergence Thesis is true. If happiness is contemplation, as the Monist Constraint requires, but contemplation can occur without ethically virtuous activities, then happiness can occur without ethically virtuous activities. If happiness can occur without ethically virtuous activities, then ethically virtuous activities are not necessary parts of happiness. Therefore, on the supposition that the Divergence Thesis is true, ethically virtuous activities are not necessary parts of happiness, contra the Pluralist Constraint. (The Pluralist Constraint requires that ethically virtuous activities be necessary parts of happiness because it says that happiness *is* a composite that includes ethically virtuous activities as parts. If pluralists thought that ethically virtuous activities were not necessary parts of happiness then they would, contrary to fact, not raise the immoralist objection against monists that I mentioned in 1.3.2.) From the other direction: If ethically virtuous activities are necessary parts of happiness, as the Pluralist Constraint requires, but contemplation can occur without them, then contemplation can occur without happiness. If contemplation can occur without happiness, then it could not be true that happiness is contemplation except in a contingent predicative sense of 'is' that would be incommensurate with the aspiration to conceptual analysis on display in the Monist Constraint. Therefore, on the supposition that the Divergence Thesis is true, the Monist Constraint cannot be met while meeting the Pluralist Constraint. So, for one who believes the Divergence Thesis, that is, the claim that, for Aristotle, it is possible to possess theoretical wisdom and reliably manifest it in contemplation without possessing practical wisdom and reliably manifesting it in ethically virtuous activities, the Conjunctive Problem is unsolvable.

(2002, 48), Burger (2008, 111 and 120), Celano (2016, 36), Charles (1999, 206), Dirlmeier (1984, 501 n. 105, 30), Dirlmeier (2014, 454–455 n. 130, 1), Gadamer (1998, 39 n. 20), Gauthier and Jolif (1970, vol. 2.2, 463), Greenwood (1909, 83), Kenny (1992, 103), Keyt (1989, 18), Natali (1989, 93), Natali (2007a, 19), Nightingale (2004, 203–205), Schütrumpf (1989, 16–17), Sim (2018, 191), Thorsrud (2015, 351), and Zanatta (1986, vol. 2, 912). Current proponents of virtue epistemology who are interested in Aristotle's conception of theoretical and practical wisdom have echoed the consensus that the Divergence Thesis is correct. See, for example, Baehr (2012, 83 n. 7) and Zagzebski (1996, 211–231).

I will argue in this chapter that Aristotle does not subscribe to the Divergence Thesis. The passage about Anaxagoras and Thales in *NE* 6.7 that is commonly taken to support Divergence is better understood as reporting common, but partially mistaken, opinions that Aristotle's own account regiments and explains. We can reconstruct Aristotle's reasons for believing the contradictory opposite of the Divergence Thesis: One possesses and reliably manifests theoretical wisdom in contemplation only if one possesses and reliably manifests practical wisdom. With this impediment, the Divergence Thesis, removed, we will be one step closer to solving the Conjunctive Problem.

2.2 Aristotle's Intellectual Virtues

In order to approach the passage put forth as evidence by proponents of the Divergence Thesis, it will be best to clarify some key features of its context. In *NE* 6 Aristotle is discussing the intellectual virtues. These virtues are theoretical wisdom (*sophia*) and practical wisdom (*phronêsis*), though various praiseworthy states (perhaps virtues) may be distinguished, at least in thought, as components of these.[3] Theoretical wisdom involves correct systematic understanding of first principles (*NE* 10.7, 1177ᵃ12 – ᵇ26, 10.8, 1179ᵃ29–32), the highest causes (10.7, 1177ᵃ19–27), chiefly the prime mover. It comprises the developed capacity to grasp principles intuitively (*nous*) and the developed capacity to give scientific demonstrations (*epistêmê*) (6.7, 1141ᵃ18–20, 6.3, 1139ᵇ31–32).[4] Theoretical wisdom is manifested in contemplation (*theôria*), which manifestation is best described as reflection on systematic knowledge of first principles, the highest causes (10.7, 1177ᵃ19–27).[5]

---

[3] Prantl (1852, 10) offers a spirited argument that theoretical and practical wisdom are fundamentally the only intellectual virtues according to Aristotle. He is followed by Burnet (1900, 281), Dirlmeier (2014, 445 n. 124,8), Gauthier and Jolif (1970, vol. 2.2, 450–452), Natali (1999, 504 n. 577), Rassow (1874, 124 n. 1), Reeve (2013, 127), and Zanatta (1986, vol. 2, 902–903). Those who favor this position tend to view Aristotle's recapitulation at 6.11, 1143ᵇ14–17 as strong evidence. Zeller (1879, vol. 2.2, 649 n. 2) dissents, followed by Stewart (1892, vol. 2, 32–33), on the grounds that the five states by which the soul grasps truth (6.3, 1139ᵇ15–17), including skill (*technê*), are all praiseworthy states. But evidence against the view of Zeller and Stewart is that according to Aristotle skill is not a virtue. That is because skill is concerned with production, virtue with action, and skill, but not virtue, can manifest itself in intentional errors (6.5, 1140ᵇ3–25).

[4] Kosman (2014, 294) highlights the significance of Aristotle's description of *epistêmê* as a *hexis apodeiktikê* (6.3, 1139ᵇ31–32) as designating a capacity for the *activity* of demonstration.

[5] I discussed this description of contemplation and alternatives to it in Chapter 1, Section 3.2.1.

Practical wisdom (*phronêsis*) involves reliably grasping how to act finely in the circumstance at hand. For example, the practically wise person reliably grasps that a situation calls for being generous to her neighbor, and reliably decides to give the right amount at the right time for the sake of benefiting her neighbor rather than for some ulterior purpose. Practical wisdom includes good deliberation (*euboulia*) (6.9), good comprehension (*eusunesia*) (6.10), sympathetic consideration (*sungnômê*) (6.11, 1143^{a}19–34), and a developed capacity to grasp principles intuitively (*nous*), which Aristotle describes in perceptual terms (6.11, 1143^{a}35 – ^{b}14). Crucially, one has practical wisdom if and only if one has every practical virtue.

According to Aristotle, to have any virtue of soul in the strict sense, including theoretical and practical wisdom, is to have a capacity for reliable performance of fine activity for its own sake. Virtues of soul in the strict sense thus differ from "natural virtues" (6.13), which are aptitudes that fail to meet one of these requirements. For example, a person with natural courage might be disposed to deeds of derring-do, but perhaps without a firm grasp of what the situation calls for or without a reliable tendency to perform them for the right reasons. Unless otherwise indicated, when I discuss virtues, including theoretical and practical wisdom, I have in mind virtues of soul (rather than, say, of body) in Aristotle's strict sense (rather than natural virtues). Meeting the requirements for virtue of soul in the strict sense is extremely difficult and Aristotle knows it. As already mentioned, having theoretical wisdom requires comprehensive grasp of first principles (6.7, 1141^{a}18) and correctness about invariable things (6.6, 1141^{a}2–4), such as the prime mover and the celestial order. Anyone with practical wisdom is insusceptible to vice and even to weakness of will (7.10, 1152^{a}6–7). Clearly, then, having theoretical wisdom is distinct from being able to propound ingenious explanatory systems, or even what we might call "theoretical knowledge," since those are both compatible with incompletely grasping first principles. Likewise, having practical wisdom differs from being clever, since one with cleverness could be weak-willed.

The distinctive characteristic of the practically wise person is to make reliably good deliberative decisions (*prohaireseis*) that are executed in fine activity (*eupraxia*). Since decisions have fine activity as their proper aim (6.2, 1139^{a}31 – ^{b}4), to decide well about performing activities is to decide to perform fine activities. Reliably deciding upon and performing fine activities requires a stable capacity to do so, which capacity Aristotle says is practical wisdom (6.5, 1140^{b}4–5, 20–21). Practical wisdom, moreover, is concerned with coordinating and performing these fine activities in such a way as to live well in general and to attain the highest human good achievable in action (6.5, 1140ᵃ28, 6.7, 1141ᵇ12–14). In short, it is concerned with the performance of the fine activities that make one happy (6.12, 1143ᵇ19–21), where such performance is contingent, indeed voluntary.

Can the aim associated with theoretical wisdom, contemplation, be reliably achieved without those associated with practical wisdom? According to proponents of the Divergence Thesis, the answer is "yes": One can have theoretical wisdom and reliably manifest it in contemplation without having and reliably manifesting practical wisdom. Proponents of the Divergence Thesis rely on a single passage for support. This passage appears to claim that one can have theoretical wisdom without practical wisdom and to give a reason why (6.7, 1141ᵇ2–16). But the evidential value of this passage fades away on closer inspection. Section 3 presents a close reading of it that shows that the claim at issue is a report of others' opinions that Aristotle does not fully endorse, but the appeal of which he wants to explain, and that he takes the alleged reason for the claim to support a much weaker thesis.[6] The purported evidence for Divergence, then, does not in fact support it. Section 4 adduces textual evidence for the contradictory opposite of the Divergence Thesis. Aristotle thinks that reliably manifesting practical wisdom is necessary for reliably manifesting theoretical wisdom and furnishes the ingredients of an explanation for why this is so.

2.3 Apparent Evidence for Divergence

The passage that allegedly suggests Divergence is this:

T1 (*NE* 6.7, 1141ᵇ2–16)

> (1) It is clear from what has been said that theoretical wisdom (*sophia*) is a combination of the capacity to give scientific demonstrations (*epistêmê*) and the capacity to grasp principles intuitively (*nous*) concerning things that are by nature most worthwhile. (2) That is why people say (*phasin*) that

---

[6] Walker (2018, 212–214) also thinks that the passage reports others' opinions that Aristotle does not fully endorse, but for a different reason. Walker addresses neither the Divergence Thesis nor how this passage bears on it. His concern is instead to rebut the initial impression that Aristotle thinks that the theoretical knowledge that Anaxagoras and Thales possess is useless for guiding their practical deliberations and actions. My thoughts about this passage are closer to the brief remark of Kraut (1993, 370 n. 4) in his review of Broadie (1991), where he says that Aristotle need not be committed to agreeing with the report about Anaxagoras and Thales, but rather to the claim that "whether they had this virtue or not, we can learn something about the distinction between practical and theoretical wisdom by noticing that the latter virtue but not the former is attributed to them."

Anaxagoras and Thales and others like them have theoretical but not practical wisdom whenever they see them as ignorant of what is to their own advantage, and say that they know things that are extraordinary, marvelous, difficult, and divine, but also unprofitable (*achrêsta*), since they do not seek human goods. (3) Now, practical wisdom (*phronêsis*) is concerned with human things, specifically those things about which it is possible to deliberate. (4) For we say (*phamen*) that the characteristic activity of the practically wise person is most of all to deliberate well, and nobody deliberates about things that cannot possibly be otherwise, or about things that fail to have as an end a good achievable in action. (5) Now, the one who deliberates well without qualification is the one who aims in accordance with reason at those things that are the best for a human being among those achievable in action. (6) Neither is practical wisdom concerned with universals only, but rather it must also recognize particulars since it is concerned with action and action is concerned with particulars.

This passage is standardly interpreted as offering examples of people (Anaxagoras and Thales) who exhibit theoretical, but not practical, wisdom, and giving the reason why such examples are possible: Each kind of wisdom is concerned with different things.[7] However, there is good reason to doubt the standard interpretation. Sentence (2) seems to refer to the opinions of others, the appeal of which Aristotle's own account will explain. He reports what people say (*phasin*) about Anaxagoras and Thales in sentence (2). Aristotle customarily treats others' opinions as data that a developed theory will regiment, systematize, or modify. The final theory is typically not identical with the sum of the contents of these opinions, but rather explains their allure. The chief point of this report of others' opinions, indicated by the scope of 'that is why' in sentence (2), is to cite an opinion harmonizing with the definition of theoretical wisdom in sentence (1), specifically the part that says that theoretical wisdom is concerned with what is "most worthwhile." The appeal of the opinion about Anaxagoras and Thales is seen by recognizing that theoretical and practical wisdom are concerned with different things, a claim for which Aristotle argues in sentences (3)–(6). Theoretical wisdom is concerned with things that are by nature most worthwhile. This explains why people say that Anaxagoras

---

[7] Albertus Magnus (*Ethica* 6.2.22.439[b]), Aquinas (*Quaestio Disputata de Virtutibus Cardinalibus* 2 ad 8), Burger (2008, 111 and 120), Celano (2016, 36), Charles (1999, 206), Dirlmeier (2014, 454–455 n. 130,1), Gadamer (1998, 39 n. 20), Gauthier and Jolif (1970, vol. 2.2, 463), Kenny (1992, 103), Natali (1989, 93), Nightingale (2004, 203–205), Thorsrud (2015, 351), and Zanatta (1986, vol. 2, 912) say that Aristotle means Anaxagoras and Thales to be such examples. Of these, Aquinas says most explicitly that one can have theoretical without practical wisdom "because they are concerned with different kinds of things."

and Thales know things that are extraordinary, and so on, even if such things have no obvious connection to practical affairs. The point in which Aristotle is interested is that something can be extraordinary, and so on, without being something with which practical wisdom is characteristically concerned. Granted this point, Aristotle can claim that his contention in this passage, namely that theoretical and practical wisdom are concerned with different things, harmonizes with others' opinions.[8] Now, Aristotle thinks that if x and y are concerned with different things, they are distinct at least in account, if not in number. This passage, then, supports his view that theoretical and practical wisdom are virtues that are distinct at least in account.

Notice, however, that Aristotle does not need to endorse all of sentence (2) in order to make the point that theoretical and practical wisdom are distinct states. Specifically, the claim that one can have theoretical wisdom without having practical wisdom is significantly stronger than the claim that each sort of wisdom is concerned with different things. The latter claim is the only new claim that Aristotle needs in order to argue that they are distinct states. This is because of his general account of virtue-individuation, which is that virtues are defined by their activities and the things with which they are concerned (4.2, 1122^{b}1–2).[9] He can make his argument without claiming that it is possible to have theoretical wisdom without practical wisdom.

Another reason for regarding the claims in sentence (2) that would favor the Divergence Thesis as expressing only the opinion of others is that Aristotle elsewhere disbelieves these claims. Sentence (2) includes the following claims:

i. Anaxagoras and Thales "know things that are extraordinary, marvelous, difficult, and divine."
ii. Anaxagoras and Thales have theoretical wisdom.
iii. Anaxagoras and Thales are "ignorant of what is to their own advantage" and their knowledge is "unprofitable."
iv. Anaxagoras and Thales lack practical wisdom.

---

[8] It is after introducing the difference in the things with which theoretical and practical wisdom are concerned that Aristotle says "we say." The fact that he distinguishes between the first and third person forms of the verb across (4) and (2), respectively, is some evidence that he is careful here about which view is whose, though neither form of the verb would have decided the issue on its own.

[9] See also *De anima* 2.4, 415^{a}16–22 for the account of how to individuate psychic powers in general.

Those whose opinions Aristotle cites believe (i)–(iv), evidently inferring (ii) from (i) and (iv) from (iii). There is no reason to doubt that Aristotle believes (i) and (iv), but he elsewhere denies (ii) and (iii). He can coherently do so because on his view (i) is not sufficient for (ii) and (iii) is not necessary for (iv). He denies (ii) because having theoretical wisdom in his strict sense involves being correct about what the first principles are (*NE* 6.7, 1141ª18) and precludes being deceived about invariable things (6.6, 1141ª2–4). But Anaxagoras and Thales both fail in this regard, for they are mistaken about first principles and the nature of invariable things (*Phys.* 3.4, 203ª16 – ᵇ15, *DC* 2.13, 294ª28 – ᵇ30, *Metaph.* 1.3, 983ᵇ6 – 984ᵇ22). So, they could be theoretically wise in a loose, popular sense, but not in Aristotle's strict sense. A proponent of the Divergence Thesis might think that if these philosophers fail Aristotle's strict official criteria for having theoretical wisdom, then the criteria are too strict: Aristotle does not really hold to the criteria and is getting a bit carried away when he announces them. I respond that denying that Aristotle means what he so explicitly says will be a significant cost for the standard interpretation that mine avoids.

Not only does Aristotle deny the part of sentence (2), namely (ii), that says that Anaxagoras and Thales have theoretical wisdom, but he also denies (iii) of sentence (2), at least in the case of Thales, the part that says that Anaxagoras and Thales are ignorant of their own advantage and that their knowledge is unprofitable:[10]

T2 (*Pol.* 1.11, 1259ª9–18)

> People reproached [Thales of Miletus] for his poverty, claiming that philosophy was useless. According to the story, he realized from his astronomical research that there would be a good olive harvest. While it was still winter and he had a little money to spare, he put down deposits for all of the olive presses in Miletus and Chios, procuring them for a low price because nobody outbid him. But when the time of the harvest came, and many people sought the presses suddenly and simultaneously, he rented them out at whatever price he wished. He made a lot of money, thus demonstrating that it is easy for philosophers to become rich if they wish, but this is not their real ambition.

---

[10] Walker (2018, 212–214) also thinks that Aristotle denies (iii) of sentence (2) and cites the same passage that I cite as evidence. However, as already mentioned, he does not discuss the Divergence Thesis, but rather is interested in this passage because of its connection to the question of whether practical thought depends on theoretical thought.

Aristotle here recounts how Thales created a profitable olive-press monopoly precisely by using the knowledge that some had ridiculed as useless (ᵃ9). Aristotle expresses no doubt that the story is true, but stresses that Thales's success is to be regarded as an example of a general phenomenon, profiting through a monopoly, of which he provides a further instance in the lines that follow. The important point for now is that Aristotle is aware that many doubted the utility and profitability of Thales's astronomical researches and thinks them mistaken in doing so, even though he thinks that Thales lacks practical wisdom. It is therefore unlikely that he would endorse (iii) of sentence (2). Rather, he wants to show how his view explains why sentence (2) might have seemed appealing in its entirety to those who endorse it.

The Divergence Thesis has it that, in the passage about Anaxagoras and Thales, Aristotle commits himself to the claim that one can have theoretical wisdom without practical wisdom in the strict sense of each. As we have seen, though, he here commits himself only to the much weaker claim that they are not the same virtue (since they are concerned with different things).

One might think that the point that interpreters standardly try to extract from the passage about Anaxagoras and Thales can still be gotten from *NE* 6.2, where Aristotle says:[11]

> Of the kind of reason (*dianoia*) that is theoretical rather than practical or productive the good and the bad are truth and falsity, for this is the work (*ergon*) of everything dianoetic. But of that which is practical and dianoetic it is truth in agreement with correct desire. (1139ᵃ27–31)

This passage is notoriously mysterious, and the ordering of the surrounding text uncertain (Greenwood, 1909, 174–175), but one might suppose that it supports the following argument:

1. The work (*ergon*) of theoretical reason, truth, is separable from the work of practical reason.
2. Since something's virtue depends on its work (1139ᵃ17), theoretical reason's virtue is also separable from that of practical reason.

---

[11] Thanks to Gabriel Richardson Lear for discussion of this point.

3. Since theoretical reason's virtue is theoretical wisdom and practical
    reason's is practical wisdom, theoretical wisdom is separable from
    practical wisdom.
∴ The Divergence Thesis is true.

Such an argument trades on unclarity about the kind of separability at issue and about what things are supposed to be separable from one another.[12]
Aristotle recognizes multiple ways of being separable (*chôriston*). The two
most relevant for current purposes are the capacity for separate existence
and separability in essence.[13] As an example of the former, Aristotle says
that a Platonic Form of the Good is supposed to exist separately from particular good things, such that it can exist without them (1.6, 1096^{b}33).[14]
An example of the latter is that general justice and the whole of virtue
are separate in essence, though they cannot exist separately (5.1, 1130^{a}12).
The same goes for practical wisdom and political wisdom (6.8, 1141^{b}23–
24).[15] The argument above for the Divergence Thesis requires Aristotle to
have the capacity for separate existence in view in the passage quoted, but
there is no evidence that he does. He more likely means that the work of
theoretical reason, and therefore its virtue, is distinct from that of practical reason in some weaker way, for example, definable without reference
to desire, unlike the work, and therefore the virtue, of practical reason.[16]
The passage about Anaxagoras and Thales, we have already seen, supports
the claim that theoretical and practical wisdom are distinct virtues. If in
the argument above we substitute 'distinct,' 'separable in essence,' 'separable in account,' or other designations that do not entail the capacity for
separate existence, the conclusion clearly does not follow. Furthermore,

---

[12] Aristotle does not speak explicitly of separability in the passage. It is left implicit that there is a
   distinction of some sort between the work of theoretical and practical reason. Formulating the argument in terms of separability gives us the best chance of appreciating why such an argument might
   have initially seemed plausible to those who would use this passage as evidence for the Divergence
   Thesis.

[13] Peramatzis (2011) discusses the difference between these kinds of separability in detail. See also Reece
   (ms.).

[14] Fine (1984) provides an extensive treatment of this kind of separability.

[15] Jagannathan (2019) offers a thorough discussion of the relationship between practical and political
   wisdom.

[16] Note that by saying this I am not committed to Aristotle thinking that the relation between theoretical reason and practical reason is like that between general justice and the whole of virtue, or
   between practical and political wisdom, in any respect other than being separable in a way that
   underpins definitional distinctness but not the capacity for separate existence. For further examples
   of such separability and the subtle differences between them, see Irwin (1988, 582–583 n. 21).

even if it is possible to get theoretical truth without getting practical truth, this would not be tantamount to having and reliably manifesting theoretical wisdom in reflection on a systematic grasp of first principles without getting practical truth. For these reasons, I do not think that 6.2 motivates the Divergence Thesis.

In the next section, I will show why, for Aristotle, one cannot have theoretical wisdom without practical wisdom.

2.4   The Connection between Theoretical and Practical Wisdom

The standard interpretation of the passage about Anaxagoras and Thales has prevented commentators from appreciating textual evidence that Aristotle regards practical wisdom as necessary for theoretical wisdom. On his view, practical wisdom is manifested in acting rightly and nobly, and at the end of *NE* 10.8 he tells us that the theoretically wise person acts rightly and nobly most of all:

T3 (*NE* 10.8, 1179^{a}22–32)

> (1) The one who is active in accordance with intellect (*nous*) and attends to it seems to be both in the best condition and most loved by the gods. (2) For if the gods in some way care about human affairs, as they are thought to do, then it would be reasonable to suppose both that they delight in what is best and most akin to them, namely intellect (*nous*), and that they benefit those who most love and honor this, for caring for the things that the gods love and acting both rightly (*orthôs*) and nobly (*kalôs*). (3) It is clear that all of these attributes belong most of all (*malista*) to the person with theoretical wisdom (*sophos*). (4) This person, therefore, is the one most loved by the gods. (5) This same one is likely also to be happiest. (6) So, in this way, too, the person with theoretical wisdom (*sophos*) will more than any other be happy.

Sentence (3) of this passage indicates that acting rightly and nobly, an attribute listed in sentence (2), is something that belongs to the theoretically wise person *most of all.* Such a person is preeminent in acting rightly and nobly. But since so acting is the characteristic aim of practical wisdom, this could not belong to anyone *most of all* if that person fell short of reliably acting in accordance with practical wisdom. Anyone who could manage to act rightly and nobly without reliably acting in accordance with practical wisdom would still not do so to the extent that one who reliably acts in accordance with practical wisdom does, and therefore would not act rightly and nobly most of all.[17] So, the theoretically wise person must reliably act in accordance with practical wisdom.[18]

A fragment of Aristotle's *Protrepticus* contains a very similar point to that made in sentences (2)–(3). In a discussion of the significance of the philosopher having his eyes fixed on what is divine, he says that "to the philosopher alone among craftspeople belong laws that are stable and *actions that are right and noble*" (ap. Iamblichus, *Protrepticus* ch. 10, 55.24–25).[19] Here, as above, the idea is that it is peculiarly characteristic of philosophers, those who in virtue of theoretical wisdom approximate the divine as closely as possible, to act rightly (*orthôs*) and nobly (*kalôs*). Devereux (2014, 163–164) argues on the basis of this passage and its context that at the time of writing the *Protrepticus* Aristotle believed that theoretical and practical wisdom, though distinct states, are biconditionally related. However, as is standard, Devereux (2014, 167–168) believes that Aristotle denies this in the *NE*. He does not address the striking similarity between the *Protrepticus* passage and sentences (2)–(3) of T3.[20]

---

[17] One might argue that Aristotle here means simply to affirm that contemplation is the activity that is most *kalon* (noble, fine), and being *kalon* need not have any particular relationship to being ethically virtuous. However, he uses 'καὶ ὀρθῶς τε καὶ καλῶς πράττοντας,' emphasizing that the theoretically wise person *acts* rightly *and* nobly most of all. The connection with *praxis* and the conjunction of 'rightly' and 'nobly' make it unlikely that Aristotle here refers to some non-ethical kind of nobility. I know of only two other passages in which he explicitly connects acting, rightness, and nobility in this way: 4.1, 1120ᵃ24–25 and the passage that I will discuss in the next paragraph of the main text. In both of those cases, it is clear from the context that he has in mind ethical rightness and nobility. Thanks to Timothy Roche for helpful discussion of this point.

[18] Commentators have tended to neglect this implication of the passage, focusing instead on the important and puzzling theological issues raised therein, of which Aufderheide (2020, 224–227) and Zanatta (1986, vol. 2, 1112–1113 n. 11) have useful summaries. Broadie (2003), for example, devotes most of her paper to an analysis of this passage, but says nothing about the aspect of it that I discuss. I will address such theological issues in Chapter 4. (In short, my position on the theological remarks in this passage is as follows: These remarks are endoxic. But, as Aristotle sometimes does, he here embeds a point made in his own voice within an *endoxon*, showing that his view can vindicate an important part of that *endoxon* even if not the whole. In this case, the core of the *endoxon* that he deems worth saving is that the godlike person exhibits what is in fact the most divine sort of activity, which has turned out to be contemplation, as well as standardly recognized markers of piety, namely acting rightly and nobly. Those who hold the *endoxon* did not recognize that the most divine sort of activity is contemplation as Aristotle specifies it. Neither did they have in view a systematic account of virtue that would enable them to explain in Aristotle's preferred way what it is to act rightly and nobly. They were right that divine activity and standardly recognized markers of piety are concomitant – this is the part of the passage in which I am interested – but their mistaken theology gave them the wrong explanation for their concomitance. Thanks to Anthony Price for discussion of this passage.) The Byzantine commentator Michael of Ephesus (*In EN* 604.1–10) is a rare exception, though even he does not say much about the overall significance of this point for the relationship between theoretical and practical wisdom.

[19] The Greek for the part that I italicize is "πράξεις εἰσὶν ὀρθαὶ καὶ καλαί."

[20] According to Hutchinson and Johnson (2014, 401–407) *everything* in *NE* 10.7–8 is recycled from *Protrepticus* except the lines that open 10.8, which I will discuss in the next chapter, and 1179ᵃ17–22, the lines that immediately precede T3.

T3, like the *Protrepticus* passage, supports not only the claim that theoretical wisdom requires practical wisdom, but also the claim that practical wisdom requires theoretical wisdom. The view expressed in T3 is that the theoretically wise person is the same as the one who acts rightly and nobly most of all, and we know from Aristotle's descriptions of practical wisdom and ethical virtue that the practically wise person is the same as the one who acts rightly and nobly most of all. So, according to Aristotle in the *NE*, theoretical and practical wisdom belong to the same people. The claim that practical wisdom requires theoretical wisdom is worth highlighting and explaining, though I will do so only briefly since various commentators have already defended it.[21]

First, consider the fact that one who would deny that practical wisdom requires theoretical wisdom is in the following awkward position: Such a one must suppose, since according to T3 the theoretically wise person acts rightly and nobly most of all, that there is a practically wise person who falls short, for some reason of cognition or character, of acting rightly and nobly most of all. This reason could not be practical wisdom itself, or practical wisdom would be the cause of somehow not acting rightly and nobly, which is absurd. If practical wisdom is not the reason for his failure, then the failure cannot be one about cognizing practical particulars, for practical wisdom involves excellent cognition of practical particulars. The failure also cannot be due to a deficiency in character, for the practically wise person has none. What about a deficiency in *epistêmê*, *nous*, or supposition of practical universals? That would make him wicked (3.1, 1110^{b}28 – 1111^{a}2). What about a failure in *epistêmê* and/or *nous* of non-practical universals? Now one begs the question, for those are what theoretical wisdom involves. In short, what Aristotle says about practical and theoretical wisdom makes it difficult to explain coherently how the practically wise person could fail to meet the description of the theoretically wise person given in T3 as the one who acts rightly and nobly most of all.

As I mentioned above, according to Devereux (2014) Aristotle is committed in the *NE* to denying that practical wisdom requires theoretical wisdom. This, Devereux alleges, is a striking departure from his view in

---

[21] See, for example, Broadie (1991, 389), Baracchi (2007, 209–214), Walker (2018, esp. 212–214), and Wood (2011). Müller (2020) argues for the weaker thesis that, given Aristotle's oft-repeated principle that nature does nothing in vain, there can be no organism endowed with practical reason but not theoretical reason. If, as Müller thinks, practical reason has scope to go drastically awry precisely *because of* facts about theoretical reason, one could, with a few added premises, argue that theoretical reason's excellent condition is necessary for one whose practical reason, like that of the practically wise person's, lacks scope to go drastically awry.

the *Protrepticus* and *Eudemian Ethics*. He argues that in both of those texts Aristotle holds the two kinds of wisdom distinct, as he does in the *NE*, but thinks that they are biconditionally related. Devereux's putative evidence for thinking that in the *NE* Aristotle no longer believes that practical wisdom requires theoretical wisdom comes from the passage that begins *NE* 10.8. That passage will be the subject of my next chapter, so I will not go into detail here. As I mentioned in Chapter 1, Aristotle in that passage appears to distinguish between two kinds of happiness, one in accordance with theoretical intellect and the other in accordance with practical virtue. If there is a kind of happiness that accords with practical virtue but not with theoretical intellect, Devereux thinks, then it is possible to have practical wisdom without theoretical wisdom. I will argue in the next chapter that Aristotle does not in fact distinguish between two kinds of happiness. *That* distinction is an artifact of a translation of a word that does not occur in the Greek. Aristotle draws a different distinction, one that supports, rather than undermines, the claim that practical wisdom requires theoretical wisdom. That explanation will have to wait. For now, I want to point out that it would be awkward for Aristotle to imply, as Devereux thinks that he does, in the first part of 10.8 that the claim is false, and then presuppose, as I have argued that he does, later in 10.8, namely T3, that the claim is true. It is one thing to argue that Aristotle's view changes between different works, but quite another to allege that it does so over the course of 10.8. The weight of contradiction is simply too much for a non-existent word (at the beginning of 10.8) to bear. It is unfortunate that Devereux does not address T3, despite its very close similarity to the *Protrepticus* passage that he uses as his evidence for Aristotle's view in that work. I will now mention some of the reasons why Aristotle would affirm in T3, as he does in the *Protrepticus* and *EE*, the claim that practical wisdom requires theoretical wisdom. This part of the discussion will overlap partially with some of Wood's (2011) arguments.

Recall from earlier in this chapter that practical wisdom is concerned with coordinating and performing fine activities in such a way as to attain the highest human good achievable in action (6.5, 1140^a28, 6.7, 1141^b12–14). In other words, it is concerned with the voluntary performance of the fine activities that make one happy (6.12, 1143^b19–21). If one fails to perform the fine activities that make one happy, or botches their coordination, with the result that the highest good achievable in human action is not attained, then one has missed that at which practical wisdom aims. Fine activities include not only ethically virtuous activities, but also theoretical wisdom's manifestation, contemplation, which Aristotle explicitly calls "*eupraxia*" (*Pol.* 7.3, 1325^{b}14–23). But contemplation is not just any sort of *eupraxia*; it is either the highest human good achievable in action or at least a part of it (*NE* 1.7, 1098^{a}16–18, 1.8, 1099^{a}29–31, 6.7, 1141^{a}16–22, 6.13, 1145^{a}6–11, 10.7, 1177^{a}12–21). Practical wisdom cannot coordinate fine activities in such a way as to attain the highest human good achievable in action without this particular kind of fine activity occurring.[22] It is for this reason that practical wisdom "provides for theoretical wisdom's emergence" and "prescribes for its sake" (6.13, 1145^{a}6–9). The aims associated with practical wisdom, then, cannot be reliably achieved without achieving theoretical contemplation.

According to Aristotle, one is good (*agathon*) if and only if one is practically wise (*phronimos*) (6.12, 1144^{a}36 – 1144^{b}1, 6.13, 1144^{b}30–32). The good (*agathon*) and wise (*emphrona*) person is always (*aei*) such as to act (*prattein*) in the noblest (*kallista*) ways (1.10, 1100^{b}35 – 1101^{a}3). Since the good person and the practically wise person are the same, the practically wise person is always such as to act in the noblest ways. This makes it very difficult to deny that the practically wise person is most of all such as to act rightly and nobly, which is what T3 affirms of the theoretically wise person.

Furthermore, Aristotle tells us that the practically wise person enjoys, loves, and hates correctly (10.1, 1172^{a}21–26; *Pol.* 8.5, 1340^{a}14–18). One could hardly be a comprehensive "lover of the noble," as the practically virtuous person is said to be (*NE* 1.8, 1099^{a}7–26), if one did not enjoy and love the most noble things, which Aristotle says are precisely those eternal, invariable things with which theoretical wisdom is concerned.[23] But enjoying and loving eternal, invariable things is not something that practical wisdom can do, for it is concerned with variable things. So, the practically wise person must have a theoretical ability that involves enjoying and loving eternal, invariable, noble things correctly. This ability is theoretical wisdom.[24]

---

[22] This is not like saying that you cannot be courageous or generous if your action fails to achieve the intended external result. In those cases, but precisely not in the case of contemplation, the good external result of the action is at least part of what the agent intends in performing it. On external results and the aims of virtuous actions, see for example, Brown (2006, 249–252), Heinaman (1993), Hirji (2018), Jimenez (2016), Müller (2018, 168–175), and Whiting (2002).

[23] One might allege that Aristotle's claims about enjoying and loving the noble are meant to be restricted to the domain of variable particulars. That would be ad hoc, though, since nothing about Aristotle's remarks suggests such a restriction.

[24] This has some similarities with one of Wood's (2011) arguments, according to which the practically wise person's grasp of how it is best to act in the circumstance depends on his grasp of invariable principles, such as the nature of the noble. He says: "Such principles are certainly practically

These are some of the reasons for which Aristotle would think, as T3 reveals that he does, that practical wisdom implies theoretical wisdom. Even if Devereux's (2014) interpretation of the beginning of *NE* 10.8 were correct, it would not undermine these reasons. Neither would it undermine the reason that Aristotle gives in *EE* 8.3, 1249^{b}16–21, namely that anything less than what most of all (*malista*) brings about the contemplation (*theôria*) of the god is base (*phaulê*), a designation most uncharacteristic of the practically wise person. But one might think that Devereux could martial more textual evidence in his favor: Perhaps Aristotle regards Pericles as a counterexample, someone who might appear to be practically wise (6.5, 1140^{b}7–10) even while – let us suppose, though Aristotle does not comment – lacking theoretical wisdom. But there is no reason to believe that Aristotle takes him to have practical wisdom in his full technical sense, for that requires having all of the ethical virtues.[25] *Politics* 2.12, 1273^{b}28 – 1274^{a}22 and *Athenian Constitution* 27, like Plato's *Gorgias* 515E – 516D, represent Pericles as having introduced conditions that predictably made the Athenians more susceptible to a degenerate democracy that featured bribery and other such problems. Aristotle does not follow Plato's Socrates as far as saying that Pericles was a bad politician, but there is more reason to suppose that Aristotle shared at least some of his hesitation about Pericles than there is to interpret him as lauding Pericles as a possessor of every ethical virtue. It is plausible that Aristotle's point in bringing up Pericles is far more limited, namely to warm his audience up for the idea that practical wisdom extends more widely than does cleverness in achieving aims peculiar to oneself or to a specific domain of one's own affairs.

I have been discussing the implication of T3 that practical wisdom requires theoretical wisdom. I now return to my argument for the converse. Aristotle claims in T3 that the theoretically wise person most of all acts rightly and nobly, which is what the practically wise person does. He expresses a similar idea in *NE* 6.12, though it requires more unpacking to see:

---

relevant in the sense that they are meant to bear on action and guide practical reasoning, but in themselves they are not practical, because as unchanging principles they are grasped by the scientific faculty and need not have any practical application at all. Aristotle repeatedly reminds his readers (or auditors) that they *should* be put into practice precisely because it is possible to grasp them *without* putting them into practice, which is to say, merely 'theoretically' (cf. I.3, 1095a5–6; II.2, 1103b27–29)." (Wood, 2011, 401, emphasis in original)

[25] See Irwin (2019, 280) and Kraut (1993, 370 n. 4), who distance Aristotle from the remark about Pericles and portray it as endoxic, as well as Reeve (2013, 158–159), who argues more fully that Pericles does *not* have practical wisdom in Aristotle's full technical sense.

T4 (*NE* 6.12, 1144^{a}3–9)

> (1) Next, [theoretical and practical wisdom] do produce something: theoretical wisdom (*sophia*) produces happiness not in the way that the art of medicine produces health, but rather in the way that health produces health. (2) For since it is part of the whole of virtue it makes [one happy by being possessed and activated (*energein*).]^{26} (3) Furthermore, our work (*ergon*) is performed in accordance with practical wisdom and with ethical virtue. (4) For virtue makes the aim correct, and practical wisdom what conduces to it.

Disputes abound regarding sentence (4) of this passage, and to some extent regarding sentences (1)–(2), but sentence (3) has received far less attention. Since Aristotle regards the manifestation of theoretical wisdom in contemplation as our work (*ergon*), or at least part of it, sentence (3) of this passage implies that the manifestation of theoretical wisdom is in accordance with practical wisdom and with ethical virtue.^{27} This should not surprise us, since shortly after giving the *ergon* argument he insists that his theory of happiness can vindicate the claims that happiness accords with theoretical wisdom and that it accords with practical wisdom (1.8, 1098^{b}22–25).^{28} If this is the correct interpretation of T4, there is a straightforward explanation for its correctness, namely the same as that which I have given for T3: The theoretically wise person must reliably act in accordance with practical wisdom because attaining the characteristic aim of theoretical wisdom requires attaining that of practical wisdom.^{29}

So far in this section I have argued that, contrary to the Divergence Thesis, Aristotle thinks that theoretical wisdom requires practical wisdom. But more remains to be said about Aristotle's reasons for this. What is it about theoretical wisdom that makes practical wisdom relevant in this way?

---

^{26} The part of the translation of sentence (2) enclosed in square brackets, which translation is standard, corresponds to Greek marked by the OCT as corrupt.

^{27} Some doubt that the manifestation of theoretical wisdom in contemplation is, or is part of, our work (*ergon*) because they doubt that the ability to contemplate is peculiar to humans. I will address these doubts directly in Chapter 4. I have already done so in Reece (2020b). One might attempt to interpret sentence (3) as saying that only a part of our work (*ergon*), the practical part, accords with practical wisdom. But then sentence (3) becomes trivial and introduces an unexplained, unmotivated scope restriction that fits poorly with sentence (2) – it is theoretical wisdom that is "part of the whole of virtue" – and with Aristotle's use of '*ergon*' in *NE* 1.7, 1098^{a}16–18.

^{28} Long (2011, 103–104) highlights the importance of this fact. See my earlier note (p. 19 n. 36) on this passage.

^{29} While there are various ways in which 'in accordance with' ('*kata*') can be used, examples of which are discussed by Walker (2018, 19–20), I require only that it here have the minimal implication that if *x* is *kata y*, then one could not act *kata x* without acting *kata y*.

We can begin to answer this question, which I will approach in two stages, by considering a passage in which he says that practical wisdom provides for theoretical wisdom's emergence:

T5 (*NE* 6.13, 1145^{a}6–11)

> But practical wisdom is not superior to theoretical wisdom or to the better part, just as medicine is not superior to health. For practical wisdom does not make use of theoretical wisdom, but rather provides for its emergence. Practical wisdom prescribes for theoretical wisdom's sake, but does not prescribe to it. Again, to say that practical wisdom is superior to theoretical wisdom would be like saying that the political craft rules the gods because it prescribes with regard to all of the affairs of the city.

I take the emergence of theoretical wisdom to be the emergence of a state that is reliably manifested in contemplation (in Aristotle's strict sense of 'contemplation' discussed above). But what does providing for such emergence involve?[30] Is it a matter of A) merely facilitating the acquisition and manifestation of theoretical wisdom, where something else might have facilitated it? Or is it rather that B) without practical wisdom humans could not acquire and manifest theoretical wisdom at all? A proponent of the Divergence Thesis must opt for (A) over (B). She must say that practical wisdom, *if it is present*, facilitates the acquisition of theoretical wisdom, but theoretical wisdom could be acquired without it. Otherwise, practical wisdom would be necessary for theoretical wisdom, which the Divergence Thesis denies. We can adjudicate between (A) and (B) by answering two questions:

1.   What necessary concomitants of theoretical wisdom does practical wisdom provide *when practical wisdom is present*?
2.   Could anything that can be present without practical wisdom, such as mere cleverness or mere strength of will (*enkrateia*), provide them?[31]

---

[30]   If x provides for y's emergence, this does not imply that x is fully present and active in temporal precedence to y. It may be, for example, that their emergence is contemporaneous and x, as it emerges, facilitates y's emergence. It is in this sense that practical wisdom provides for the emergence of justice, and temperance for the emergence of courage, but none of these is present in its full form without the others. Aristotle describes situations of this kind in *NE* 2.4 and 6.13. Thanks to an anonymous referee for this point.

[31]   Charles (1999, 206 n. 1) thinks that mere cleverness would suffice. Lear (2004, 198–199) aims the question about *enkrateia* at those who think that practical virtue might somehow be instrumental for contemplation. Callard (2017) has recently argued that *enkrateia* is never present without practical wisdom. If this is right, then *enkrateia* need not be considered for answering question (2). But since most interpreters think that the enkratic lacks practical wisdom, I will operate under that assumption in this section. Cooper (1975, 164–165) believes that only a pseudo-virtue, such as a

If the answer to (2) is negative, then reliably manifesting theoretical wisdom in contemplation requires reliably manifesting practical wisdom, and the answer to (1) can help us to understand why.

I address question (1) first. Practical wisdom, when present, makes the development and manifestation of theoretical wisdom behaviorally feasible for us as embodied and socially situated beings. It allows us to manage our affairs so as to make it possible to develop theoretical wisdom and manifest it in contemplation. Recall that for Aristotle contemplation is reflection on one's firmly possessed, systematic grasp of the highest causes. One who has theoretical wisdom reliably engages in this.[32] (Keep in mind that to figure in happiness in the way that Aristotle says that it does, namely, as a manifestation of theoretical wisdom that characterizes an appropriately long life, contemplation must be reliably performed.)[33] Such reliable engagement requires reliably well-ordered passions, for one cannot reliably reflect on one's systematic grasp of the highest causes if one is apt to be distracted by fear, anger, or pleasure.[34] Aristotle says at *NE* 1.3, 1095^{a}2–8 that those who

disposition that approximates temperance in allowing one to control one's appetites just enough to make contemplation behaviorally feasible, is required. He is pressed into this position by his claim that the contemplator *cannot* have genuine ethical virtues. I take it that Cooper is assuming that it would be because of cleverness or *enkrateia* that the pseudo-virtuous person he imagines is able to control himself and figure out how to contemplate, so I will not discuss his case separately from cleverness and *enkrateia*. My argument will have the result that nothing short of genuine ethical virtue is materially sufficient for contemplation. Notice that if anything short of genuine ethical virtue were materially sufficient for contemplation, then, according to the argument that I gave at the beginning of this chapter, the Conjunctive Problem of Happiness would be unsolvable.

[32] As I mentioned (p. 31 n. 1), reliability in this context is not a matter of absolute frequency. Thanks to Gabriel Richardson Lear for discussion of this point.

[33] On this point, see especially Kraut (1989, 71–73 and 171) and Lear (2015).

[34] The author of the *Magna Moralia* 1.34, 1198^{b}9–24 explains providing for theoretical wisdom's emergence in terms of procuring leisure by keeping one's passions in order. (Inwood 2014, 31–32 comments on ways in which the *Magna Moralia* differs from the *Eudemian Ethics* and the *Nicomachean Ethics* on issues concerned with the relationship between theoretical and practical wisdom.) Michael of Ephesus (*In EN* 578.23–35) says that contemplation requires reliably well-ordered passions. Adkins (1978, 301) insists that disordered passions would distract one from contemplation. Tuozzo (1995, 145) thinks that ethically virtuous actions secure leisure for contemplation by "effecting an absence of action-oriented passion." The point made by these authors by itself does not answer question (2) and therefore does not adjudicate between (A) and (B). Halper (1999) argues that any virtuous activity, including contemplation, requires that all of one's passions be well-ordered, and therefore requires what he calls "psychic virtue" but not "proper virtue." "Proper virtues" are individuated by actions of a particular type (generosity, for example, is a settled disposition to perform generous actions knowingly, reliably, and for the right reason), and are the virtues standardly recognized as being Aristotle's focus, whereas "psychic virtue," a lower grade, is a matter not of performing actions of a particular type but rather of having all of one's passions in order. Thus, one could exhibit "psychic magnanimity," for example, by *refraining* from magnanimous action provided that one's passions are in order (141). For Halper, having "psychic virtue" is necessary and sufficient for having practical wisdom of a weak sort, which can be developed through the exercise of only one proper virtue. One could perform properly generous actions, say, and have all of

act in accordance with passions, whether they do so because they are young or merely because they are immature, are not equipped for the systematic study of political science. Such study is not the same as contemplation, but the reasons are similar for regarding unregulated passions as disruptive to both. *NE* 6.5, 1140^{b}11–19 argues that the person who is temperate, and therefore also has practical wisdom, is guarded against the distorting effects of pleasure and pain on one's perception of what is to be done and for what reason. The point is that, for Aristotle, unregulated passions impede one's access to truth, whether theoretical or practical, in part because they pervert our conception of what is important and worthy of attention. In the case of theoretical truth, the welter of pleasures and pains associated with unregulated passions is incompatible with the "marvelously pure and stable" pleasure that is a necessary concomitant of reflection on the highest principles (10.7, 1177^{a}22–27).

Practical wisdom, when present, makes contemplation behaviorally feasible because it involves having well-regulated passions. Now we turn to question (2): Could this be true not only of practical wisdom, but also of mere cleverness, *enkrateia*, or anything short of virtue? Not according to Aristotle, who thinks that the best good is apparent only to the person who has practical wisdom (6.12, 1144^{a}29–36). Recall that according to T3, the theoretically wise person, the one who engages in contemplation in Aristotle's technical sense, acts rightly and nobly most of all. But it is false that the merely clever person and the enkratic person act rightly and nobly most of all, for there is one who is more excellent in this respect than they are: the practically wise person. Since the theoretically wise person has a property that merely clever or enkratic people necessarily lack, they cannot be the same. But *why* does Aristotle think that acting rightly and nobly most of all, as the person with practical wisdom does and those who are merely clever or enkratic do not, is required for manifesting theoretical wisdom? In saying why, rather than merely reporting that, he thinks this, some of the details must involve speculative reconstruction.

one's passions in order, but never perform (or even be capable of performing) properly courageous or temperate actions, and this would suffice for practical wisdom in Halper's sense (142). So, Halper would deny that having theoretical wisdom in the strict sense requires having practical wisdom in the strict sense, if practical wisdom in the strict sense is biconditionally related to virtues individuated with reference to actions of a particular type (which I and most others think that it is). His position on this issue is motivated by the view that Aristotle's commitment to the reciprocity of practical wisdom and all of the ethical virtues is misguided if practical wisdom and ethical virtue are understood in their strict and proper senses, but not misguided if they are understood in Halper's more permissive way. Neither Halper nor the other authors leverage the aforementioned points to argue against the Divergence Thesis.

The clever person has the deliberative abilities to discover means conducive to his ends, so there is perhaps some reason to think him capable of effective management of his affairs. However, the merely clever person can be weak-willed, succumbing to base appetites or wild passions (7.10, 1152ª10). Cleverness, then, does not involve the sort of regulation of passions that is required for contemplation's behavioral feasibility. What about *enkrateia*? It is an action-type that involves standing by the result of one's deliberations under the influence of strong passions. Interpreters disagree about whether it is also a stable condition, such that one could *habitually* resist strong passions in this way.[35] If it is not stable, then *enkrateia* could not, like practical wisdom, make reliable contemplation behaviorally feasible by properly regulating the passions. Even if it is stable, Aristotle might think that persistently having bad appetites and strong passions, as a stable enkratic would, even if one does not in the end act to satisfy them, would be sufficiently disruptive to forestall the development and reliable manifestation of theoretical wisdom in contemplation.[36] These might impede one's concentration, absorb one's time and other resources in efforts to overcome them, or prevent one from taking the sort of "marvelously pure and stable" pleasure (unmingled with the pain that the enkratic experiences in acting against appetite according to *EE* 2.8, 1224ª33–36) in reflection on the highest principles that necessarily attends contemplation in Aristotle's strict sense (*NE* 10.7, 1177ª22–27).[37] So, it is far from clear that *enkrateia* could involve, as practical wisdom does, passions reliably well-ordered in such a way as to make contemplation feasible. Indeed, Aristotle argues in *Politics* 7–8 that a contemplative life requires properly managed leisure, which in turn requires temperance to forestall inappropriate passions (7.15, 1334ª24–34). It is for this reason that he recommends that temperance be developed by training the bodily appetites through athletic activity before undertaking serious study (8.3, 1338ᵇ4–8). But since the enkratic person does not have temperance, he will not meet the standard of properly managed leisure that Aristotle proffers. Even if he did, there is

---

[35] For example, Callard (2017, 43) thinks that it is a stable condition and Woods (1986, 152) denies this.

[36] Since Aristotle does not explicitly settle the issue of whether *enkrateia* is a stable condition, he also does not explicitly pronounce on whether *enkrateia* involves stable passions that are disruptive in the way that this sentence describes. So, this is a speculative reconstruction of what Aristotle might say if we asked him to justify the position that he takes in T3 and T4 by adopting the aforementioned explanation of T5 *while assuming* that *enkrateia* is a stable condition. Thanks to an anonymous referee for urging clarity on this point.

[37] Coope (2012) argues that *enkrateia* involves a failing of the rational part of the soul, specifically a cognitive failure to appreciate fineness, that makes it incompatible with practical wisdom.

a deeper explanation of the connection between theoretical and practical wisdom that will reveal why theoretical wisdom requires nothing short of practical wisdom and genuine ethical virtue.

Before turning to the deeper explanation, I want to mention an indirect reason to favor the conclusion that contemplation requires practical wisdom, not some inferior state like cleverness or *enkrateia*. I treat this reason separately because it is indirect. Its force derives from the need that at least some will feel to resist an argument given by one who disagrees with my thesis in this chapter, namely Nightingale (2004, 220–222). I quote her summary with gaps, retaining her emphasis:

> Clearly, Aristotle wanted to argue that *theoria* is intrinsically nonutilitarian and nonproductive. But, for this to be the case, there would have to be something in the nature of *theoria* and/or the objects of theoretical thought that invariably and necessarily affects the individual in such a way that he could never choose to theorize for the wrong reasons. In other words, theoretical activity would have to have a determinate and invariable effect on the person's practical reasoning. It is not enough to say that the theorizer *should* opt to engage in this activity for the right reasons. He must necessarily do so, and this must be a direct result of the activity of contemplation. Otherwise, it would always be possible for a person to engage in *theoria* for the utilitarian purposes – to make theorizing useful instead of useless in the practical sphere... And it is always possible that a gifted theorizer may not have perfected all the practical virtues and that he will therefore approach his theoretical activities in a fashion which is not completely disinterested... *Theoria*, in sum, is not intrinsically nonutilitarian and nonproductive... Let me emphasize that Aristotle himself would have disagreed with this argument. He clearly wanted to say that *theoria* is intrinsically nonutilitarian and nonproductive – it is not just one activity among many but rather the final end of all activities (like happiness).

Nightingale is correct that Aristotle would dispute the conclusion of her argument. How would he avoid it? Since the conclusion threatens a centrally important claim of the *NE*, Aristotle urgently needs to deny a premise (assuming that Nightingale has offered a valid argument). Nightingale's textual support for the premise that, according to Aristotle, it is always possible for the contemplator to lack practical virtue comes from her interpretation of the passage about Anaxagoras and Thales. I have argued that her interpretation of that passage is incorrect, so the textual evidence for this premise is gone. If instead Aristotle believes that one cannot have theoretical wisdom and reliably manifest it in contemplation without also having practical wisdom, as I am urging, then he has an easy way out of

Nightingale's conclusion. If Nightingale's argument is valid and her other premises are true, then avoiding the anti-Aristotelian conclusion is an indirect reason to attribute to Aristotle the position that I have argued that he holds instead of the position for which the textual evidence has vanished.

I turn now to the deeper explanation of the connection between theoretical and practical wisdom that I prefigured before mentioning Nightingale's argument. Recall that theoretical wisdom is not the mere possession of a static body of knowledge, but rather a stable capacity to perform well a certain sort of *activity*, contemplation.[38] For humans, unlike for Aristotle's prime mover, performing activities requires us to do something that we might not have done or might have done differently.[39] We must decide whether, when, and how to perform them. According to Aristotle, contemplation, as a voluntarily performed activity of our theoretical intellect, implies activity of our practical intellect. Consider his discussions of voluntary activity (*NE* 3.1) and the voluntariness of contemplation (*DA* 2.5). I quote those about the latter:

DA 2.5, 417ª21–29

One must also distinguish different senses of potentiality and actuality. Just now we were speaking of them simply. One way in which something can be a knower (*epistêmon*) is that in which we would call a human a knower, because humans are within the class of beings that know and have knowledge. A second way is that in which we say directly that the one who has grammatical knowledge is a knower. Each of these has a potentiality in a different way: the one, because his genus and matter are of this kind, and the other, because he can contemplate (*theôrein*) if he wishes (*boulêtheis*),[40] provided that nothing external prevents him. A third sort of knower is the one who is already (*êdê*) contemplating (*theôrôn*), being in actuality and knowing (*epistamenos*) in the strict sense (*kuriôs*) this *A*.

---

[38] Neither of the constituents of theoretical wisdom – the capacity to grasp principles intuitively (*nous*) and the capacity for scientific demonstration (*epistêmê*) – is mere possession of a static body of knowledge. Kosman (2014, 296) emphasizes contemplation's status as an activity. Zagzebski (1996, 211–231) argues that we today should think that practical wisdom is necessary for performing intellectually virtuous activities in general because they are *activities*, though she supposes, in accordance with the Divergence Thesis, that Aristotle would have denied this.
[39] Aufderheide (2015, 54) mentions that the very fact that we must *develop* our capacity to engage in such activity is another significant difference between humans and the prime mover.
[40] Even if in *DA* 2.5 Aristotle uses 'contemplation' in something other than his full technical sense, a manifestation of theoretical wisdom, his remarks indicate that the sort of thinking that he there describes would share the relevant property, voluntariness, with contemplation in his full technical sense. That is because in these passages contemplation, unlike perception, does not depend on the immediate physical presence of some particular external object. Rather, one activates one's state whenever one chooses to do so.

DA 2.5, 417ᵇ18–25

Actively perceiving is spoken of similarly to contemplation (*theôrein*). But there is a difference, namely that the things productive of the activity (i.e., perceiving) are external: the visible and the audible, and likewise for the other perceptibles. The reason is that active perception is of particulars, whereas knowledge (*epistêmê*) is of universals, and the latter are in a way in the soul itself. That is why thinking (*noêsai*) is up to oneself, whenever one wishes,⁴¹ but perceiving is not up to oneself, since the perceptible must be present.

These two passages reveal that Aristotle thinks that activating theoreti-cal intellect in contemplation, unlike perceiving, is voluntary.⁴² Voluntary activations of theoretical intellect do not depend on the presence of exter-nal particulars. Neither are they random or passive. Rather, they are up to us to engage in whenever we wish. Voluntarily activating theoretical intellect implies an attitude, paradigmatically decision (*prohairesis*), that we can have about things that are up to us to do. After all, contempla-tion is something achievable in action (*prakton*) and everything achievable in action (*prakton*) is decidable (*prohaireton*) (*Metaph*. 6.1, 1025ᵇ24). Any such attitude in turn implies an application of practical intellect, not the-oretical intellect as such. To see why, consider what Aristotle says about the conditions for voluntary activity in *NE* 3.1. Voluntariness requires "being aware of the particulars in which the act consists" (1111ᵃ22–24).⁴³ Such particulars include what one is doing and how and why one is do-ing it (1111ᵃ2–6). We can see from Aristotle's examples that one is aware of such particulars (or not) under specific qualifications. It is for this reason that my speaking, *qua* conversing, might be voluntary, but *qua* divulging a secret, non-voluntary. For contemplating to be voluntary, I must be aware of contemplation at least *qua* something in which I can engage even though I am not always doing so. It is a contingent, variable, particular, human activity that is up to me to perform.⁴⁴ Awareness of such things is characteristic of practical intellect, not theoretical intellect (6.7, 1141ᵇ8–21). So, every case of human contemplation implies activity of practical intellect.

---

⁴¹ ἐπ' αὐτῷ, ὁπόταν βούληται
⁴² This paragraph draws substantial inspiration from Corcilius (2009).
⁴³ εἰδότι τὰ καθ' ἕκαστα ἐν οἷς ἡ πρᾶξις
⁴⁴ Contemplation's status as such an activity is discussed by Bostock (2000, 19 n. 33), Nightingale (2004, 219–220), Price (2011, 71) and (2014, 34), and Thorsrud (2015, 352).

As I have already mentioned, to figure in happiness in the way that Aristotle says that it does, namely, as a manifestation of theoretical wisdom that characterizes an appropriately long life, contemplation must be reliably performed. Reliable contemplation implies reliable activity of practical intellect.

Aristotle tells us that contemplation is fine activity (*eupraxia*), and therefore that its instances are practical (*praktikas*) (*Pol.* 7.3, 1325^{b}14–23).[45] Voluntary, reliably performed, fine activities implying the application of practical intellect meet Aristotle's criteria for acting virtuously (*NE* 2.4, 1105^{a}30–33) and thus imply manifestations of practical virtue. (On his view, reliably choosing and performing fine activity requires reliably selecting and using the correct means for achieving the correct end. Aristotle thinks that it is impossible reliably to decide upon or perform fine activity unless one has practical virtue (6.12, 1144^{a}6–9, ^{a}20, 6.13, 1145^{a}4–6).[46] But on his view having any practical virtue requires having all of them. The merely clever person and the enkratic lack temperance, at least, and therefore, Aristotle thinks, they cannot reliably select and use the correct means for achieving the correct end.[47])

The conclusion of the foregoing argument is that the manifestation of theoretical wisdom in contemplation, insofar as it is a voluntary, reliably performed, fine activity implying the application of practical intellect, implies the manifestation of practical virtue. I want to emphasize that this is not merely to claim that contemplation implies that practically virtuous activity has occurred at some time or other in the past, but rather that it implies reliable, ongoing practically virtuous activity.[48] Aristotle's view as I interpret it thus contrasts not only with recent interpretations

---

[45] This does not mean that theoretical wisdom is somehow subordinate to practical considerations, as Aristotle reminds us (T5: *NE* 6.13, 1145^{a}6–11).

[46] There is no indication in these passages Aristotle is restricting the scope of activities and ends at issue to fine ethical activities and ends. He seems, rather, to be arguing on the basis of facts about the structure of decision quite generally. We would need strong evidence that he has in mind facts about domain-restricted decision in order to assert that the sort of fine activity at issue here excludes the fine activity that contemplation is (according to *Pol.* 7.3, 1325^{b}14–23), or that his views about fine activity in *NE* 6 and *Pol.* 7 conflict. Furthermore, aside from whether one calls contemplation "fine activity," one can still think that contemplation is at least part of the correct end for human beings (*NE* 1.7, 1098^{a}16–18, 10.7, 1178^{a}5–8) and that one will not reliably have, or act for the sake of, the correct end without practical virtue.

[47] The boorish (*agroikos*) person also lacks temperance and so, for the reasons just mentioned, will not reliably engage in fine activity, including contemplation. He has appetites, but not the right ones (and so is deficient), and does not take the appropriate pleasure in fine activity and will stubbornly avoid it (against reason) if it thwarts some other appetite or pleasure (7.9, 1151^{b}4–32).

[48] Discussion with Gabriel Richardson Lear was especially helpful for clarifying this feature of my account.

according to which one can contemplate without ever having been practically virtuous, but also with the view of Plotinus, who thinks that having once manifested the practical virtues, we can subsequently dispense with such activities and focus on contemplation (*Enneads* 1.2.7).[49] Furthermore, my claim is not that contemplation requires practically virtuous activity as an instrument.[50] The relationship is much closer than that, as the second stage of my argument above showed. Most fundamentally, it is because contemplation is a voluntary, reliably performed, fine activity implying the application of practical intellect that it implies practically virtuous activity, not simply because of facts about the human behaviors that conduce to or impede contemplation.[51]

The argument of this section has been as follows: In T3, Aristotle indicates that one with theoretical wisdom acts rightly and nobly *most of all*, and therefore must have practical wisdom rather than something less than that, such as mere cleverness or *enkrateia*. This claim is at least partially anticipated in T4 and echoes a fragment of Aristotle's *Protrepticus*. We gain insight into *why* Aristotle might think this if a certain interpretation of T5 is true, namely, an interpretation according to which practical wisdom is implied in the emergence and manifestation of theoretical wisdom because contemplation implies that one's passions and pleasures are such as only the practically wise person's are, and is voluntary, reliably performed, fine activity that implies the reliably excellent application of practical intellect.

---

[49] Thanks to Caleb Cohoe for pointing out the contrast between Plotinus's view and my interpretation of Aristotle's. This difference is illuminating in a further way: Nightingale (2004, 231–232) argues that Aristotle consciously disagrees with Plato, Isocrates, and Xenophon on the issue of whether theoretical wisdom is practically useful. According to Nightingale, Aristotle thinks that it is practically useless, whereas the others think that it is supremely practically useful. I think that we can state the disagreement in a more nuanced way, one that is compatible with a wider range of textual evidence (e.g., Aristotle's *Protrepticus*), if to this picture we add Plotinus, who thinks (*Enneads* 1.2.7) that the theoretically wise person lives impractically. As I interpret Aristotle, he holds that theoretical wisdom is practically useless insofar as it does not in its own right further some practical objective beyond its own manifestation, but also that the theoretically wise person lives very practically insofar as he acts rightly and nobly most of all. Nightingale cannot accept this more subtle account of Aristotle's disagreement with other ancient philosophers on this subject because she assumes (203–205) that he regards Anaxagoras and Thales as possessors of theoretical wisdom but also as practically useless.

[50] Kraut (1989, 179–180), for example, gives an instrumentalist account of why temperance is needed for contemplation.

[51] This should not be taken to suggest that contemplation inherits its fineness from practical features, for example its timing. Thanks to Anthony Price for pushing for clarification about this.

2.5 The Availability of Wisdom and the Nature of Practical Science

Two charges might be made against me for urging rejection of the Divergence Thesis, as I have done in this chapter: By rejecting Divergence I have made Aristotle's account of happiness unduly restrictive and empirically false. I will clarify and address these charges in order.

I have presented evidence that according to Aristotle theoretical and practical wisdom are biconditionally related. If happiness requires one kind of wisdom, then it requires the other. Happiness would have been hard enough to achieve if only one kind of wisdom were required. Who, then, can be happy? It is difficult to say.

Curzer (2012, 393 and 399) would allege that I have made it *too* difficult to say. According to him, happiness should not require the package of virtues that I have described. His evidence is as follows, in his translation with his brackets. I have provided the Greek for comparison.

NE 1.9, 1099^{b}18–20

[Happiness is] very generally shared; for all who are not maimed as regards their potentiality for virtue may win it by a certain kind of study and care.	εἴη δ' ἂν καὶ πολύκοινον· δυνατὸν γὰρ ὑπάρξαι πᾶσι τοῖς μὴ πεπηρωμένοις πρὸς ἀρετὴν διά τινος μαθήσεως καὶ ἐπιμελείας.

It will be noticed that the part that Curzer brackets does the heavy lifting. 'Happiness' does not appear as the explicit subject. Perhaps it is the implicit subject. It occurred six lines previously. Or perhaps something more complex, such as 'the potential for happiness' (as Curzer later seems to suppose on p. 399), is the implicit subject. Furthermore, the verb that Curzer translates as 'is' is an optative, '*eiē.*' I do not propose to rule out Curzer's translation, though most translators here impart to '*eiē*' the role of signaling that Aristotle is saying that this *will* or *would* follow *if* the assumptions about divine dispensation and luck that he had just been mentioning in the previous sentence were correct. In any case, Aristotle is clear a few lines later that his own view is that happiness is not a matter of luck (1099^{b}24), but rather of virtuous activity, the manifestation of "perfect virtue" (*aretês teleias*, 1100^{a}4), and other goods associated with happiness will be associated with it only insofar as they are involved in the performance of virtuous activity. In short, happiness is as widely shared as perfect virtue is. And in fact, Aristotle tells us several times that neither virtue nor happiness is widely shared (1.5, 1095^{b}14–17, 3.11, 1118^{b}22–25,

9.8, 1168^{b}15–25, 10.9, 1179^{b}10–18).[52] Perhaps it is the case that happiness *could have been* widely shared – this is compatible with taking the implicit subject to be 'the potential for happiness' – but at least most of us have squandered the opportunity by living wrongly.

To the first of the two charges that I mentioned earlier, I therefore reply as follows: I do indeed have the audacity to suggest that happiness, which Aristotle says is the highest thing achievable in action for human beings, might come with great difficulty and rarity, if at all.

The second charge was that rejecting the Divergence Thesis does violence to the empirical data. These data, allegedly, are that paragons of theoretical excellence exhibit ethical behavior that is no better, and perhaps worse, than the average person's is. This would seem to conflict with Aristotle's assertion that the same people are theoretically wise and practically wise. The data that I have in mind are amassed in such papers as Schwitzgebel et al. (2012) and numerous others by the same authors. The gist of these studies is that professional philosophers, especially ethicists, misbehave at alarming rates, whether it be by slamming doors at conferences, being unresponsive to emails, or failing to live up to dietary commitments.

I do not believe that these data impugn Aristotle's theory as I have interpreted it. What they show, at most, is that the intellectual achievements of the sample of professional philosophers have little relationship to their ethical behavior. But those intellectual achievements are not the same as what Aristotle calls "theoretical wisdom," *sophia*. A philosopher might have been expected to have love for *sophia*, but is there any good reason to think that those who are called "philosophers" because of their occupation have such love in fact? Do professional academics, as a group, really have a systematic grasp of the highest principles of reality?[53]

Aristotle, then, invites us to consider an extremely lofty intellectual and ethical standard. One who would use the aforementioned empirical data to argue for Divergence makes the same assumption that underlies Curzer's remarks. Such would liberalize the standard. I mentioned in Chapter 1 that Curzer (2012, 401), for this reason, takes "the objects of contemplation to be primarily the matters of ordinary human life," rather than the highest

---

[52] I obtain all but the first citation from Broadie's (2002, 282) note on this passage. Müller (2020) discusses the significance of the passage from 10.9, as well as that of Aristotle's reference to the many as "base" (*phauloi*) in 9.4, 1166^{b}2–3. Heinaman (1993, 44) also adduces various passages from the *EE* and *Politics* regarding the limited distribution of virtue and happiness within the human population.

[53] Hitz (2019) offers extensive general reflection on these kinds of questions.

principles. We will have done something similar if we take the intellectual achievements of professional philosophers (or other academics) to be the standard. If we liberalize the standard, we lose the opportunity to conform to a better one. I see no reason to think that academics are peculiarly well suited to grasp the highest principles of reality. Why not think, as Aristotle does, that anyone who has done so would be found among those who have grasped how to act rightly?

To the second allegation, then, I reply that even if the empirical phenomena call into question the relationship between a certain kind of intellectual achievement and a certain kind of ethical achievement, they do not countervail Aristotle's view about the relationship between theoretical and practical *wisdom*.

I will tie together my responses to these two charges. Both charges reveal a temptation to de-idealize what Aristotle regards as the supreme principle of practical science: the highest good achievable in action, happiness. Such de-idealization is perhaps a precondition for conducting surveys of large numbers of actual humans, as the research agenda of Schwitzgebel et al. requires, or for depicting the highest good as achievable for large numbers of actual humans, as Curzer prefers. But de-idealization of the supreme principle of practical science, whether as an assumption in empirical investigation or out of a desire to broaden the attainability of the highest human good, comes at an enormous cost for an Aristotelian: that of disqualifying practical science from counting as scientific. Aristotle describes the subject of his *Nicomachean Ethics* as practical science (1.2), but also says that the principles of science are invariable (6.3, 1139^{b}20–25).[54] Witt (2015) argues that Aristotle is committed to the variability of ethical kinds and that this disbars them from being properly scientific principles. I think that if, contrary to fact, Aristotle had been committed to the variability of the supreme principle of practical science, then Witt would have been correct. But Aristotle thinks that the supreme principle of practical science, happiness, indeed is invariable in the way that such a principle of *practical* science should be: it is invariably good to achieve in action. Plato's Form of the Good was meant to confer goodness invariably, but Aristotle argues in 1.6 that it is the wrong kind of principle for *practical* science because it

---

[54] Even those who, like Polansky (2017), believe that the principles of practical science must be grasped only by practical wisdom can agree that such principles are invariable in the way that I am describing, provided that they think, as Polansky does, that practical wisdom grasps not only particulars, but also universals. See Karbowski (2019) and Scott (2015) for recent, in-depth studies of Aristotle's conception of the nature and methods of practical science.

is not *prakton*, achievable in action (1.6, 1096ᵇ31–35).[55] Aristotle's inquiry concerns the highest good achievable in action. But it is not a fit principle for practical *science* if it is, to transpose Moore's (1903) leitmotif from a Platonic to an Aristotelian register, an *open question* whether it is good to achieve it in action. The main reason to find the research of Schwitzgebel et al. interesting, surprising, disturbing, or otherwise important is precisely that it is an open question whether it is good to achieve in action what the subjects of their experiments have achieved. If professional academics misbehave with such frequency, might the good that they have attained be less worthwhile than we had thought, or than other goods? Likewise, the immoralist objection to monist interpretations of Aristotle's account of happiness, which I discussed in Chapter 1, derives its force precisely from the fact that it is an open question whether an immoral contemplator's achievement is invariably something good to achieve in action. If Aristotle's commitment to practical *science* is to abide, his candidate for the highest good achievable in action must be invariably good to achieve in action. Only if the Divergence Thesis is false has Aristotle proposed such a candidate. I have suggested that the scientific status of Aristotle's ethical theory is at stake in questions about how high the standard for our highest good should be. We should expect that a standard high enough to vouchsafe practical science as science will be so high that its achievability will be called into question.[56]

2.6 Conclusion

Aristotle is standardly regarded as being committed to the Divergence Thesis, namely that one can have and reliably manifest theoretical wisdom without practical wisdom. If he is committed to the Divergence Thesis, the Conjunctive Problem cannot be solved. The Divergence Thesis is motivated by a passage in *NE* 6.7 that appears to suggest that Anaxagoras

---

[55] This is not his only criticism of the Form of the Good. For example, Shields (1999, 194–216) and (2015a) discusses his complaint that the postulation of such a Form would lead us to expect the univocity of goodness, whereas we in fact find non-univocity, and argues that Aristotle's complaint threatens his own ability to draw cross-categorial comparisons between goods.

[56] Some, such as Augustine (*Civ. Dei* 19.4 and 19.19) and Aquinas (*ST* 1a2ae q. 3, a. 2, ad 4), have agreed with Aristotle that our highest good comprises activity in accordance with full intellectual and ethical virtue, and they explicitly argue that our full happiness will never be attained in this life. They have reasons other than Aristotle's, of course, for thinking that the particular sort of "seeing" of the highest principles that Aristotle calls "*theôria*" would require perfect ethical virtue: "Blessed are the pure in heart: for they shall see God." (μακάριοι οἱ καθαροὶ τῇ καρδίᾳ, ὅτι αὐτοὶ τὸν θεὸν ὄψονται.) (Matthew 5, William Tyndale's modernized translation from the *Modern Reader's Middle English Bible of the 1530's*, prismcp.com)

and Thales have theoretical wisdom without practical wisdom. In point of fact, though, that suggestion is demonstrably endoxic. Aristotle believes no such thing – indeed, he could not do so on pain of contradicting his explicit claims about their attainments – but his own account of theoretical and practical wisdom is meant to explain the intuitions that might have led someone to that conclusion. These are distinct virtues on his view, but they are not independently acquired or manifested. In particular, contemplation, the manifestation of theoretical wisdom, implies practical wisdom in two ways. First, it implies a passional and hedonic profile unique to the practically wise person. Second, it is voluntary, reliably performed, fine activity, and so implies the reliably excellent application of practical intellect.

The impediment that the Divergence Thesis has long been to arriving at an interpretation of Aristotle's theory of happiness that would solve the Conjunctive Problem has now been cleared away. But it is only one of three such impediments. I now move to the next.

CHAPTER 3

Are There Two Kinds of Happiness?

3.1 The Duality Thesis

In this chapter I will address a second thesis, held by numerous interpreters, that thwarts solving the Conjunctive Problem of Happiness:

Duality Thesis

Aristotle thinks that there are two kinds of happiness, one corresponding to theoretical contemplation and the other corresponding to ethically virtuous activities, and the former kind is superior to the latter.

This thesis is widely believed, but also standardly recognized as problematic for various reasons that I will discuss. Although, as I will soon argue, the Duality Thesis thwarts solving the Conjunctive Problem, one might at first wonder whether it holds some promise of *helping* to solve that problem. It would do this, the thought goes, by saying that 'happiness' as it occurs in the Pluralist Constraint has a different sense from 'happiness' as it occurs in the Monist Constraint. But the Pluralist Constraint and Monist Constraint are supposed to be constraints on a dialectically satisfactory account of the main subject about which they disagree, namely happiness. If the word designating that main subject, 'happiness,' had a different sense in each constraint, then pluralists and monists would simply be failing to engage with each other about their main subject. I do not think that they are doing so. That is why I said in Chapter 1 that solving the Conjunctive Problem requires affirming the Pluralist Constraint and Monist Constraint of the same kind of happiness. This is one reason that the Duality Thesis thwarts solving the Conjunctive Problem: it denies that the Pluralist and Monist Constraint apply to the same kind of happiness and thus prevents affirming both of the same kind of happiness.[1] But it is possible to be more specific about how the Duality Thesis

---

[1] Thanks to Gabriel Richardson Lear for discussion of this point.

thwarts solving the Conjunctive Problem. Consider the possible ways of spelling out what the virtuous activities involved in the two kinds of happiness mentioned in the Duality Thesis would be (I exclude obvious non-starters):

A. Both kinds involve contemplation and ethically virtuous activities, with one kind featuring more or less emphasis on the former or the latter.

B. The primary kind involves contemplation but not ethically virtuous activities, whereas the secondary kind involves ethically virtuous activities but not contemplation.

C. The primary kind involves contemplation and ethically virtuous activities, whereas the secondary kind involves ethically virtuous activities but not contemplation.

D. The primary kind involves contemplation but not ethically virtuous activities, whereas the secondary kind involves contemplation and ethically virtuous activities.

(A) is very difficult to derive from the text. Its comeliness derives from the unattractiveness of the others. Furthermore, it merely pushes the Conjunctive Problem back a step, for now we must explain *how* both kinds of happiness, or at least the first kind, could involve contemplation and ethically virtuous activities in a way that respects the Pluralist Constraint and Monist Constraint that I discussed in Chapter 1. (B) and (C) are awkward for familiar reasons:[2] Contemplation is at least part of the human *ergon* and is required for happiness to be perfect and self-sufficient. Unless we are prepared to attribute to Aristotle the view that there is a kind of human happiness that does not fulfill the human *ergon* and is neither perfect nor self-sufficient, (B) and (C) cannot work. (D) pushes the Conjunctive Problem back a step for the second life and violates the Pluralist Constraint for the first. That constraint is supposed by pluralists to apply to anything that counts as happiness. So, (D) makes the Conjunctive Problem unsolvable. Furthermore, if primary and secondary happiness are envisioned as available to different people (rather than it being required that both kinds of happiness are always possessed by the same people), then (B) and (D)

---

[2] See, for example, Bush (2008, 51–60), Cooper (1975, 165–167), Curzer (2012, 392), and Whiting (1986, 93–94 n. 50). Lear (2004, 193–194) finds it odd that Aristotle does not explicitly spell out or attempt to justify why the second kind of happiness is supposed to count as happiness at all. On the interpretation that I will offer, Aristotle's silence on this matter is completely unsurprising: Aristotle gives no separate defense for why a life in accordance with ethically virtuous activities counts as happy because it is not a separate kind of happy life at all.

also entail the Divergence Thesis, which we saw in Chapter 2 makes solving the Conjunctive Problem impossible. Since all of the possible ways of spelling out the Duality Thesis put a solution to the Conjunctive Problem further out of reach, we should explore how plausible the thesis is in the first place.

The Duality Thesis is motivated by a way of understanding the first line of *NE* 10.8 that was implemented in every published translation of which I am aware until that of Aufderheide (2020), who takes account of Reece (2020a), on which latter the current chapter is based. Aristotle appears to claim that there are two kinds of happy life: one in accordance with contemplation, the other with ethically virtuous activities. The standard way of translating this passage is as follows:

NE 10.7, 1178ᵃ6 – 10.8, 1178ᵃ10

Life in accordance with intellect is proper to a human being, since intellect is a human being most of all. So, this life also is happiest. Life in accordance with the other kind of virtue is ⟨happiest/happy⟩ in a secondary way, for activities in accordance with this kind of virtue are properly human.

καὶ τῷ ἀνθρώπῳ δὴ ὁ κατὰ τὸν νοῦν βίος, εἴπερ τοῦτο μά- λιστα ἄνθρωπος. οὗτος ἄρα καὶ εὐδαιμονέστατος. Δευτέ- ρως δ' ὁ κατὰ τὴν ἄλλην ἀρε- τήν· αἱ γὰρ κατὰ ταύτην ἐνέρ- γειαι ἀνθρωπικαί.

In the passage thus translated, Aristotle appears to make the bewildering announcement that the life of ethically virtuous activity ("life in accordance with the other kind of virtue") that he has heralded throughout the rest of the work is happiest (or happy) in a secondary way, subordinate to the supremely happy life of contemplative activity ("life in accordance with intellect"). His point here is standardly taken to be that there are two lives, one in accordance with theoretical intellect and the other in accordance with ethical virtue, and that both count as happy but the former in a superior way to the latter. Such a point is widely regarded as discordant with the rest of the *Nicomachean Ethics* (and with the *Protrepticus*, *Eudemian Ethics*, and *Politics*), or at least thoroughly unexpected.[3] It also invites various embarrassing questions: If happiness is self-sufficient and final, as Aristotle says it is, how could there be two kinds of it, one of which is superior to the other? Why would Aristotle lead us in the entirety of the

---

[3] One might think that it is anticipated by Aristotle's discussion in *NE* 1.5 of three popular candidates for the highest good, which are supposed to be the ends of three types of life: the life of sensory pleasure, the life of political honor, and the life of contemplation. I join Gauthier and Jolif (1970, vol. 2.2, 860) in questioning the degree of relevance *NE* 1.5 has to the claim currently under discussion, namely that there are two lives, one in accordance with theoretical intellect and the other in

NE to expect only one kind of happiness, a single aim (1.2, 1094ᵃ18–22), a *highest* good achievable in action, and then frustrate this expectation without offering any reason why the original reasons for it no longer apply? Why would he resume speaking, for the rest of the *NE* and throughout its sequel, the *Politics*, as if there is only one kind of happiness if he here asserts that there are two? Even more specifically, why would he on the next Bekker page (10.8, 1179ᵃ29–30, which I discussed in the previous chapter) affirm a biconditional relationship between theoretical wisdom and ethical virtue if he thinks that each is characteristic of a different kind of happiness?[4]

---

accordance with ethical virtue, and that both count as happy but the former in a superior way to the latter. First, Aristotle cites the same classification of three lives in *EE* 1.5, 1216ᵃ28–37 and clearly feels no pressure from it to make in the rest of the *EE* the claim that I have just mentioned. It is one thing to say that Aristotle's views have developed between the *EE* and the *NE*, but it is another thing to insist that a connection that Aristotle simply did not see, and indeed would have denied, in the *EE* is incumbent upon us to recognize in the *NE*. A second reason for doubting that *NE* 1.5 anticipates 10.7–8 in the way that I have mentioned is that it is controversial whether a life of political honor and a life in accordance with ethically virtuous activity are meant to be the same. See, for example, Brown (2014, 111–114), Kraut (1989, 17–19), Lear (2004, 178–181), Roche (2014b), and Roche (2019, 36–48). Third, a life of contemplation need not exclude a life in accordance with ethically virtuous activity. Indeed, my previous chapter argued that according to Aristotle precisely the same people contemplate and engage in ethically virtuous activities. Fourth, it is not obvious that Aristotle regards the standard options discussed in 1.5 as correctly described or individuated. He introduces them at a very early stage in his discussion. There is very little reason to expect that his eventual account of happiness will be beholden to popular ways of partitioning the options, since he unhesitatingly rejects Theognis's threefold partition in his famous inscription at Delos (*EE* 1.1, 1214ᵃ7–8, *NE* 1.8, 1099ᵃ24–25). In *NE* 1.8 he lists various popular opinions about happiness that he does aim to vindicate at least partially, and nothing about this list indicates that he intends to respect the partition on display in 1.5 in his official theory. On the contrary, the list shows that his theory will explain how happiness is in accordance with theoretical wisdom and with practical wisdom (1.8, 1098ᵇ22–25). See Long (2011, 103–104) for a further explanation of the importance of this fact. Such an explanatory ambition is far from suggesting the kind of divergence between theoretical and practical virtue often assumed to be on display in 10.7–8. I agree with Irwin (2019, 209) that Aristotle's real interest in discussing the lives of sensory pleasure, political honor, and money-making in 1.5 is in exhibiting his formal criteria for the highest good. Thanks to Eric Brown for encouraging me to discuss this issue. He thinks (Brown, 2014, 111–114) that 1.5 is relevant to 10.7–8, but does not directly argue that it anticipates the distinction between two kinds of happiness that Aristotle is standardly taken to draw there. In fact, his point is that the distinction is surprising, and is grounded in an equally surprising distinction between two kinds of self-sufficiency.

4 In this chapter I use 'kinds of happiness' and 'kinds of happy life' interchangeably. These are not always interchangeable, as many commentators have argued. The typical point of distinguishing between these is that the life can involve more than the activity does. But Aristotle in these lines focuses on two different kinds of virtuous activities, theoretical and practical. The alleged difference in lives is grounded entirely in the alleged difference between the activities that characterize those lives. Aristotle gives no indication here that the difference in lives, to the extent that there is one, is supposed to be one grounded in some other factor. So, while the distinction between a happy life and the activity of happiness is important for other reasons, it does not impact the argument that I will make. Since the current chapter is concerned with the question of whether Aristotle distinguishes two kinds of happy lives that are made distinct and made happy by two kinds of

We have seen that the Duality Thesis creates various problems for achieving a coherent interpretation of Aristotle's theory, some of which are commonly recognized, and that it thwarts solving the Conjunctive Problem. In this chapter I will argue that the passage that has motivated the Duality Thesis does not in fact commit him to that thesis. The interpretation that I offer makes better sense of the progression of Aristotle's argument in the immediate context, and of the connection between this passage and a parallel passage in *NE* 10.5, than does the standard interpretation. My interpretation does not commit Aristotle to an abrupt and surprising distinction between two kinds of happiness, but rather to a more minimal distinction that the standard distinction presupposes and for which readers of the *NE* are significantly better prepared. Furthermore, it brings us closer to, rather than further from, a solution to the Conjunctive Problem of Happiness.

3.2   The Proposal in Context

I begin by situating the passage in its context, initially leaving a blank in the translation at the point disputed between me and other interpreters:

NE 10.7, 1178ᵃ2 – 10.8, 1178ᵃ23

Each ⟨human being⟩ would in fact seem to be this (i.e., the best thing in us, intellect), since it is the determinative and better ⟨part⟩. So, it would be bizarre if one did not choose a life characteristic of oneself, but rather a life characteristic of something else. What was said previously applies now, too. For what is proper by nature to each thing is best and most pleasant to each thing. Indeed, life in accordance with intellect is proper to

δόξειε δ' ἂν καὶ εἶναι ἕκαστος ᵃ2 τοῦτο, εἴπερ τὸ κύριον καὶ ἄμει- νον. ἄτοπον οὖν γίνοιτ' ἄν, εἰ μὴ τὸν αὑτοῦ βίον αἱροῖτο ἀλλά τινος ἄλλου. τὸ λεχθέν τε πρό- τερον ἁρμόσει καὶ νῦν· τὸ γὰρ 5 οἰκεῖον ἑκάστῳ τῇ φύσει κρά- τιστον καὶ ἥδιστόν ἐστιν ἑκά- στῳ· καὶ τῷ ἀνθρώπῳ δὴ ὁ κατὰ τὸν νοῦν βίος, εἴπερ τοῦτο μάλι-

happiness, it will often be convenient to speak directly of these alleged kinds of happiness. Also, when I speak of 'kinds of happiness,' I do not intend to suggest that all of the traditional answers to the foregoing questions are committed to there being two ways of being happy that are actually achievable. Broadie (1991, 430), for example, thinks that what Aristotle calls "life in accordance with intellect" is actually happiest, but what he calls "life in accordance with the other kind of virtue" is potentially happiest. I mean merely that standard translations tend to encourage interpreters to think that there are two kinds of happiness, ways of being happy, relations to happiness, or at least that the two lives are somehow of a different status specifically with respect to happiness. This last claim is all that is needed to surprise readers and to thwart the project of solving the Conjunctive Problem of Happiness.

a human being, since this is a human being most of all. So, this ⟨life⟩ also is happiest. ⟨Life⟩ in accordance with the other kind of virtue is _____ in a secondary way, for activities in accordance with this ⟨kind of virtue⟩ are properly human. For just acts, courageous acts, and acts in accordance with the other kind of virtue are such that we perform them in relation to each other, observing what is fitting for each in our dealings and affairs and in various actions and passions. All of these appear to be properly human. Some ⟨of these acts⟩ seem also to result from the body, and in many ways ethical virtue seems to be associated with the passions. Practical wisdom, in turn, is closely united with ethical virtue, and it with practical wisdom, since on the one hand the starting-points of practical wisdom are in accordance with the ethical virtues, and on the other the rightness of ethical virtues is in accordance with practical wisdom. Since ⟨the ethical virtues⟩ are also associated with the passions, they will be concerned with the compound. The virtues of the compound are properly human. So too, then, are the life and the happiness in accordance with these. The ⟨virtue⟩[5] of the intellect is sep-

στα ἄνθρωπος. οὗτος ἄρα καὶ εὐδαιμονέστατος.

Δευτέρως δ' ὁ κατὰ τὴν ἄλ- 9
λην ἀρετήν· αἱ γὰρ κατὰ ταύτην ἐνέργειαι ἀνθρωπικαί. δί- 10
καια γὰρ καὶ ἀνδρεῖα καὶ τὰ
ἄλλα τὰ κατὰ τὰς ἀρετὰς πρὸς
ἀλλήλους πράττομεν ἐν συναλ-
λάγμασι καὶ χρείαις καὶ πράξε-
σι παντοίαις ἔν τε τοῖς πάθεσι
διατηροῦντες τὸ πρέπον ἑκά-
στῳ· ταῦτα δ' εἶναι φαίνεται
πάντα ἀνθρωπικά. ἔνια δὲ καὶ
συμβαίνειν ἀπὸ τοῦ σώματος 15
δοκεῖ, καὶ πολλὰ συνῳκειῶσθαι
τοῖς πάθεσιν ἡ τοῦ ἤθους ἀρετή. συνέζευκται δὲ καὶ ἡ φρό-
νησις τῇ τοῦ ἤθους ἀρετῇ, καὶ
αὕτη τῇ φρονήσει, εἴπερ αἱ μὲν
τῆς φρονήσεως ἀρχαὶ κατὰ τὰς
ἠθικάς εἰσιν ἀρετάς, τὸ δ' ὀρ-
θὸν τῶν ἠθικῶν κατὰ τὴν φρό-
νησιν. συνηρτημέναι δ' αὗται
καὶ τοῖς πάθεσι περὶ τὸ σύνθε- 20
τον ἂν εἶεν· αἱ δὲ τοῦ συνθέ-
του ἀρεταὶ ἀνθρωπικαί· καὶ ὁ
βίος δὴ ὁ κατὰ ταύτας καὶ ἡ
εὐδαιμονία. ἡ δὲ τοῦ νοῦ κεχω-

---

[5] The majority of recent translations and commentaries understand 'virtue' ('ἀρετή') rather than 'happiness' ('εὐδαιμονία') as the referent of the feminine definite article here, despite the proximity of 'happiness.' Exceptions include Bartlett and Collins (2011), Bodéüs in Pellegrin (2014), Joachim (1951, 287 n. 4), Lawrence (1993, 21), Rackham (1947), Sachs (2002), Scott (2015, 130), and Tricot (2007), none giving an argument. Cooper (1975, 174 n. 26), Dirlmeier (2014, 594), and Ramsauer (1878, 700) argue that since the subject that is assumed here in ª22 must also be the subject of ª23–25, and the latter must be 'virtue' ('ἀρετή') on pain of saying both that happiness requires external goods and that it does not, then the former should be, as well. Cooper stresses that the main subject for the sentence preceding ª22 is 'αὗται,' which refers to 'the virtues' ('αἱ ἀρεταί'). Dirlmeier adds that understanding 'virtue' here makes good sense of Aristotle's claim in light of what he has just been arguing: Ethical virtues are associated with the passions, but the virtue of the intellect is separate from the passions. Aufderheide (2020, 198–199), Frede (2020, 970), and Reeve (2014, 347–348) offer further explanations, drawing on other parts of Aristotle's philosophy, for why it is correct to read 'virtue' here.

arate. Let that much be said about it.[6] To treat it precisely is beyond the scope of the present topic.

ρισμένη· τοσοῦτον γὰρ περὶ αὐτῆς εἰρήσθω· διακριβῶσαι γὰρ μεῖζον τοῦ προκειμένου ἐστίν.

The primary focus of this chapter will be on ᵃ9, which is where standard interpretations locate Aristotle's announcement that there is a second kind of happiness. I have left a blank in the translation to indicate that while Aristotle does say that the life in accordance with ethical virtue is somehow secondary, there is no explicit specification of the respect in which this life is secondary. Translators have assumed that the elided predicate must be the superlative adjective 'happiest' ('*eudaimonestatos*'), which occurs in the previous sentence but is awkward in conjunction with 'in a secondary way' ('*deuterōs*'),[7] or 'happy' ('*eudaimōn*'), which is not explicitly present in the immediately surrounding text but is understood as implicit in 'happiest.'[8] It is precisely this decision to understand 'happiest' or 'happy' as the elided predicate that generates the Duality Thesis, which encumbers any attempt

---

[6] The manuscript reading, retained by Susemihl (1887), is 'τοσοῦτον γὰρ περὶ αὐτῆς εἴρημαι' ('for so much has been said'). That is what Irwin (2019) translates. His comment on the back-reference that this would imply is that "Aristotle probably refers to vi 7 on *sophia*." If so, this would lend powerful additional support to understanding 'virtue' as the referent in ᵃ22, as I discussed in the previous note.

[7] '*Deuterōs*' occurs more than 400 times in the ancient Greek corpus, and I know of no clear occurrence of the word in its subordinating sense (as opposed to one in which it merely marks a new point, say) directly modifying a superlative adjective. On the contrary, there are many cases in which '*deuterōs*' explicitly *contrasts* with a superlative. Anthony Price points out in conversation that at *Pol.* 4.2, 1289ᵃ35 – ᵇ5 '*deutera*' and '*deuteron*' (adjectival cousins of '*deuterōs*') occur after superlatives. I suspect that these are most naturally read in the ordinary way, namely as indicating an ordinal position, where in this case the preceding superlative has determined the nature and direction of the ranking scheme. Robinson (1995) translates as follows: "It remains to deal with the constitution that is called by the common name, and with the other constitutions, oligarchy and democracy and tyranny. Now it is plain with regard to these perversions also which is worst and which second. The perversion of the first and most divine must be worst; and kingship must either be kingship merely in name and not also in fact, or else depend on great superiority in the man who is reigning. Hence tyranny, being worst, is farthest removed from a constitution; oligarchy is second (aristocracy is very far from this constitution); and democracy is the most moderate." Robinson translates '*deutera*' and '*deuteron*' simply as 'second,' which I think is most natural. Aristotle's discussion in this context is about three perverse forms of government: tyranny, oligarchy, and democracy. Since he establishes the ranking of tyranny and democracy with opposite superlatives, he needs no more exotic description of oligarchy than that it is the second in the series of three, since that is where it must fall if the other two are the extremes in the series. The ordinary meaning of the adjective suffices.

[8] This has been the situation since the earliest extant Greek paraphrase of and commentary on *NE* 10, by 'Heliodorus' and Michael of Ephesus, respectively, as well as the ninth- through tenth-century Arabic translation (Akasoy and Fidora, 2005) and the middle commentary of Averroes. The first full translation of the *NE* into Latin by Robert Grosseteste, and the revised version of it by William of Moerbeke, are as indeterminate as the Greek is, but the paraphrase of Albertus Magnus and commentary by Aquinas, which are based on Grosseteste's translation and written shortly afterward, both understand '*felix*' as implicit.

to solve the Conjunctive Problem. A different proposal for the elided predicate is possible, and it lacks this unhappy result. I propose that it is possible to fill in the blank with 'proper to a human being,' which occurs in ᵃ6 and has its sense fixed by 'proper' (*'oikeion'*) in the preceding clause. On this proposal, ᵃ9–10 would be understood as follows:

Proposal

⟨Life⟩ in accordance with the other kind of virtue is ⟨proper to a human being⟩ in a secondary way, for activities in accordance with this ⟨kind of virtue⟩ are properly human.[9]	Δευτέρως δ' ὁ κατὰ τὴν ἄλλην ἀρετήν ⟨οἰκεῖος τῷ ἀνθρώπῳ⟩· αἱ γὰρ κατὰ ταύτην ἐνέργειαι ἀνθρωπικαί.

Like 'happiest' (*'eudaimonestatos'*) but unlike 'happy' (*'eudaimôn'*), 'proper to a human being'[10] is present in the immediately preceding lines.[11] In fact, 'proper to a human being' is no further back than is 'life' (*'bios'*), which occurs in the same clause and must be the referent of the definite article in ᵃ9. One might wonder why Aristotle would use the superlative, 'happiest,' in ᵃ8 if he were not claiming in ᵃ9 that there is a secondary sort of happiness. Of the six uses of 'happiest' in Aristotle's extant works, two besides this one are in his own voice (*EE* 7.12, 1245ᵇ11 and *NE* 10.8, 1179ᵃ31). These passages identify the one who is happiest with the one who is best (1245ᵇ11, 1179ᵃ23) and most loved by the gods (1179ᵃ24, ᵃ30). In neither of the passages is there any suggestion that one could be happy in any other way, let alone that activity in accordance with ethical virtues makes for a

---

[9] After writing and submitting a draft of Reece (2020a), on which this chapter is based, I discovered that Green's (2016, 142–154) PhD dissertation and his talk given for the Society for Ancient Greek Philosophy session in March 2017 suggested understanding 'human being' (*'anthrôpos'*) from ᵃ7 as what has been elided. While I agree with Green in preferring an alternative to the traditional proposals, and in recognizing that doing so permits one to deny that there are two kinds of happiness mentioned in these lines, I regard his suggestion and the argument for it as less plausible. Anthony Price, who in personal correspondence with me in June 2017 proposed independently of Green (but does not endorse) the possibility of saying that *'anthrôpos'* is what has been elided, offers the following reason for rejecting that proposal: If *'anthrôpos'* were what had been elided, then the meaning of ᵃ6–7 should be that life in accordance with intellect is a human being most of all and of ᵃ9–10 that life in accordance with ethical virtue is a human being in a secondary way, but the meaning of ᵃ6–7 is instead that *intellect* is most of all a human being. I also have qualms about Green's main argument for his proposal, which is that the surrounding context of ᵃ9 expresses the monist view that the highest good includes only contemplation and supplying *'anthrôpos'* would fit this purportedly monist context better. By contrast, the arguments that I give for understanding 'proper to a human being' as the elided predicate do not presuppose monism.

[10] '⟨οἰκεῖος⟩ τῷ ἀνθρώπῳ'

[11] Although οἰκεῖος is not directly predicated of 'βίος' in its explicit occurrence at ᵃ5, I take it to determine the sense of 'τῷ ἀνθρώπῳ' in ᵃ6, which is directly predicated of 'βίος.'

life that is happy but not happiest.[12] In fact, the second of these passages shows that Aristotle would resist such a suggestion, for he there insists that the happiest person acts rightly (*orthôs*) and nobly (*kalôs*) most of all (*malista*). This echoes his willingness elsewhere to call 'best' people who, or lives that, are happy in accordance with ethical virtues (*NE* 4.3, 1123^{b}26–30, *Pol.* 7.1, 1323^{b}21 – 1324^{a}4). The relevance of these latter passages depends on whether or not 'best' in these passages is relative to the same comparison class as it is at *EE* 7.12, 1245^{b}11 and *NE* 10.8, 1179^{a}23. On my reading of *NE* 10.7–8, 'happiest' is a correlate of 'best and most pleasant' (cf. *EE* 1.1, 1214^{a}7–8, *NE* 1.8, 1099^{a}24–25) in the preceding general claim (^{a}5–6) that is then applied to the case of human beings. Aristotle's point is that a life that is proper to a human being is happiest for a human being, just as what is proper to anything else is best and most pleasant for that thing. A life characteristic of grazing animals, for example, would not be happiest for a human being. He continues in ^{a}9 with the claim that life in accordance with ethical virtue, and not only life in accordance with intellect, is proper to a human being. So, it is perfectly sensible for Aristotle to use the superlative in ^{a}8, but it would be awkward to use it in ^{a}9 in conjunction with 'in a secondary way' ('*deuterôs*'). 'Proper to a human being' lacks this awkwardness.

Understanding 'proper to a human being' as the elided predicate makes ^{a}9 adhere more closely to the parallel structure of

… life in accordance with intellect is proper to a human being, since ⟨intellect⟩ is a human being most of all.	… καὶ τῷ ἀνθρώπῳ δὴ ὁ κατὰ τὸν νοῦν βίος, εἴπερ τοῦτο μάλιστα ἄνθρωπος. ^{a}ᵉ

'Proper to a human being' is drawn from a clause that is explained or expanded, and understood as the elided predicate in a clause that is explained

---

[12] The same goes for a different superlative formed from '*eudaimon*,' namely '*eudaimonikôtatê*,' and its corresponding comparative, '*eudaimonikôtera*,' which occur at 10.8, 1178^{b}23 and 10.6, 1177^{a}6, respectively. These suggest a comparison *of some sort* between contemplation and other activities, but not one that requires multiple kinds of happiness. The comparison that they suggest is compatible with there being precisely one kind of happiness with different activities being more or less characteristic of it, conducive to it, and so on. (See my p. 22 n. 40 on the translation of such words.) It is unclear whether *NE* 1.10, 1101^{a}6–8 distinguishes blessedness from happiness as being higher in degree – Nussbaum (2001, 329–333), Roche (2014a, 45–59), and White (1992, 120 n. 16), for example, argue that it does not – and whether 1.8, 1099^{b}2–6, 1.10, 1100^{b}22–29, or 3.9, 1117^{b}9–11 commits Aristotle's official view to degrees of happiness. (*Politics* 7.8 speaks of different degrees of happiness, but for groups of people.) Even if they do, the passages that feature 'happiest' do not, and so the presence of that word in our passage tells us nothing about Aristotle's commitment or lack thereof to degrees of happiness. Furthermore, the passages that some have taken to support degrees of happiness certainly do not support the claim that one degree of happiness is associated with intellectually virtuous activity and another with ethically virtuous activity, where these degrees of happiness in association with each sort of activity are separately available as different lives, which is the relevant issue for our passage. Thanks to Anthony Price for discussion of these points.

or expanded in a parallel fashion. (By contrast, 'happiest' is imported from what looks like a conclusion to a clause that is explained or expanded en route to that conclusion.) This is important, since the clauses that explain or expand display a similar pattern to each other:

...since (intellect) is a human being most of all.	... εἴπερ τοῦτο μάλιστα ἄνθρω-πος.	[a]7
...for activities in accordance with this ⟨kind of virtue⟩ are properly human.	... αἱ γὰρ κατὰ ταύτην ἐνέργειαι ἀνθρωπικαί.	[a]9–10

The similarity is this: Both support a claim that a certain sort of life C (life of contemplative activity, life of ethically virtuous activity) has a certain property A_1 (being proper to a human being) by saying that the defining activity B (contemplative activity, ethically virtuous activity) of that life has a certain property A_2 (being human most of all, being properly human). That is to say, both sentences are of the form: A_1 belongs to all C, since A_2 belongs to all B and B belongs to all C.[13] This makes best sense, of course, if for A_1 in either case we substitute 'being proper to a human being,' for then if Aristotle thinks that being human most of all and being human are ways of being proper to a human, A_2 will in each case be an instance of A_1. Since substituting anything other than 'being proper to a human being' for A_1 in the case of [a]9 would disrupt the otherwise closely parallel structure of the two sentences, there is some pressure to understand 'proper to a human being' as the elided predicate in [a]9, as I am urging. If we do so, the comparison will be between life in accordance with intellect and life in accordance with the other kind of virtue,[14] where the former is proper to a human being since a human being is most of all his or her intellect, and the latter is proper to a human being (in a secondary way) since activities in accordance with the other sort of virtue are properly human. The upshot of the two parallel claims will be that there are two ways in which something can be proper to a human being. One way of being proper is to be in accordance with what is a human being most of all, and the other is to be in accordance with what is a human being in another way.[15]

---

[13] The claim that I am representing by '$A_2 a B$' is not directly stated, but clearly implicit, in [a]6–7.

[14] ὁ κατὰ τὸν νοῦν βίος and ὁ κατὰ τὴν ἄλλην ἀρετήν βίος

[15] I will have much more to say about the two ways of being proper to a human being in Chapter 5. There are multiple ways of being proper to a human being rather than one way of being proper that happens to be complex since there is an ordering in properties that human beings have in virtue of which something could be proper to them. This ordering is encoded in '*deuterôs*.' (If Aristotle had intended a non-ordered distinction, he could have used '*allôs*' or '*heterôs*,' both of which are vastly

The distinction between two ways of being proper to a human being is the reason why ᵃ9–10 is not redundant:[16]

⟨Life⟩ in accordance with the other kind of virtue is ⟨proper to a human being⟩ in a secondary way, for activities in accordance with this ⟨kind of virtue⟩ are properly human.

In this sentence, the explanandum is that the life in accordance with the other kind of virtue is proper to a human being *in a secondary way*. In other words, what needs to be explained is not only that such a life is proper to a human being, but also that it is proper in a way that differs from the primary way mentioned in ᵃ6–7. The explanans that follows 'for' (*'gar'*) is that even though ethically virtuous activities are not proper to humans in the way in which theoretical intellect is proper (since theoretical intellect has a unique claim to being a human being most of all), ethically virtuous activity is proper in some way, implicitly different from the first, to humans.

In addition to revealing the parallel reasoning in ᵃ6–7 and ᵃ9–10, understanding 'proper to a human being' as the elided predicate imputes to Aristotle a significantly less surprising distinction than does understanding 'happiest' or 'happy.' On the standard interpretations, Aristotle is here distinguishing between two kinds of happiness. On my proposed interpretation, he distinguishes between two ways of being proper to a human being. Whereas the former distinction has frequently been rightly regarded as entirely foreign to Aristotle's comments about happiness in the rest of the *NE* and other works, and therefore as puzzling, the latter distinction emerges naturally from one that he draws at the end of *NE* 10.5, where he discusses the connection between human nature, virtue, and pleasure as a segue to his remarks on happiness in 10.6–8:

10.5, 1176ᵃ26–29

Each kind of animal is thought to have a pleasure proper to it, just as it has an *ergon* proper to it: ⟨the pleasure proper to it⟩ is the one that is in accordance with its activity. This is apparent if we look at each kind, for a horse's	δοκεῖ δ' εἶναι ἑκάστῳ ζῴῳ καὶ ἡδονὴ οἰκεία, ὥσπερ καὶ ἔργον· ἡ γὰρ κατὰ τὴν ἐνέργειαν. καὶ ἐφ' ἑκάστῳ δὲ θεωροῦντι τοῦτ' ἂν φανείη· ἑτέρα γὰρ

more common in his works. Thanks to Brad Inwood for this point.) Cf. 10.5, 1176ᵃ26–29, which I discuss in the next paragraph. I will address this matter further in the following chapter, as I did in Reece (2020b).

[16] Thanks to Gabriel Richardson Lear for encouragement to make this feature of my account explicit.

pleasure differs from a dog's or a human's... Of those ⟨pleasures⟩ that are thought to be good, what sort, or which one, should be said to be characteristic of a human being? Or is this not clear from the activities, since the pleasures accompany these? So then, whether one or more ⟨activities⟩ are ⟨characteristic⟩ of the complete/perfect and blessed man, the pleasures that complete these ⟨activities⟩ will be called pleasures of a human being in the primary way, whereas the rest ⟨will be called pleasures of a human being⟩ in a secondary or even more remote way, as will the activities.

ἵππου ἡδονὴ καὶ κυνὸς καὶ ἀν-θρώπου... τῶν δ᾽ ἐπιεικῶν εἶ-ναι δοκουσῶν ποίαν ἢ τίνα φατέον τοῦ ἀνθρώπου εἶναι; ἢ ἐκ τῶν ἐνεργειῶν δῆλον; ταύ-ταις γὰρ ἕπονται αἱ ἡδοναί. εἴτ᾽ οὖν μία ἐστὶν εἴτε πλεί-ους αἱ τοῦ τελείου καὶ μακα-ρίου ἀνδρός, αἱ ταύτας τελει-οῦσαι ἡδοναὶ κυρίως λέγοιντ᾽ ἂν ἀνθρώπου ἡδοναὶ εἶναι, αἱ δὲ λοιπαὶ δευτέρως καὶ πολ-λοστῶς, ὥσπερ αἱ ἐνέργειαι.

In this passage Aristotle ties together various threads. As we know from *NE* I.7, humans have an *ergon* (work, function, characteristic activity) that is proper to them as the kind of living thing that they are. Pleasures accompany activities. The pleasure proper to humans will be the pleasure that accompanies their functioning well, virtuous rational activity. This is why Aristotle's point of reference for the pleasure proper to humans is the complete/perfect and blessed man. But there are different kinds of virtuous rational activities and therefore different pleasures accompanying each. Each is proper to humans, but is there one that is most proper to them? Aristotle defers this question, saying that it will be clear from consideration of the good activities that those pleasures accompany. He seems to have confidence that regardless of how diverse the pleasures proper to humans are, we can clarify matters by referring those pleasures to the corresponding activities, each of which will be more or less closely associated with what kind of thing a human being is. He goes on to consider these activities in 10.7–8, as well as the issue of what a human being is most of all. The explanatory projects set forth in this passage in 10.5 are, then, those that are completed in 10.7–8.[17]

---

[17] Thus Aufderheide (2020, 149) on the connection between these lines of 10.5 and the passage that is my main concern in this chapter: "In X.7–8, Aristotle takes up the task of identifying the best activity by comparing theoretical reflection with virtuous action. Do both the intellectual aspect of virtuous action and purely theoretical thought yield pleasures that can be called with equal right 'primarily human', or does one top the other? The answer requires thinking further on what it is to be human – which Aristotle does at X.7.1177b26 – X.8.1178b32. In other words, the question of which pleasures count as primarily human depends on which life counts as primarily human (and the best human life). Thus, Aristotle sees the discussion of pleasure, or at least one important question, as continuous with the discussion of the best life in X.7–8."

Importantly for our purposes, 10.5 introduces, in a context that could hardly be more relevant, the idea that things proper to humans can be called proper to them in primary, secondary, and perhaps other ways. On my interpretation of 10.7–8, it explicitly draws a distinction between things proper to humans that are called proper to them in primary and secondary ways. Both passages mark the distinction with 'in a secondary way' ('*deuterôs*'), which is notable since it appears in only two other passages in Aristotle's extant works (*NE* 8.7, 1158^{b}30–33 and *Metaph.* 5.11, 1022^{a}18).[18] Aristotle's suggestion in 10.5 that things proper to humans can be called proper to them in primary, secondary, and perhaps other ways is set down to be picked back up again in 10.7–8 as part of an explanation of the sort to which 10.5 pointed. Unless Aristotle specifies in 10.7–8, as I have said that he does, two kinds of lives, activities, virtues, and pleasures that are proper to humans in primary and secondary ways, an important question raised by 10.5 using closely corresponding terminology will have been left unanswered. A distinction in 10.7–8 between primary and secondary ways of being proper to humans is not just unsurprising, but positively called for. By contrast, the distinction between two kinds of happiness that is usually attributed to Aristotle in 10.7–8 is not just surprising, but implicitly contradicted before and after its alleged occurrence.

The standard way of interpreting 10.7–8 agrees with me that part of the intention of those chapters is to answer the question from 10.5 that I have just been discussing. In other words, it agrees that 10.5 calls for a further elaboration of primary and secondary ways of being proper to humans, one that is grounded in further details about human nature and the different kinds of virtuous activities associated with it. That is because the distinction usually drawn between two sorts of happiness *presupposes* the distinction between two ways of being proper to humans. On the standard interpretation, each kind of happiness is characteristic of a life that is proper to humans in a different way. If they were proper to humans in the same way, it would be difficult to see how, given his pattern of reasoning at the end of 10.7, he could think that each is characteristic of a different kind of happy life. The standard interpretation alleges that in 1178^{a}9 Aristotle makes a claim about a secondary kind of happiness that is supported by a claim in ^{a}10 about a way of being proper to humans that is distinct

---

[18] Broadie (1991, 430 n. 75), Green (2016, 147–148), Lawrence (1993, 20 n. 22), Ramsauer (1878, 698), and Scott (1999, 233 n. 21) also note the similarity of the primary/secondary distinctions in 10.5 and 10.8. I do not claim that '*deuterôs*' functions in exactly the same way in both passages, but only that its presence in conjunction with other commonalities between the two passages suggests that 10.5 should inform our interpretation of 10.7–8 in the way that I suggest.

from the way of being proper to humans that had been mentioned in ᵃ6–7. My proposal, by contrast, is that in ᵃ9 Aristotle makes a claim about a way of being proper to a human being that is distinct from that mentioned in ᵃ6–7, which is then explained or expanded in ᵃ10. The standard interpretation already commits Aristotle to an implicit distinction between two ways of being proper to a human being. My proposal is merely that this implicit distinction is encoded here in ᵃ9, precisely where the absence of an explicit predicate calls for something implicit, and precisely where the verbal echoes of the end of 10.5 would make natural the explication of the distinction for which that chapter had led us to wait expectantly. The standard interpretation commits him to much more. This is important, since the additional commitment that it foists upon him is widely regarded as one of the most puzzling and unexpected in all of Aristotle's works.

3.3 A Reconstruction of Aristotle's Argument

In order to show how my proposal for the elided predicate affects the interpretation of the passage as a whole, I provide here a reconstruction of Aristotle's argument.

1. What is proper to a human being is best and most pleasant to a human being (ᵃ5–6).
2. What is best and most pleasant to a human being is happiest.
3. So, a life that is proper to a human being is happiest (from 1–2).
4. What is a human being most of all is proper to a human being.
5. Intellect is a human being most of all (ᵃ7).
6. Life in accordance with what is a human being most of all is proper to a human being.
7. So, life in accordance with intellect is happiest (ᵃ7–8, from 3–6).

Understanding the elided predicate as 'proper to a human being,' as I have proposed, has Aristotle continue to argue for two conclusions (10) and (20) as follows:

8. If a set of activities is properly human, then the life and the happiness associated with them are proper to a human being.
9. Activities in accordance with the other kind of virtue are properly human since they have to do with our relations to each other, actions, and passions (ᵃ10–14).

10. Therefore, the life and the happiness associated with activities that are in accordance with the other kind of virtue are proper to a human being (^{a}20–22, from 8–9).

11. Activities in accordance with the other kind of virtue have to do with passions (^{a}13, from 9).

12. Passions are of the compound (of body and soul).

13. So, activities in accordance with the other kind of virtue have to do with the compound (^{a}19–20, from 11–12).

14. Activities of intellect (and thus the virtue of intellect) do not have to do with the compound (they are separate) (^{a}22).

15. So, activities in accordance with the other kind of virtue are not the activities of what is a human being most of all (intellect) (from 13–14).

16. So, it is not the case that what is a human being most of all is the sort of thing that engages in activities in accordance with the other kind of virtue (from 5 and 15).

17. If it is not the case that the sort of thing that engages in activities in accordance with the other kind of virtue is what is a human being most of all, then a life in accordance with the other kind of virtue cannot be proper to a human being in the same way in which life in accordance with intellect is proper to a human being.

18. So, it is not the case that life in accordance with the other kind of virtue is proper to a human being in the same way in which life in accordance with intellect is proper to a human being (from 16–17).

19. If something is proper to a human being, but not proper to a human being in the same way in which life in accordance with intellect is proper to a human being, then it is proper to a human being in a secondary way.

20. Therefore, life in accordance with the other kind of virtue is proper to a human being in a secondary way (^{a}9, from 18–19).

On this reconstruction of Aristotle's argument, one conclusion (10) is found in ^{a}21–22, and another (20) is given in the first clause of ^{a}9. (20) is a more precise version of one of the conjuncts of (10), the one having to do with a life. (20) is thus the analog of (6). (10) has no analog in the preceding part of the argument, the part about life in accordance with intellect. However, we might take (10) to license an analog of (7): [Therefore, life in accordance with the other kind of virtue is also happiest.] This will follow only if being proper to a human being even in a secondary sense is enough to satisfy (3).[19] The argument thus construed, with or without the analog of (7), does not at any point imply that there are two kinds of happiness. Only if one has already included in ᵃ9 the claim that there are two kinds of happiness by understanding the elided predicate to be 'happiest' or 'happy,' or if one adds premises linking kinds of happiness with ways of being proper to a human being, will one be tempted to see two kinds of happiness being expounded in the rest of the argument.[20]

One may still ask what, if I am right, would be the point of concluding (20) in addition to (10). An attractive answer is that Aristotle does so

[19] There are multiple interpretive options at this point that would be compatible with the argument as I have construed it so far. The one that best coheres with my overall argument in this book is that in this passage Aristotle is not saying that there are two *separately livable* happy lives, but rather one happy life that has two dimensions, aspects, or spheres of life. This is the view of Crisp (1994, 133), Engberg-Pedersen (1983, 108–111), Gauthier and Jolif (1970, vol. 2.2, 862), Gurtler (2003, 825 n. 36), Heinaman (1988, 32–33), Keyt (1983, 386) and (1989), Pakaluk (2005, 320–328), Scott (1999, 236 n. 27), Stewart (1892, vol. 1, 59–62 and vol. 2, 443–444), and Zanatta (1986, vol. 2, 1107 n. 2). On such accounts, my proposal will have the effect that the one happy life's theoretical dimension is proper to a human in the primary sense, and its practical dimension is proper to a human in the secondary sense, but since both dimensions are proper to a human, both count as dimensions of one happy human life. Cooper (1975, 159–160) and (1987, 207 n. 14), by contrast, maintains that there must be two separately livable happy lives. He is echoed, though less vociferously, by Broadie (1991, 429) and White (1992, 101 n. 17). On this view, (3) can be satisfied by both kinds of lives that are proper to a human being only if we are willing to say that two separately livable lives could be happiest, a possibility presupposed by understanding 'happiest' as the elided predicate at ᵃ9, which Broadie (1991, 429) does. This second view introduces two kinds of happiness, which is precisely the impediment to solving the Conjunctive Problem of Happiness that I am dealing with in this chapter. So, the first view is preferable if we are to solve that problem. Note, however, that even the first view does not much mitigate the surprise that a reader feels upon encountering ᵃ9 unless it is combined with my proposal. That is because the traditional translations of ᵃ9 support taking Aristotle's point to be that there are two lives, one in accordance with intellect and the other in accordance with ethical virtue, and that both count as happy, but the former counts as happy in a superior way to the latter. This is surprising even if the two lives are aspects of one person's overall life rather than separately livable lives, for Aristotle would then be claiming that one person's contemplative life is happy, and her ethical life is happy, and the happiness of the former is superior to that of the latter. When combined with my proposal, though, understanding the two lives as aspects of one person's overall life yields the claim that one of these aspects is proper to a human in a primary way, the other in a secondary way, and leaves open what the aspect proper in a secondary way has to do with that person's happiness (which matter I will address in Chapter 5) rather than attempting to combine two happy lives in one life. This claim is much less surprising than is the one that results from the usual proposals.

[20] Since (2), (4), (5), (6), and (7) feature superlatives, one might be tempted to add to Aristotle's argument as I have construed it two premises to the effect that there are degrees of happiness that track degrees of being proper to a human being, *and* that such degrees of happiness count as distinct ways of being happy. This would allow one to derive the claim that there is more than one sort of happiness. I do not see any good reason for doing so and I have given a reading of the argument that does not demand doing so. The fact that the Duality Thesis would impede solving the Conjunctive Problem gives a reason for *not* doing so, as do various other considerations mentioned in this chapter.

in order to show that it is possible both to affirm his claims about the relationship of ethically virtuous activity to happiness from *NE* 1–9 and to adhere to his psychological view, mentioned at the beginning of our *NE* 10 passage, that a human being is most of all his or her (theoretical) intellect. If Aristotle can conclude both (10) and (20) from a consistent and plausible set of premises, then this will have been accomplished. This is a very different result from the one that Cooper (1975) claims to see, which is that in our passage Aristotle abruptly rejects the view about the relationship of ethically virtuous activity to happiness that he has been expressing throughout most of the *NE* (and indeed in the *Protrepticus* and *Eudemian Ethics*) precisely in order to give an account of human happiness that adheres to the psychological view of a human being as most of all his or her intellect. I will discuss this at length in Chapter 5.

A doubt may still linger about the difference that my proposal actually makes. Even if my proposal is correct, and therefore ^a9 does not commit Aristotle to two kinds of happiness, or at least to two lives that differ in status with respect to happiness, does the rest of 10.7–8 not already commit him to that? After all, Aristotle makes the following claims in these chapters:

i. Happiness is contemplative activity.
ii. The person with theoretical wisdom (of which contemplation is the activity) is happier than any person lacking it.
iii. Contemplation as an activity meets the formal requirements of happiness to a greater extent than ethically virtuous activity does.

However, it simply does not follow from (i)–(iii), or from anything else in the rest of 10.7–8, that there are two kinds of happiness, or two lives that differ in status with respect to happiness, unless we add the claim that corresponds to the traditional interpretation of ^a9, namely that one life is happy (or happiest) in the primary way, and another in a secondary way. For all that Aristotle has said in the rest of 10.7–8, it might be true that there is one happy life (and one way of being happy). The traditional understanding of ^a9 gratuitously attributes a distinction between two kinds of happiness to him, whereas mine does not do so. My interpretation thus leaves the door open for a solution to the Conjunctive Problem of Happiness, which solution I will describe in Chapter 5.

But one might still wonder whether a commitment to two kinds of happiness is derivable in the following way: If from the fact that contemplative activity is proper to humans in a primary way we can infer that it is happiness, can we not also from the fact that ethically virtuous activities are proper to humans in a secondary way infer that they are happiness, but of a secondary kind? In short, no. Even if being the activity that is proper to humans in a primary way is sufficient for that activity to be human happiness, this does not entitle us to conclude that a difference in activities' ways of being proper to humans suffices for a difference in kinds of happiness corresponding to those activities. For example, the activities might have different relationships to the same kind of happiness. I will say more about such matters in Chapter 5.[21]

3.4 Conclusion

I have argued that there are good reasons to understand 'proper to a human being'[22] as the elided predicate at *NE* 10.8, 1178^a9 instead of the almost universally adopted 'happiest' ('*eudaimonestatos*') or 'happy' ('*eudaimôn*'), and that doing so permits an interpretation of the passage that, unlike the Duality Thesis, does not impede solving the Conjunctive Problem of Happiness. My proposal for the elided predicate is preferable to the traditional ones because it makes better sense of the structure of Aristotle's argument and commits him to less than they do: The standard distinction between two ways of being happy presupposes the distinction between two ways of being proper to a human being, but not vice versa. In Chapter 5 I will explain what these two ways of being proper to a human being are. In Chapter 4 I will address whether theoretical intellect is proper to a human being at all, for there is yet another notorious problem that stands in the way of a solution to the Conjunctive Problem of Happiness.

---

[21] This paragraph is due to helpful discussion with Gabriel Richardson Lear.
[22] '⟨οἰκεῖος⟩ τῷ ἀνθρώπῳ'

CHAPTER 4

Is Contemplation Proper to Humans?

4.1 The Divinity Thesis

At various points in the *Nicomachean Ethics* Aristotle argues or assumes
that we can infer the nature of human happiness by identifying some activity that is proper (*idion, oikeion*) to human beings. His *ergon* argument
in *NE* 1.7 relies on such an inference, and there he rejects as candidates
for happiness activities like self-nourishment, growth, and perception on
the grounds that they are shared by beings other than humans.[1] As we saw
in the last chapter, his argument in *NE* 10.7–8 depends on claims about
what is proper to human beings. This argument eventually culminates in
the conclusion that human happiness is "a kind of contemplative activity" (*theôria tis*). The reason given for this is that the life characterized by
contemplative activity is most proper to a human being. Aristotle is rely-
ing on the claim that only human beings are capable of contemplation.
But many scholars have thought that his recognition that divine beings
contemplate creates a problem. Their worry is expressed by the following
argument:

---

[1] There is an issue here that is worth mentioning although it does not affect my argument: Aristotle
indicates that the *erga* of different species of non-human animals are peculiar to them (10.5, 1176ᵃ3–
12), echoing Plato's point in *Rep.* 1, 352E, but he does not satisfy our thirst for examples of such
erga. How does a horse's *ergon* differ from a dog's? He offers an answer at 2.6, 1106ᵃ15–24, but it
introduces a new complication: His description there of a horse's *ergon* is in terms of how the horse is
useful to humans. We are left with the question of what the *ergon* of a horse could be independently
of human interests. *Politics* 1.8, 1256ᵇ15–22 might tempt us to despair of an answer, for it says that
plants are for the sake of animals and the latter for the sake of humans. Then there is *GA* 1.23,
731ᵃ24–34, which speaks of the *erga* of plants and animals as if they were generic: reproduction for
plants and perception for animals. All of this leaves us wondering how Aristotle can generalize and
consistently deploy his peculiarity requirement for *erga* in the case of plants and animals. In any case,
Aristotle is very clear that, at least in the context of identifying the human good, the human *ergon*
must be peculiar to humans. Thanks to Gabriel Richardson Lear for encouraging me to mention
this issue as an interesting aside.

80

Argument from Divine Contemplation

1. If contemplation is proper to human beings, then only human beings are capable of contemplation.
2. If divine beings are capable of contemplation, then it is false that only human beings are capable of contemplation.
3. Divine beings are capable of contemplation.
4. So, it is false that only human beings are capable of contemplation.
∴ Contemplation is not proper to human beings.

This argument encapsulates what I will call "the Divinity Thesis."

Divinity Thesis
Contemplation is not proper to human beings, for divine beings engage in it, too.

The Divinity Thesis, like the Divergence Thesis and the Duality Thesis that I considered in the previous two chapters, thwarts solving the Conjunctive Problem. It makes it impossible to affirm the Monist Constraint, according to which happiness is a single activity, theoretical contemplation, while adhering to Aristotle's basic commitment that our *ergon*, and therefore our happiness, is proper to us.

Many commentators have addressed the Argument from Divine Contemplation.[2] Some accept the conclusion, attributing various degrees of inconsistency in thought or expression to Aristotle. Those who wish to reject the conclusion on his behalf have standardly denied premise (1). I will discuss these interpretations and their shortcomings in Section 2. In Section 3 I will survey the most relevant apparent evidence for premise (3), the texts that describe divine contemplation. Section 4 contends that the Argument from Divine Contemplation is invalid because it equivocates on 'contemplation.' According to Aristotle, divine and human contemplation cannot be type-identical activities.[3] This way of responding to the

---

[2] Among those who have discussed this problem, but without arguing for the solution that I will advocate, are Ackrill (1974, 352), Aufderheide (2015, 54), Bush (2008, 65), Cagnoli Fieeconi (2019), Charles (2017a,b), Curzer (1990, 426–428) and (2012, 411–412), Dahl (2011, 78), Joachim (1951, 50), Keyt (1983, 385), Kraut (1979) and (1989, 312–319), Lear (2004, 189–193), Nagel (1972, 255), Reeve (1992, 145–149), and Whiting (1988, 37–38). Lawrence (2001, 445) mentions the problem but does not offer a solution. Wilkes (1978, 557–566) argues that Aristotle does not have a solution and his theory of happiness is therefore internally inconsistent.

[3] This directly contradicts the assumption of several of the commentators mentioned above, as well as that of certain interpreters who discuss divine and human contemplation without explicitly addressing the problem with which I am concerned. These include Bodéüs (1992, 46), Bordt (2006, 116), Burnyeat (2008, 43), Keyt (1989, 17–18), Lear (1988, 297–298), McCready-Flora (2019, 44), and

Argument from Divine Contemplation closely parallels Aristotle's explicit response to a structurally similar argument dealing with animals, as Section 5 argues. There is, then, some reason to believe that he would have adopted the strategy that I elaborate if he had been confronted with the Argument from Divine Contemplation. That argument thus gives us no reason to disbelieve Aristotle's claim that contemplation is proper to human beings. The impediment that the Divinity Thesis presents to solving the Conjunctive Problem will be cleared away.

4.2   The Views of Other Commentators

Three sets of responses have been offered to the Argument from Divine Contemplation. The brief arguments that I offer against them, some of which have been given before, are not meant to show that they are unworkable, but rather to indicate that they are sufficiently controversial and disruptive to the project of solving the Conjunctive Problem to motivate the response to the argument that I will advocate in Section 4.

4.2.1   Transhumanism

Transhumanists accept the conclusion, (5). They think that contemplation is not proper to human beings as such, but only to the divine.[4] There are multiple subspecies of transhumanist. For example, Ackrill (1974, 352), giving a slightly more detailed statement of the claim expressed by Joachim (1951, 50), thinks that since contemplation is not a good candidate for something that is proper to human beings, ethically virtuous activities, which are more fitting candidates, must be the activities that Aristotle has in mind in the *ergon* argument of *NE* 1.7, and indeed in *NE* 1–9. He of course realizes that *NE* 10.7–8 upsets this picture, seemingly prioritizing contemplation. At the other extreme, Nagel (1972, 255) thinks that the Argument from Divine Contemplation pushes us to admit that Aristotle has the apparently paradoxical view that the human good is not the human good, but rather the divine good. To live well as human beings, we must transcend living as human beings at all. Whereas Ackrill's view favors a reading of the

---

Norman (1969, 67). Gauthier and Jolif (1970, vol. 2.2, 897) are not explicitly addressing the Argument from Divine Contemplation or the problem that underlies it, though they say, as I do, that divine and human contemplation are type-distinct. See my p. 92 n. 21 and the section of the main text to which it refers for three differences between their comment and my proposal.

[4] Proponents of this view include Ackrill (1974, 352), Bush (2008, 65), Charles (2017a,b), Curzer (1990, 426–428), Joachim (1951, 50), Keyt (1983, 385) and (1989, 17–18), Nagel (1972, 255), and Reeve (1992, 145–149).

ergon argument that makes *NE* 10.7–8 a non sequitur, Nagel's prioritizes a reading of *NE* 10.7–8 that comes as a severe shock to readers of the *ergon* argument. The problem with any version of transhumanism is that it requires us to think that contemplation, whether it is part, all, or one kind of human happiness, is not part, all, or one kind of it in virtue of being proper to a human being. But both the *ergon* argument and *NE* 10.7–8 have standardly been taken to suggest that the human good ought to count as the human good in virtue of being proper to those beings whose good it is.[5] A response to the Argument from Divine Contemplation that lacked this problem would be desirable.[6]

4.2.2   Composite Essence

Another view, advocated principally by Whiting (1988, 37–38) and adopted in various forms by Aufderheide (2015, 54), Cagnoli Fiecconi (2019), Curzer (2012, 411–412), Dahl (2011, 78), and Lear (2004, 189–193), is that contemplation considered in its own right is not proper to human beings, but considered as part of a composite set of activities it is proper to human beings.[7] That is because, according to this view, the human essence is

---

[5] Whiting (1986, 88–90) inveighs against a position that she calls "the transcendental account," the view that Aristotle is interested in the human good in the *ergon* argument, but in a good that transcends the human good in *NE* 10, on the grounds that such an account threatens the coherence of the *NE* (particularly since, as she points out, *NE* 10.5, 1176ᵃ3–4 seems to refer to the *ergon* argument). Thorsrud (2015, 355–356) highlights this threat with reference to *NE* 1.5, 1096ᵇ31–35, which suggests that the object of investigation in the *NE* is a good that human beings are capable of achieving. Unlike Whiting, Thorsrud thinks that Aristotle's account does not escape the threat, and that is because Aristotle is genuinely pulled in two different directions and is honest about this.

[6] Charles (2017a,b), who articulates a particularly nuanced version of transhumanism, would presumably contravene the common interpretation according to which the human good ought to count as the human good in virtue of being proper to those beings whose good it is. Charles thinks that what is proper to human beings is a whole pattern of life activities, considered as a whole, and that only some of these activities, including contemplation, are part of the human *ergon*. Contemplation, considered as an activity in its own right, is not proper to human beings, according to Charles. Interpreters will disagree with Charles if they think that the answer to Aristotle's question, "What, then, would this *ergon* (work, function, characteristic activity) ⟨of a human being⟩ be?" (*NE* 1.7, 1097ᵇ33), is constrained by his claim in the next line that "we seek what is proper (*idion*) ⟨to a human being⟩" (1097ᵇ34), and is given first in general form as "a kind of active life of the part that has reason" (1098ᵃ3–4) and then more specifically as "activity of the soul in accordance with virtue, and if there are multiple virtues, then in accordance with the best and most complete/final/perfect" (1098ᵃ16–18). An interpreter who takes this to be Aristotle's pattern of reasoning will think that there is no room for Charles's distinction between the set of proper life activities of a human being described in this passage and the human *ergon*. I am grateful to him for helpful conversations about this.

[7] The idea that in the *ergon* argument Aristotle appeals to a composite set of activities that is proper to a human being, even though individual activities in that set might not be, echoes

composite, including the capacities for intellectually and ethically virtuous activities, and the human *ergon* is the manifestation of these essential capacities. So, it is true in a way that contemplation is proper to human beings since it is part of the human essence and that in turn is proper to human beings. But it is false that only human beings contemplate because divine beings contemplate, too. The composite essence view, then, denies premise (1) of the Argument from Divine Contemplation and thus avoids the conclusion.

There are several problems for this view. First, if one accepts that humans have a composite essence, that the human essence determines the human *ergon*, and that the human *ergon* determines human happiness, one will be prevented from solving the Conjunctive Problem because one will have violated the Monist Constraint, according to which happiness is a single activity, theoretical contemplation.[8]

Charles raises a problem for it in his (2017a, 107) and (2017b, 96), a problem that is partially anticipated by Nagel (1972, 259): The view that humans have a composite essence gives no principled way of including theoretical intellect in the composite essence, and therefore contemplation as part of the excellent performance of the composite *ergon* of such an essence, without also including the perceptive part of our soul in our essence and perceptual activity in our *ergon*. Interpreters ought to have a principled explanation for such an exclusion, though, since Aristotle decisively excludes perception from our *ergon* (*NE* 1.7, 1098^{a}1–3). A proponent of the composite essence view might respond that the human essence is restricted to the rational soul and excludes perceptual capacities for that reason, but monists would presumably regard such a response as unprincipled and as complicated by Aristotle's discussion of practical intellect in perceptual terms in *NE* 6.8 and 6.11.

A third problem for the composite essence view is that even if it succeeded as an interpretation of the *ergon* argument, it would struggle to account for the way in which Aristotle argues in *NE* 10.7–8 that contemplation is proper to human beings, which I examined in the previous chapter. That is because he argues there that contemplation is proper to human beings in a primary way and ethically virtuous activities are proper to them in a secondary way. But if, as the composite essence view has it,

---

Irwin (1980, 49): "If x can do A, B, and C, and nothing else can do C, but other things can do A and B, we might describe x's peculiar function either as 'doing A, B, and C' or as 'doing C.' Now it is fairly clear that Aristotle understands the peculiar activity of man in the first, inclusive way."

[8] Bush (2008, 65 n. 23) thinks that the composite essence view assumes that happiness essentially includes ethically and intellectually virtuous activities.

contemplation and ethically virtuous activities are part of the human *ergon* because the capacities for these activities are all equally part of the human essence, then it is difficult to see what could ground the primary/secondary distinction.[9] Each would be a manifestation of capacities that are part of the human essence, and thus proper to human beings in the same way.[10] A response to the Argument from Divine Contemplation that made good sense not only of the *ergon* argument but also of *NE* 10.7–8 would be preferable.

4.2.3 Relativism

A third view, advocated by Kraut (1979) and (1989, 312–319), urges a relativistic rendering of 'proper.'[11] According to Kraut, whereas Aristotle sometimes uses 'proper' in what we might think of as the more standard, absolute sense according to which it restricts a property to items of a given kind, in the *ergon* argument and other parts of the *NE* he uses it to mean "proper to humans relative to all lower forms of life." That is to say, in the relevant contexts Aristotle means only to identify properties that humans have but animals and plants do not, regardless of whether divine beings have them, too. In this relativistic sense of 'proper,' it is true to say that contemplation is proper to human beings since lower forms of life cannot

---

[9] As I mentioned in the previous chapter, Aristotle uses '*deuterôs*' to mark this distinction, rather than the vastly more common '*allôs*' or '*heterôs*,' which makes it unlikely that both of the things called 'proper' have coordinate status. Rather, one is proper in a primary sense, and the other is proper in a way subordinate to, or dependent upon, that. In thinking that the composite essence view struggles to account for a distinction between what is proper to us in a primary way and in a secondary way, I follow Scott (1999, 231–235), though as Chapter 3 revealed I disagree with Scott's further claim that such a distinction grounds a further distinction between a primary and secondary kind of happiness.

[10] An anonymous reviewer for *Ergo: An Open Access Journal of Philosophy* wonders whether this problem could be addressed by distinguishing two levels of analysis, such that at one level the capacities are all equally part of the human essence and at another, finer level a primary/secondary distinction is discernible. I worry that even if such a distinction in levels of analysis of a composite human essence could be derived from the *ergon* argument and *NE* 10.7–8, and if some suitable ground for the distinction that is compatible with the composite essence view could be specified, the Argument from Divine Contemplation would reemerge at the finer level of analysis. If divine beings contemplate, it will be at least as problematic to say, at whatever level of analysis, that contemplation, rather than ethically virtuous activity, is proper to humans in a primary way (as Aristotle says in *NE* 10.7–8) as it is to say that contemplation, rather than ethically virtuous activity, is proper to humans. In short, I worry that the composite essence proponent's ability to respond to the Argument from Divine Contemplation depends on the impossibility of isolating contemplation in its own right as being proper (or proper in a primary way) to humans at any level of analysis, but the possibility of such isolation is central to the most plausible interpretations of *NE* 10.7–8, as well as to the possibility of solving the Conjunctive Problem.

[11] What I here call "relativism" is not the same as what I called "relativism" in Chapter 1 since the *relata* are different.

contemplate, but false that only humans contemplate since divine beings do so, too. Thus, like the composite essence view, the relativist view avoids the conclusion of the Argument from Divine Contemplation by denying premise (1).

The problem with relativism is that it would be very difficult to divine such a meaning of 'proper' from the text of the *NE*,[12] and there would be little motivation to do so unless one had been confronted with the Argument from Divine Contemplation. This view thus seems ad hoc and should therefore be an interpretation of last resort.

4.3 Divine Contemplation

Having discussed existing responses to the Argument from Divine Contemplation, I will survey the most relevant apparent evidence for premise (3) of that argument. There are two main texts that might appear to suggest that human and divine contemplation are type-identical. In this section I will contend that these texts are inconclusive and are most conservatively interpreted as saying merely that human and divine contemplation are similar in certain respects that are important for Aristotle's arguments in each context.[13] In the next section I will argue that Aristotle cannot intend to describe human and divine contemplation as type-identical.

T1 (*NE* 10.8, 1178[b]7–32)

It would appear from the following considerations, too, that perfect happiness is a contemplative sort of activity. We suppose the gods most of all to be blessed and happy. But what kind of actions ought to be ascribed to them? Actions that are just? Or will they not appear ridiculous entering into contracts, returning deposits, and all such things? Courageous actions, enduring fearful things and facing danger

ἡ δὲ τελεία εὐδαιμονία ὅτι θεω- [b]7
ρητική τις ἐστὶν ἐνέργεια, καὶ ἐν-
τεῦθεν ἂν φανείη. τοὺς θεοὺς γὰρ
μάλιστα ὑπειλήφαμεν μακαρίους
καὶ εὐδαίμονας εἶναι· πράξεις δὲ
ποίας ἀπονεῖμαι χρεὼν αὐτοῖς;   10
πότερα τὰς δικαίας; ἢ γελοῖοι φα-
νοῦνται συναλλάττοντες καὶ πα-
ρακαταθήκας ἀποδιδόντες καὶ ὅ-
σα τοιαῦτα; ἀλλὰ τὰς ἀνδρείους

---

[12] Curzer (1990, 427 n. 17) replies to Kraut as follows: "If Aristotle wanted the reader to take *idion* [proper] as relative to something, then he would have specified which something. Since he did not do so, we must take *idion* in an absolute sense." Reeve (1992, 126 n. 35) argues on the basis of *Top.* 1.5, 102[a]24–28 that Kraut's relativistic sense of 'proper' cannot be the correct one for the *ergon* argument since if it were, then because the relativistic sense of 'proper' cannot reveal something's essence, the human *ergon* would not have the relationship to the human essence that Aristotle supposes it to have.

[13] This conclusion about the passages' status agrees with that of Herzberg (2013, ch. 4), though my analyses of the passages, particularly of the first, differ in detail from his.

because doing so is noble? Or generous actions? To whom will they give? It would be odd for them to have money or anything of that sort. And what would their temperate actions be? Or would not such praise be cheap since they do not have base appetites? If we were to go through all of the things concerned with such actions, it would appear that they are trivial and unworthy of gods. But all suppose them to be alive and therefore active, for surely they cannot suppose them to be sleeping like Endymion. So then, if acting (and still more, producing) is removed from living, what is left besides contemplation? The result would be that the activity of the god, exceeding in blessedness, is contemplative. And indeed, among human activities the one that is most akin to this is the most characteristic of happiness.[14] An indication of this is that the other animals do not share in happiness, being completely deprived of this sort of activity. For in the case of the gods the whole of life is blessed, whereas in the case of human beings this is so only so far as there is some semblance of this sort of activity. But among the other animals none is happy since none shares in contemplation in any way. Indeed, happiness extends as far as contemplation does, and to those to whom it more belongs to contemplate, it more belongs also to be happy, not accidentally, but rather in accordance with the contemplation, for this is valuable in itself. The result would be that happiness is a type of contemplation.

* * ὑπομένοντας τὰ φοβερὰ καὶ κινδυνεύοντας ὅτι καλόν; ἢ τὰς ἐλευθερίους; τίνι δὲ δώσουσιν; ἄτοπον δ' εἰ καὶ ἔσται αὐτοῖς νόμισμα ἤ τι τοιοῦτον. αἱ δὲ σώφρονες τί ἂν εἶεν; ἢ φορτικὸς ὁ ἔπαινος, ὅτι οὐκ ἔχουσι φαύλας ἐπιθυμίας; διεξιοῦσι δὲ πάντα φαίνοιτ' ἂν τὰ περὶ τὰς πράξεις μικρὰ καὶ ἀνάξια θεῶν. ἀλλὰ μὴν ζῆν γε πάντες ὑπειλήφασιν αὐτοὺς καὶ ἐνεργεῖν ἄρα· οὐ γὰρ δὴ καθεύδειν ὥσπερ τὸν Ἐνδυμίωνα. τῷ δὴ ζῶντι τοῦ πράττειν ἀφαιρουμένου, ἔτι δὲ μᾶλλον τοῦ ποιεῖν, τί λείπεται πλὴν θεωρία; ὥστε ἡ τοῦ θεοῦ ἐνέργεια, μακαριότητι διαφέρουσα, θεωρητικὴ ἂν εἴη· καὶ τῶν ἀνθρωπίνων δὴ ἡ ταύτῃ συγγενεστάτη εὐδαιμονικωτάτη. σημεῖον δὲ καὶ τὸ μὴ μετέχειν τὰ λοιπὰ ζῷα εὐδαιμονίας, τῆς τοιαύτης ἐνεργείας ἐστερημένα τελείως. τοῖς μὲν γὰρ θεοῖς ἅπας ὁ βίος μακάριος, τοῖς δ' ἀνθρώποις, ἐφ' ὅσον ὁμοίωμά τι τῆς τοιαύτης ἐνεργείας ὑπάρχει· τῶν δ' ἄλλων ζῴων οὐδὲν εὐδαιμονεῖ, ἐπειδὴ οὐδαμῇ κοινωνεῖ θεωρίας. ἐφ' ὅσον δὴ διατείνει ἡ θεωρία, καὶ ἡ εὐδαιμονία, καὶ οἷς μᾶλλον ὑπάρχει τὸ θεωρεῖν, καὶ εὐδαιμονεῖν, οὐ κατὰ συμβεβηκὸς ἀλλὰ κατὰ τὴν θεωρίαν· αὕτη γὰρ καθ' αὑτὴν τιμία. ὥστ' εἴη ἂν ἡ εὐδαιμονία θεωρία τις.

---

[14] See my p. 22 n. 40 on the translation of, '*eudaimonikôtera*,' the comparative form of the adjective that here appears in superlative form.

According to what I will call an "identity reading," T1 commits Aristotle to the claim that human and divine contemplation are type-identical. On what I will call a "similarity reading," it commits him only to the claim that they are similar. If one has an identity reading, one might suppose that Aristotle argues roughly as follows, deducing the general nature of happiness from the nature of divine happiness as contemplation:

i. The gods are happy, alive, and active, but they do not engage in ethically virtuous activities.
ii. If the gods are happy, alive, and active, but do not engage in ethically virtuous activities, then the only activity remaining for them would be contemplation.
iii. So, the only activity for gods is contemplation.
iv. If something is an activity for the gods, then it is happiness.
∴. Happiness is contemplation.

The idea that human and divine contemplation are type-identical is supposed to gain support from Aristotle's argument thus interpreted. However, there is a problem: Either happiness for gods and happiness for humans are type-identical or they are not. If they are not, then the passage licenses no inference to the claim that divine and human contemplation are type-identical. We would have to assume that gratuitously. If happiness for gods and happiness for humans are type-identical, however, it would be completely superfluous to mention that animals do not share in happiness or contemplation. The argument simply would not require mentioning them at all.

It remains possible to read Aristotle as giving this argument in the passage, with the result that he would be committed to human and divine contemplation being type-identical. But attributing such a commitment to him should be an interpretation of last resort since, as we have seen already, Aristotle is elsewhere committed to contemplation being proper to human beings. Fortunately, similarity readings of the passage are possible, and these do not commit Aristotle to the type-identity of human and divine contemplation.[15] One interpretation of his argument in this passage that would involve a similarity reading construes the argument as

---

[15] If one adopts a similarity reading of T1, one can do so also for *NE* 10.7, 1177^{b}31–34 and 10.8, 1179^{a}22–32. I discussed the latter in Chapter 2 and will discuss the former in Chapter 5. The first enjoins us to "cast off mortality (*athanatizein*) and go to all lengths to live a life in accordance with what is highest in us." The second leverages popular opinions that there are providential gods who most love contemplators – Aristotle does not regard these opinions as literally true, as I will discuss in Section 4, though Bodéüs (1992) disagrees – to argue that contemplation is the noblest activity and

an appeal to the best explanation of various opinions of others: People say that all gods are happy, some humans are, and no animals are. But gods engage in no ethically virtuous activities, which we might have been tempted to identify with happiness. The best explanation for these claims is that – and now we move to Aristotle's official view rather than the imprecise terms of the opinions[16] – all gods are happy in a way peculiar to them because they all engage in a sort of contemplation peculiar to them, some humans are happy in a way peculiar to them because they engage in a sort of contemplation peculiar to them but similar to that in which the gods engage, and no animal is happy since no animal engages in any sort of contemplation. If this is right, Aristotle can then make both the extensional claim and the causal claim that, for human beings, happiness extends just as far as (human) contemplation does and the happiness is because of the contemplation. This makes human happiness similar to the happiness of the gods. The nexus of similarity is that both kinds of happiness are what they are because of the contemplation. The happiness of the gods is what it is because of divine contemplation, and the happiness of humans is what it is because of human contemplation. Contemplation of whatever sort plays a similar role in happiness of whatever sort. In this way of interpreting the argument of T1, the final two sentences (^{b}28–32) apply only to human happiness, and no premise in the argument asserts the type-identity of human and divine contemplation. Rather, Aristotle means to say only that human contemplation is "most akin" to divine contemplation (^{b}23) and that happy humans must engage in "some semblance of this sort of activity" (^{b}27). It is preferable to adopt an interpretation of T1 that has these features if possible since Aristotle elsewhere is committed to the claim that contemplation is proper to humans.

T2 (*Metaph.* 12.7, 1072^{b}13–30)

The heavens and nature depend on this sort of principle. And this principle's occupation is like the best that we for a short time engage in. For it is always thus occupied (whereas	ἐκ τοιαύτης ἄρα ἀρχῆς ἤρτη- ^{b}13 ται ὁ οὐρανὸς καὶ ἡ φύσις. δι- αγωγὴ δ' ἐστὶν οἵα ἡ ἀρίστη 15 μικρὸν χρόνον ἡμῖν (οὕτω γὰρ

the most characteristic of happiness. Neither passage suggests type-identity (rather than similarity) between human and divine contemplation.

[16] Bodéüs (1992, 239) thinks that this passage is Aristotle's only exposition of theology. This is surprising. What is not surprising is that Bodéüs also thinks that this passage says that divine and human contemplation are type-identical (1992, 46). Gauthier and Jolif (1970, vol. 2.2, 897) have a sharply contrasting view: Aristotle's remarks in this passage about the gods are ad hominem.

we cannot be), since its activity is also pleasure (and because of this wakefulness, perception, and thinking are most pleasant, whereas
hopes and memories are so with reference to
these). Thinking in its own right is of what
is best in its own right, and what is most of
all thinking is of what is best of all. Thought
thinks itself in partaking of thought's object,
for it becomes an object of thought in making contact with and thinking the object of
thought, with the result that thought and the
object of thought are the same. For thought
is what is capable of receiving the object of
thought, viz., the essence/substance, and it is
active when it has it, with the result that the
latter more so than the former is the divine
thing that thought seems to have, and contemplation is what is most pleasant and best.
If, therefore, the god is always doing well in
the way that we sometimes are, that is marvelous, but if the god is doing well in a better
way, that is yet more marvelous. The latter
is the case. Life also belongs to the god, for
thought's activity is life, and the god is that
activity. The god's activity in its own right is
life that is best and eternal. We say, then, that
the god is a living being, eternal, and best,
with the result that life and continuous and
eternal duration belong to the god, for this is
the god.

ἀεὶ ἐκεῖνο· ἡμῖν μὲν γὰρ ἀδύ-
νατον), ἐπεὶ καὶ ἡδονὴ ἡ ἐνέργεια τούτου (καὶ διὰ τοῦτο ἐ-
γρήγορσις αἴσθησις νόησις ἥ-
διστον, ἐλπίδες δὲ καὶ μνῆμαι
διὰ ταῦτα). ἡ δὲ νόησις ἡ καθ'
αὑτὴν τοῦ καθ' αὑτὸ ἀρίστου,
καὶ ἡ μάλιστα τοῦ μάλιστα.
αὑτὸν δὲ νοεῖ ὁ νοῦς κατὰ με-   20
τάληψιν τοῦ νοητοῦ· νοητὸς
γὰρ γίγνεται θιγγάνων καὶ νο-
ῶν, ὥστε ταὐτὸν νοῦς καὶ νοη-
τόν. τὸ γὰρ δεκτικὸν τοῦ νοη-
τοῦ καὶ τῆς οὐσίας νοῦς, ἐνερ-
γεῖ δὲ ἔχων, ὥστ' ἐκείνου μᾶλλον τοῦτο ὃ δοκεῖ ὁ νοῦς θεῖον
ἔχειν, καὶ ἡ θεωρία τὸ ἥδιστον
καὶ ἄριστον. εἰ οὖν οὕτως εὖ
ἔχει, ὡς ἡμεῖς ποτέ, ὁ θεὸς ἀεί,   25
θαυμαστόν· εἰ δὲ μᾶλλον, ἔτι
θαυμασιώτερον. ἔχει δὲ ὧδε.
καὶ ζωὴ δέ γε ὑπάρχει· ἡ γὰρ
νοῦ ἐνέργεια ζωή, ἐκεῖνος δὲ
ἡ ἐνέργεια· ἐνέργεια δὲ ἡ καθ'
αὑτὴν ἐκείνου ζωὴ ἀρίστη καὶ
ἀΐδιος. φαμὲν δὴ τὸν θεὸν εἶναι ζῷον ἀΐδιον ἄριστον, ὥστε
ζωὴ καὶ αἰὼν συνεχὴς καὶ ἀΐδιος ὑπάρχει τῷ θεῷ· τοῦτο   3ᴄ
γὰρ ὁ θεός.

The motivation for an identity reading of T2 comes mostly from its second sentence. On such a reading, Aristotle's point in this passage would be
that human and divine contemplation are the same in type and differ only
with respect to continuity and duration: human contemplation is intermittent and of finite duration, whereas divine contemplation is continuous
and of eternal duration. The second sentence of T2 considered in its own
right is ambiguous between an identity reading and a similarity reading, so
it could mean this. However, the seventh and eight sentences (ᵇ25–26), at
least on one plausible interpretation, disambiguate the second sentence in

favor of the similarity reading.[17] The god's activity is of a type that is better than, and therefore distinct from, the human activity. The fourth sentence (^{b}18–19) opens the possibility that the distinction might have something to do with differences in object of thought.[18] The god's thinking is always and necessarily directed at the highest object, whereas our thinking is apt to be diverted in a variety of ways. Even the third sentence (^{b}15–18) can be interpreted as foreshadowing the claim in the seventh and eighth (^{b}25–26) that human and divine contemplation are merely similar. It depends on what Aristotle means in the third by "we cannot be" (^{b}16). He could mean that we cannot be perpetually engaged in the same activity as the god is, or that we cannot be engaged in the same activity at all. The identity reading requires the first of these two options. The reasons why human and divine contemplation are distinct in type will be clearer when we come to Aristotle's more substantive description of divine contemplation in *Metaph.* 12.9. For now, it is enough to note that there is a way of reading T2 that has this result.

On the similarity reading of T2, how are human and divine contemplation similar? At the very least, both have an intelligible object (^{b}19–24) and are associated with the highest pleasure that each sort of being can experience and are the best activities in which each can engage, as Aristotle argues in the third, fourth, and sixth sentences (^{b}15–24). Further respects in which they are similar or different are difficult to describe precisely on any interpretation of T2.

We have seen that T1 and T2 can both be interpreted as saying that human and divine contemplation are similar in certain respects (being that which principally constitutes the happiness of each, having an intelligible object, and being associated with the highest pleasure that each can experience) rather than that they are type-identical. In the next section I will argue that Aristotle cannot consistently think that they are type-identical.

4.4 The Type-Distinctness of Divine and Human Contemplation

In this section I will contend that the Argument from Divine Contemplation, which I presented in Section 1, is invalid because it equivocates

---

[17] This is also argued by Herzberg (2013, 147) and (2016, 164 and 174–175), as well as by Laks (2000, 233).
[18] Laks (2000, 234) suggests something similar.

on 'contemplation.' There are two type-distinct kinds of contemplation at issue in the argument, one human and one divine. Furthermore, as I will argue in Section 5, there is evidence that Aristotle would prefer this way of responding to the Argument from Divine Contemplation if he had been presented with it. Parts of my argument that divine and human contemplation are different in type have been given, at least in cursory form, in literature on *Metaphysics* and *De anima*.[19] However, this literature does not argue, as I will, on the basis of a consideration internal to Aristotle's *Nicomachean Ethics*, the context in which type-identity would generate the problem with which I began. My argument is that human and divine contemplation must be distinct in type because only the former is a manifestation of theoretical wisdom (*sophia*) as Aristotle describes it in the *NE*. This distinctive way of arguing permits an otherwise unavailable response to a powerful objection that I will discuss in Section 5. Furthermore, the arguments in the existing literature tend to focus on the differences between the prime mover and human beings, leaving largely unexplored whether divine beings other than the prime mover might contemplate in the way that we can.[20] Finally, the existing considerations have not been directed toward addressing the Argument from Divine Contemplation.[21] Indeed, there has not been much interaction between the literature that addresses that argument and the literature that discusses in detail the nature of divine contemplation. This is unfortunate since, as will emerge in what follows, consideration of both issues together promotes a more accurate understanding of each.

[19] The following either state that, according to Aristotle, human and divine contemplation are distinct in type or give arguments on the basis of which this can be concluded: Aquinas (*In Metaph.* 2613–2615), Averroes (*In Metaph.* 1700–1708), Beere (2010, 27–30), Brunschwig (2000, 296–301), Cohoe (2014, 599) and (2020), Gerson (1990, 127 and 284 n. 87), Herzberg (2013, ch. 4) and (2016), Kosman (2000, 311), Menn (2012, 446–447), Modrak (1991, 770), Ross (1924, vol. 2, 379), Segev (2017, 109), Silverman (2010, 92–93), and Wedin (1988, 229–245).

[20] Cohoe (2020), Rapp (2019), and Segev (2017, ch. 3) are partial exceptions. Cohoe focuses not on whether divine beings other than the prime mover contemplate in the way that we can, but rather on demonstrating that such beings are alive but lack souls. His argument has implications for certain issues that I discuss, such as whether celestial bodies have imagination (*phantasia*). Rapp is principally concerned with a problem about whether the observed heterogeneity of activities of celestial and human beings accords with what we might have expected given antecedent assumptions about the orderliness of the cosmos. Segev more directly discusses the relationship between the cognitive activities of humans and of divine beings, but is more hospitable than I am to the conclusion that these activities possess "essential commonality" (2017, 120).

[21] Each of these three descriptions of remarks in existing literature applies to the comment by Gauthier and Jolif (1970, vol. 2.2, 897), which I have already mentioned as being broadly similar to the view that I adopt in denying that divine and human contemplation are type-identical.

4.4.1   How to Distinguish Types of Activities

Not every difference between two activities is a difference in type. There are significant differences between, for example, plant nutrition and human nutrition, as well as between animal perception and human perception. Plant nutrition involves roots, human nutrition mouths. Lizard vision is mediated by hard eyes, human vision by soft. Humans smell by inhaling through the nose, whereas bloodless animals do not. But Aristotle thinks that such differences are not in type (DA 2.9, 421^{b}13 – 422^{a}7). Even when the activity of smelling takes place through different organs, the per se object of smelling is always the same: odor. Whereas a difference in per se objects suffices for a difference in type of activity, a difference in the material substratum (e.g., organ) affected per se by the same objects does not.

This would follow from an extension of the general account of how to determine whether two things are distinct in species that Aristotle articulates in *Metaph.* 10.8–9. (I take distinctness in species to be sufficient for distinctness in type.) On that account, x and y are distinct in species if F belongs to x in virtue of x's form, G belongs to y in virtue of y's form, and F and G are contraries. x and y are not distinct in species if F belongs to x in virtue of x's matter and G belongs to y in virtue of y's matter, regardless of whether F and G are contraries. For example, a brazen triangle and brazen circle differ in species, as do a brazen triangle and a wooden circle, but a brazen circle and a wooden circle do not. In short, contrariety due to form, which I will call "formal difference," is sufficient for difference in species, but contrariety due to matter, which I will call "material difference," is not. The *Metaph.* 10.8–9 account of difference in species does not deal directly with activities. That is because activities, as non-substances, do not have matter strictly speaking (*Metaph.* 8.4, 1044^{a}32 – ^{b}20), and therefore no difference due to matter strictly speaking. But they do have material substrata in virtue of which they can differ. If differences due to matter include differences due to the material substrata of two activities, then the *Metaph.* 10.8–9 account of difference in species can be extended to cover activities. If Aristotle is indeed extending that account in this way, it would explain why he indicates in *De anima* that a difference in per se objects suffices for a difference in type of activity, but a difference in the material substratum affected per se by the same objects does not.

In addition to, or perhaps as evidence of, having different per se objects (or more generally, being concerned with different things), activities can exhibit one or more of the following indicators of difference in type. They can differ in that one of them, but not the other, is up to us to perform by choice (*DA* 3.3, 427^{b}16–20), constantly performed (428^{a}8–9), or fallible (428^{a}11–12; *NE* 6.3, 1139^{b}14–18), or one implies another activity or state that the other does not (*DA* 3.9, 432^{b}14–26), or they are concerned with things that have a different modal status (*NE* 3.2, 1111^{b}19–23; 6.3, 1139^{b}19–24). Furthermore, Aristotle thinks that if activity *x* is concerned with more kinds of things than activity *y* is, *x* and *y* are type-distinct. For example, whereas *epistêmê* (the developed capacity for scientific demonstration from first principles) and theoretical wisdom are concerned with universals, practical wisdom is concerned not only with universals, but also with particulars, and is therefore type-distinct from the others (*NE* 6.7, 1141^{b}2–15).[22] Such differences are formal rather than material (adverting to the extension of the *Metaph.* 10.8–9 account mentioned previously) since they do not apply in virtue of the material substrata of the activities in question, but rather in virtue of the things with which they are concerned or the way in which they are concerned with them.[23] Formal differences between activities, but not material differences, will be markers of type-distinctness. In the sections that follow I will argue that divine and human contemplation exhibit various formal differences and therefore are type-distinct. We know that these differences must be formal rather than material for the following reason: The prime mover's contemplation cannot have a material substratum. On some interpretations of *De anima*, human contemplation has none. If it has none, then any difference between the prime mover's contemplation and human contemplation would have to be formal rather than material. If human contemplation does have a material substratum, then it would still differ in type from the prime mover's contemplation since the essence of one, but not the other, can be materially realized. I will assume that if the prime mover's contemplation and human contemplation differ formally in respects *F*, *G*, *H*, and so on, then differences in respects *F*, *G*, or *H* between human contemplation and contemplation performed by divine beings other than the prime mover (such as celestial bodies) are also formal differences, whether or not the other divine beings and humans contemplate in a matter-involving way.

---

[22] This need not mean that practical wisdom is concerned with the same universals as *epistêmê* and theoretical wisdom are, but only that it differs from those because it is concerned not only with some universals or other, but also with particulars. That is to say, practical wisdom is concerned with more kinds of things.

[23] For a detailed account of formal differences between, and material substrata of, activities, see Reece (2019).

4.4.2 Human Contemplation

As I discussed in Chapters 1 and 2, Aristotle thinks that any instance of human contemplation is a manifestation of the virtue of theoretical wisdom (*sophia*) in his technical sense (*NE* 10.7, 1177^{a}12 – ^{b}26, 10.8, 1179^{a}29–32),[24] which in turn includes two states: a particular sort of *nous*, the developed capacity to grasp first principles intuitively as first principles, and *epistêmê*, the developed capacity for scientific demonstration from first principles (*NE* 6.7, 1141^{a}18–20, 6.3, 1139^{b}31–32). If divine beings lacked either of these states, then they would lack theoretical wisdom in Aristotle's technical sense. But then their contemplation could not be of the same type as human contemplation is since it would not be a manifestation of the same state of capacity. So, our question is: Do the divine beings that Aristotle recognizes have the aforementioned states, namely the developed capacity to grasp first principles intuitively as first principles and the developed capacity for scientific demonstration from first principles?

4.4.3 The Range of Divine Beings

In order to answer the question with appropriate generality, we need to identify what divine beings Aristotle recognizes. Most obviously, there is the prime mover of *Metaph.* 12.[25] This being is supposed to be responsible for the fact that there is continuous motion in the universe. Disputed questions about the range of beings moved by the prime mover, and whether the prime mover moves them as both a final cause and an efficient cause, are irrelevant for my purposes here. What is relevant is that Aristotle describes the prime mover as "thinking thinking of thinking" (*Metaph.* 12.9,

---

[24] As I mentioned in Chapter 1, some advocate a more liberal view of what contemplation involves, according to which it can in some cases be virtuous inquiry, including Guthrie (1981, 396–398), Jirsa (2017), Roochnik (2009), and Walker (2017). Such a view, or the proposal that contemplation can in some cases be a manifestation of practical wisdom, would make my argument in this section easier. That is because Aristotle's divine beings clearly do not engage in inquiry or possess practical wisdom (see T1 above). I address the harder case of whether or not they have theoretical wisdom and manifest it in a comprehensive grasp rather than an inquiry. That is because I find more plausible the more conservative view of what contemplation involves. The same is true of those many who have thought the Divinity Thesis problematic and interesting enough to address in print.

[25] *Metaph.* 12.8 raises the question of how many divine unmoved movers there might be. Aristotle's view about this is notoriously unclear. I will assume that any divine unmoved movers other than the prime mover would share at least some of the features of the prime mover that I argue are individually sufficient for type-distinctness from human contemplation.

1074^{b}34–35).[26] The other divine beings in Aristotle's system are various celestial objects, including the rotating spheres that move other celestial objects, the stars, the planets, the sun, and the moon. Aristotle is clear that these are divine.[27] Each of these celestial objects is perpetually engaged in unvarying, uninterrupted movement, which movement is supposed to be explained, either directly or derivatively, by the prime mover (or at least an unmoved mover) being a final cause for it in the way that an object of thought is (*Metaph.* 12.7, 1072^{a}24–32). One might think that Aristotle's ontology includes, in addition to the prime mover and celestial objects, the gods of popular Greek religion. He does, after all, mention them frequently. However, this is no indication that he is committed to their existence; his mentions of them may reflect only popular opinions the appeal of which he wants his own theories of celestial objects to explain.[28] This is what he seems to intend in various passages.[29] Furthermore, those who take Aristotle to be committed to the type-identity of human and divine contemplation have a special reason to deny that he is committed to the existence of the gods of popular Greek religion. Recall the identity reading of the argument of T1 in Section 3. On that interpretation of Aristotle's argument, contemplation would have to be the only activity in which the gods engage. This means that the deities of popular Greek religion are ruled out. Furthermore, on any interpretation of T1, if ethically virtuous activities are somehow unworthy of true divinity, the salacious escapades of popular Greek deities are all the more unworthy. The only beings within Aristotle's system that behave in the way that he seems to envision in T1 are the prime mover and perhaps certain celestial objects, if indeed the latter contemplate at all.

With the range of Aristotle's divine beings in view, let us return to our question: Do these beings have the states involved in theoretical wisdom, namely the relevant sort of *nous* (the developed capacity to grasp first principles intuitively as first principles) and *epistêmê* (the developed capacity for scientific demonstration from first principles)?

---

[26] ἡ νόησις νοήσεως νόησις
[27] *Phys.* 2.4, 196^{a}33–34, *DC* 2.12, 292^{b}31–32, *PA* 1.5, 644^{b}24–25, *Metaph.* 12.8, 1074^{a}30–31, *NE* 6.7, 1141^{a}34 – ^{b}2.
[28] This is argued at length by Segev (2017, chs. 1 and 3). Contrast (Bodéüs, 1992, ch. 5).
[29] *DC* 1.3, 270^{b}1–24, 1.9, 279^{a}30 – ^{b}3, 2.1, 284^{a}2–14, and *Metaph.* 12.8, 1074^{b}1–14. Johnson (2005, 262) and Segev (2017, 18) cite the last in support of the idea that Aristotle does not believe in the popular Greek deities, but rather sees popular beliefs as indicating the truth that there are divine celestial objects.

4.4.4   The Prime Mover

Let us start with why the prime mover cannot have *epistêmê*.[30] First, *epistêmê* always has an object other than itself (*Metaph.* 12.9, 1074^{b}35), whereas the prime mover's thinking never does (1074^{b}25–34, 1075^{a}3–5). That is because the prime mover thinks only about its own thinking. *Epistêmê* scientifically demonstrates from first principles, which must be distinct from what is demonstrated from them. That is why Aristotle feels the need to distinguish between the objects of *nous*, which grasps first principles, and the objects of *epistêmê*, which, since it is distinct from *nous*, must have objects distinct from those of *nous* (*APo* 2.19, 100^{b}5–17). One does not have *nous* of what is demonstrated, but rather only of first principles. Likewise, one does not have *epistêmê* of first principles, but only of what is demonstrated from them. None of this would be possible if demonstration were purely reflexive. Since demonstration is not purely reflexive, *epistêmê* has an object other than itself, and therefore is incompatible with the prime mover's thinking. Since the prime mover is its thinking, the prime mover could not have *epistêmê*.

The second reason why the prime mover could not have *epistêmê* is that manifestations of *epistêmê* are complex, whereas the prime mover's thinking is not (*Metaph.* 12.7, 1073^{a}6–7; 9, 1074^{b}33–34). Manifestations of *epistêmê* are complex because demonstration requires the conjunction of distinct premises. A demonstration is a whole with parts, and thinking of such parts in the way that demonstration requires would involve change between these parts. The demonstrator must shift mentally from a premise or premises to what is demonstrated from them. But such change in thought is impossible for the prime mover. That is because if the prime mover's thinking were to shift from anything but itself, it would be thinking about something worse than it is. But then it would not be thinking about the best and most divine thing of all, and then would not be the best and most divine sort of thing (*Metaph.* 12.9, 1074^{b}21–35). Any change in the prime mover's thinking would be a change for the worse, but it cannot change for the worse.[31] So again, the prime mover cannot have *epistêmê*.

---

[30] Parts of the arguments that follow can be found in Beere (2010, 27–30), Brunschwig (2000, 296–301), Herzberg (2013, ch. 4) and (2016), Menn (2012, 446–447), Modrak (1991, 770), and Wedin (1988, 229–245).

[31] A change from thinking to not thinking would also be a change for the worse since Aristotle supposes the prime mover's thinking to be the best activity. That is why, as Thorsrud (2015, 352) mentions, human contemplation can be engaged in intermittently whereas the prime mover's contemplation cannot. The difference in duration of divine and human contemplation thus depends on a difference in type. For more on the intermittency of human thinking, see Reece (forthcoming).

Indeed, the prime mover could not even have *nous* in the sense that is required for theoretical wisdom. That sort of *nous* grasps multiple first principles of a demonstrative science (*APo* 2.19, 100^{b}5–17, *Metaph.* 1.2, 982^{a}19 – ^{b}10, *NE* 6.5).[32] But, as already mentioned, the prime mover's thought is not complex, and so it cannot grasp multiple first principles.

Furthermore, the prime mover's thinking involves no images (*phantasmata*) since it cannot involve anything but itself and it is not an image, and since interaction with images requires a perceiving soul, which the prime mover lacks. However, one might think that human grasp of first principles must involve images (*DA* 3.7, 431^{b}2–9, 3.8, 432^{a}3–9; cf. *APo* 2.19), at least while embodied (*DA* 3.7, 431^{b}17–19).[33] Precisely how it is possible (and whether it is necessary) for us to grasp first principles by way of images is controversial, but if Aristotle thinks that at least in our present condition our path to grasping first principles goes through images, whereas the prime mover's thinking cannot do so,[34] then for this reason, too, the prime mover would not have *nous* of the sort required for theoretical wisdom.

4.4.5 Celestial Objects

Let us now turn to celestial objects. The primary apparent evidence that any of them contemplates is the following passage, which explains what sort of mover is required to cause the eternal, unvarying rotation of at least the outermost celestial sphere:

[32] This is mentioned by Burnyeat (2008, 27–28), who adds that the sort of *nous* required for theoretical wisdom must involve grasping principles as principles of demonstrations, which of course the prime mover's thinking could not do. Burnyeat infers from this that *nous* in general (whether human or divine) could not be about something lacking distinguishable parts. He draws the astonishing conclusion that, in spite of the evidence of *Metaph.* 12.9, the prime mover's thinking is of something composite. This view is also held by Kahn (1981, 412–414), Lear (1988, 295), and Silverman (2010, 92–93). Beere (2010, 28 n. 47) argues that such a proposal faces grave difficulties. It would do far less violence to the text to conclude, as I do, that the prime mover's thinking does not involve the sort of *nous* required for theoretical wisdom. It is surprising that Silverman does not do so since he eventually embraces the view that immediately follows from this that human and divine contemplation are distinct not merely in duration and continuity but also in type (2010, 93).

[33] This is mentioned by Herzberg (2016, 167), Modrak (1991, 770–771), Ross (1924, vol. 2, 379), Segev (2017, 109), and Wedin (1988, 244–245) as a reason why the prime mover's thinking cannot feature *nous* considered as grasping first principles.

[34] Cohoe (2016, 352) argues that the prime mover's thinking cannot involve images. His paper as a whole discusses the extent to which, and reasons why, human thinking involves images.

T3 (*Metaph.* 12.7, 1072^{a}19–30)

Since this is possible, and unless it were so then the world would be from night and 'all things together' and from not-being, these difficulties are resolved, and there is something that always is moved with an unceasing motion, which motion is circular (and this is clear not only by argument but in fact), with the result that the first heaven would be eternal. Therefore, there is also something that moves it. Since what is moved and moves is also intermediate, there is something that moves without being moved, being eternal, a substance, and actuality. And an object of desire and an object of thought move in this way: They move without being moved. The primaries of these are the same. For the apparent good is the object of appetite, and the real good is the primary object of wish. We desire something because it seems good rather than it seeming good because we desire it, for thinking is a starting-point.

Ἐπεὶ δ' οὕτω τ' ἐνδέχεται, καὶ εἰ μὴ οὕτως, ἐκ νυκτὸς ἔσται καὶ ^{a}20 ὁμοῦ πάντων καὶ ἐκ μὴ ὄντος, λύοιτ' ἂν ταῦτα, καὶ ἔστι τι ἀεὶ κινούμενον κίνησιν ἄπαυστον, αὕτη δ' ἡ κύκλῳ (καὶ τοῦτο οὐ λόγῳ μόνον ἀλλ' ἔργῳ δῆλον), ὥστ' ἀΐδιος ἂν εἴη ὁ πρῶτος οὐρανός. ἔστι τοίνυν τι καὶ ὃ κινεῖ. ἐπεὶ δὲ τὸ κινούμενον καὶ κινοῦν [καὶ] μέσον,^{35} †τοίνυν† ἔστι τι ὃ οὐ κινούμενον κινεῖ, 25 ἀΐδιον καὶ οὐσία καὶ ἐνέργεια οὖσα. κινεῖ δὲ ὧδε τὸ ὀρεκτὸν καὶ τὸ νοητόν· κινεῖ οὐ κινούμενα. τούτων τὰ πρῶτα τὰ αὐτά. ἐπιθυμητὸν μὲν γὰρ τὸ φαινόμενον καλόν, βουλητὸν δὲ πρῶτον τὸ ὂν καλόν· ὀρεγόμεθα δὲ διότι δοκεῖ μᾶλλον ἢ δοκεῖ διότι ὀρεγόμεθα· ἀρχὴ γὰρ ἡ νό- 30 ησις.

One might suppose that Aristotle here says that the prime mover is literally an object of desire and of thought for the outermost celestial sphere ("the first heaven"). A problem for such an interpretation is that he also says that the elements and plants "desire" to share in the divine and eternal motion (*GC* 2.10, 336^{b}27 – 337^{a}7; *DA* 2.4, 415^{a}25 – ^{b}7), but on his view they do not literally desire anything.^{36} Alternatively, we might think that Aristotle is simply giving familiar examples of unmoved movers, objects of desire and objects of thought, in order to illustrate what sort of mover is required to explain the outermost celestial sphere's eternal motions, namely, something that moves without being moved. On this second interpretation, the sphere would not literally desire or think

^{35} Ross (1924, vol. 2, 374), whose text I have printed, argues that this line is textually problematic. Laks (2000, 219) thinks that the transmitted text gives all that is needed to make the argument work. My translation of this sentence follows his.
^{36} This point is made forcefully by Caston (1999, 217).

about the prime mover, and so *a fortiori* would not contemplate it.[37] Even on the first interpretation, the prime mover need be only an object of whatever sort of thought is required for it to be desired (rather than theoretical thought) for the outermost celestial sphere (*DA* 3.10, 433ᵃ15–20).[38] That Aristotle argues for a prime mover on the ground that it is necessary to explain the locomotion of celestial objects makes better sense, in fact, if the prime mover is an object of such thought for the outermost celestial sphere rather than of theoretical thought. That is because, according to him, objects of desire, and precisely not objects of theoretical thought, are causes of locomotion (*DA* 3.10).[39] Such considerations are clearly on Aristotle's mind in T3, for sentences (3)–(9) echo several passages from *DA* 3.10.[40]

T4 (*DA* 3.10, 433ᵇ13–18)

> The following three are involved in movement: first, the mover, second, that by which it moves things, and third, the moved. There are two sorts of movers, one unmoved and one that moves and is moved. The one that is unmoved is the good achievable in action (*prakton agathon*), the one that

---

[37] Simplicius (*In DC* 388.16–19) reports in his commentary on *DC* 2.2, 285ᵃ27–30 that certain respectable but unnamed ancient commentators attributed to Aristotle the view that celestial objects do not have rational souls and therefore cannot think about anything. Blyth (2015, 429 n. 5) thinks that Theophrastus and Alexander of Aphrodisias had this interpretation. For the long and complicated history of debate among Greek, Arabic, and Latin commentators on Aristotle about what sorts of psychic capacities, if any, celestial objects have, see (Wolfson, 1973). Among recent commentators, Broadie (1993, 406) argues that the prime mover does not cause the movement of any celestial object by literally being an object of thought for it. According to her, this is because the prime mover is related to the outermost celestial sphere as soul is related to body, and its causality of the movement of this sphere is efficient rather than final. Roughly this view is also articulated by Bodéüs (1992, ch. 2). Blyth (2015, 455–463) contends that no celestial object contemplates the prime mover because no celestial object has a rational soul. His conclusion is thus similar to that of Broadie and Bodéüs, but derived from premises several of which are incompatible with theirs. Blyth (2015, 456–459) thinks that T3, within its context in *Metaph.* 12.7, suggests only that the prime mover is an object of desire and thought for the thinking that is its essence. The outermost celestial sphere does not have a soul at all, let alone a rational soul, but is moved because the *aithêr* of which it is composed naturally (not intentionally) responds to the prime mover by rotating, a response that Aristotle describes in erotic terms in *Metaph.* 12.7 (2015, 460–462). Roughly this view was taken in antiquity to be supported by Aristotle's remarks about *aithêr* in *DC* 1.2, as is noted not only by Blyth (2015, 441), but also by Wolfson (1973, 23–24).

[38] See (Laks, 2000, 221).

[39] One might think that it is inappropriate to appeal to Aristotle's remarks about desire and thought in *DA* 3.10 to understand what sort of cognitive activity (if any) is characteristic of celestial objects for the reason that the cognitive activity of superlunary beings is so different from that of humans that his remarks in *DA* cannot be supposed to apply to such beings. If that is correct, then my conclusion of this section follows. Thanks to Mor Segev for discussion.

[40] Laks (2000, 220, 223–224) thinks that T3 offers a "condensed version" of parts of *DA* 3.10.

moves and is moved is the desiring part (for what is moved is moved insofar as it desires, and active desire is a sort of movement), and the one that is moved is the animal.[41]

T5 (*DA* 3.10, 433ᵃ27–29)

That is why what moves is always the object of desire, and this is either the good or the apparent good, not every good, but rather the good achievable in action (*prakton agathon*).

T6 (*DA* 3.10, 433ᵃ17–20)

As a result, these two reasonably appear to be movers, namely, desire and practical thought. For the object of desire moves, and because of this thought moves, since its starting-point is the object of desire.

So, whether one adopts the first or the second interpretation of T3, one will not have much reason to say that any celestial object engages in theoretical thought about the prime mover, let alone that any meets Aristotle's strict criteria for theoretical wisdom. In fact, even if one wants to insist that the prime mover is an object of theoretical thought for celestial objects, these objects could not have theoretical wisdom. Here is why. Either the continuous, simple, and unvarying movement of the celestial objects is explained by theoretical thinking about the prime mover or it is not.[42] If it is not, then nothing about the structure of Aristotle's argument would lead us to suppose that they engage in theoretical thought about the prime mover in the first place, since the phenomenon of their continuous,

---

[41] Bonitz (1848, 496) proposes that T4 can give insight into the original text of the third sentence of T3.

[42] This disjunction requires some clarification in the case of celestial spheres other than the outermost, which is the only one mentioned in T3, the principal source of putative textual evidence that any celestial object contemplates. The movement of the outermost sphere is comparatively easy to understand, for it simply rotates. To describe the movements of the spheres nested within the outermost sphere, Aristotle in *Metaph.* 12.8 introduces his own version of the cosmology developed by Eudoxus and refined by Callipus: The spheres nested within the outermost sphere have their proper movement, which, as in the case of the outermost sphere, is continuous, simple, unvarying rotation. However, since the spheres are nested with no void between them, they are attached, but at different angles. This means that the movement of each sphere further out will affect the movement of each sphere further in. So, as Aristotle notes in *DC* 2.12, spheres other than the outermost will have multiple movements. Nonetheless, its proper movement is rotation, and this rotation (but not whatever influences may be transmitted by spheres further out) is directly explained with reference to an unmoved mover. So, the only movement of any celestial object that an unmoved mover is supposed to explain directly is continuous, simple, unvarying rotation. Judson (2015) provides a detailed discussion of these and other aspects of Aristotle's account.

simple, and unvarying movement is what the prime mover is meant to explain. If it is explained by theoretical thinking about the prime mover, then since their movement is supposed to be continuous, simple, and unvarying, they could have neither *nous* nor *epistêmê* in the way that these figure in theoretical wisdom. Whereas the sort of *nous* that figures in theoretical wisdom grasps multiple first principles as part of a demonstrative science, the movement of any given celestial object could not be explained by its grasping multiple first principles. Else it would not be continuous, simple, and unvarying. Furthermore, no celestial object could be capable of demonstrating anything from such first principles because that would involve the potential to change from thinking about one thing to thinking about another. Since, *ex hypothesi*, its movement is explained by theoretical thinking about the prime mover, having the potential for change in object of thought would imply having the potential for change in movement. But nothing with continuous, simple, and unvarying movement could have such potentiality. Aristotle is right, then, in offering no suggestion that celestial objects are capable of scientific demonstration from first principles. So, again, celestial objects cannot have theoretical wisdom, and therefore cannot engage in contemplation of the same type as that in which human beings engage.

There is yet another reason to think that celestial objects lack the sort of *nous* required for theoretical wisdom. As mentioned above, that sort of *nous* grasps first principles of a demonstrative science by way of images (*phantasmata*). We have already seen that the prime mover is incapable of this, but what about celestial objects? To grasp first principles by way of images, one must have imagination (*phantasia*). Imagination requires a perceptive soul (*DA* 3.3, 427^{b}14–16). It is far from obvious that celestial objects have perceptive souls, though some have thought that they do.[43] Suppose for the sake of argument that they do have perceptive souls. Then, if they have desire then they would also have imagination (*DA* 3.10, 433^{b}28–29). Since imagination is regarded by Aristotle as a kind of thought

---

[43] See Cohoe (2020), Rapp (2019), Segev (2017, ch. 3), and Wolfson (1973, 34–40) for general discussion about debates concerning the psychic capacities (or lack thereof) of celestial objects. Averroes (*Magnum in DA* III, c. 5, 400–409 and III, c. 18, 438–439) believes that the active intellect and potential intellect, both of which he regards as separate, eternal, and therefore in a way divine, rely upon human imagination (*phantasia*) for abstracting and receiving intelligibles, respectively. But since, according to him, humans are *not* abstracting or receiving intelligibles in this way, human thinking is type-distinct from any sort of divine thinking. Thanks to Gabriel Richardson Lear and Stephen Ogden for discussion of this aspect of Averroes's view. I have benefited from Ogden (2021).

(*nous*) (*DA* 3.10, 433ª9–12, *MA* 6, 700ᵇ17–22), those who regard T3 as insinuating that the prime mover is literally an object of desire and thought for the outermost celestial sphere would be left with no reason to suppose that this requires the sphere to have theoretical thought.[44] After all, non-rational animals are capable of locomotion for the sake of objects of desire and thought (where imagination is the kind of thought at issue). Thus, T3 would give no support for the idea that celestial objects have the sort of *nous* required for theoretical wisdom.

The foregoing arguments show that neither the prime mover nor any other divine beings the existence of which Aristotle recognizes could engage in contemplation that is type-identical with human contemplation. If that is right, then the Argument from Divine Contemplation equivocates on 'contemplation.'

4.4.6 *Divine* Sophia *in* Metaphysics *1.2*

I have been arguing that the divine beings that Aristotle recognizes cannot, according to him, have and manifest theoretical wisdom, *sophia*, as it is described in the *NE*. Aristotle does, though, speak of divine *sophia* in *Metaph.* 1.2. There are two reasons why this is unproblematic for my argument.[45] First, as Broadie (2012) argues at length, the *sophia* that he there describes is not the virtue that he discusses in the *NE*, but rather a department of knowledge concerned specifically with answers to an array of foundational questions. So, even if the divine beings that Aristotle recognizes had this sort of *sophia*, it would tell us nothing about whether they had the virtue described in the *NE* and would therefore have no obvious tendency to generate the sort of conflict with the *ergon* argument that the Argument from Divine Contemplation encapsulates.

---

[44] One might think that there would still be a reason to suppose that the outermost celestial sphere has theoretical thought if it has any sort of thought: The sphere is divine and we are not, so its activity should be better than ours is. But if we can contemplate and the sphere cannot, but rather engages only in another sort of thought, then its activity would not be better than ours is. I reply as follows. First, Aristotle gives us no reason to suppose that a divine being's thought (of whatever sort) could not be better than a human's theoretical thought unless we assume that divine and human contemplation are type-identical. Second, the sphere's activity could be better than ours in virtue of being continuous, uninterrupted, and unforced (given that, if it is composed of *aithêr*, it does not have to exert effort the way that beings composed of the other four elements do). Being theoretical is not the only applicable determinant of being better. Thanks to Mor Segev for discussion of this point.

[45] Thanks to an anonymous reviewer for *Ergo: An Open Access Journal of Philosophy* for suggesting discussion of why this chapter is unproblematic for my view.

Second, there are reasons to believe that even this sort of *sophia* is not attributed both to humans and to the divine beings that Aristotle recognizes (rather than a divine being as commonly conceived). Human *sophia* in *Metaph.* 1.2 is understood as knowledge of causes in general of all things as far as this is possible (982^{a}8–10, ^{a}21 – ^{b}7). These causes include, but are not limited to, final causes (982^{b}9–10, 1.3, 983^{a}24–32). Indeed, they could not be limited to final causes since human *sophia* here includes knowledge of causes in mathematics (982^{a}23–28, 983^{a}15–16), which subject does not feature final causes. To the extent that Aristotle's divine beings have knowledge of causes (as such) at all, it includes neither causes in mathematics nor material causes of existing things. But Aristotle calls "this sort of knowledge," knowledge of causes in general, divine (983^{a}5–7). How, then, could he do so coherently? "This sort of knowledge" (*toiautê*), the sort called "divine," could perhaps be intended to cover two type-distinct forms of *sophia*, both of which count as divine because they are a) concerned with at least one divine cause and b) "free" in the sense that they are useless for further pursuits. Human *sophia* would be concerned with causes in general, including, but not limited to, the prime mover, and the prime mover's *sophia* would be concerned with itself exclusively. If this is what Aristotle means, then he is not committed in *Metaph.* 1.2 to the type-identity of any sort of *sophia*, let alone the sort at issue in the *NE*, possessed by humans and divine beings. If, though, Aristotle means by "this sort of knowledge" (*toiautê*) that humans and "the god" are supposed to have *sophia* of the same type, which entails that they are concerned with the same set of things, then I see no plausible way around Ross's (1924, vol. 1, 123) conclusion that he must here have in mind a god as popularly conceived, not his prime mover. That is because, as we have seen, the prime mover thinks only of itself, not of mathematics or the material causes of existing things.[46]

---

[46] Broadie (2012, 66) offers the suggestion that Aristotle's prime mover could be in view here if it thinks about itself as cause of eternal things and so do humans. This suggestion has the following weaknesses. First, there is no positive evidence that Aristotle understands the prime mover's thinking in this way. Second, even if human *sophia* concerns the prime mover as cause of eternal things, the chapter indicates that human *sophia* is concerned with other things about which the prime mover would not be thinking, such as the material causes of celestial bodies. Third, it is unlikely that Aristotle would countenance such a description of the prime mover's thought. That is because, as we have seen, he believes that the prime mover must think about what is best and nothing else. According to Broadie's suggestion, both humans and the prime mover would think about the prime mover not as an entity in itself, but rather as related to its principal effects. But if thinking of the prime mover as related to its principal effects is sufficiently different from thinking of it as an entity in itself to accommodate, as Broadie wants to do, the plurality of first principles and causes with which human *sophia* is concerned, then the prime mover, in thinking of itself as related to its principal effects, would not be thinking of what is best, namely, itself as an entity in itself. That

So, again, Aristotle would not be attributing type-identical *sophia* both to humans and to the divine beings that he recognizes.

4.5   An Aristotelian Parallel: The Argument from Animal Activities

One may wonder how likely Aristotle would be to respond to the Argument from Divine Contemplation in the way that I have suggested if he had been explicitly confronted with it. We can get some insight into this by considering the fact that Aristotle already makes a very similar move to address a parallel argument:

Argument from Animal Activities

  i. If practically wise and ethically virtuous activities are proper to human beings, only human beings are capable of practically wise and ethically virtuous activities.
 ii. If some animals are capable of practically wise and ethically virtuous activities, then it is false that only human beings are capable of practically wise and ethically virtuous activities.
iii. Some animals are capable of practically wise and ethically virtuous activities.
 iv. So, it is false that only human beings are capable of practically wise and ethically virtuous activities.
∴. Practically wise and ethically virtuous activities are not proper to human beings.

If Aristotle accepts this conclusion, then he cannot argue as he does either in *NE* 1.7 or 10.8, for both of those arguments explicitly depend on the claim that practically wise and ethically virtuous activities are proper to human beings. Aristotle clearly accepts (iii), for he attributes practically wise and ethically virtuous activities to some animals.[47] But he does not accept the conclusion; he says that mature humans alone can have virtues, and animals cannot (*NE* 7.1, 1145ᵃ25–26). Aristotle's position is consistent because he thinks that 'practically wise and ethically virtuous activities' is predicated equivocally of humans and animals (*NE* 7.6, 1149ᵇ31–32).

---

is because if something is thought of *qua* related to something else, it is thought of as having an essence mutually dependent on that to which it is related (*Cat.* 7, 8ᵃ31–32). But, as we have seen, one of Aristotle's reasons for thinking that the prime mover is best is that its essence depends on nothing else.

47 *HA* 8.1, 588ᵃ18 – ᵇ3, *Metaph.* 1.1, 980ᵇ21–22, *NE* 6.7, 1141ᵃ26–28

He thinks that some animals perform activities that he is willing to call practically wise or ethically virtuous (e.g., courageous), but in a sense that differs from that in which human beings can perform practically wise and ethically virtuous activities.[48] He distinguishes between attributing type-identical virtues and attributing merely analogous virtues, and says that we attribute the latter but not the former to humans and animals (*HA* 8.1, 588ª18 – ᵇ3).

Kraut (1979, 472–474) anticipates in broad outline the strategy of responding to the Argument from Divine Contemplation by saying that human and divine contemplation differ in type (though not for my reason for saying that they do, namely that the former but not the latter is a manifestation of theoretical wisdom), as well as its parallel with Aristotle's response to the argument from animals' practically wise and ethically virtuous activities. He gives two arguments against it. Here is the first, quoted in full:

> Is this a satisfactory way for Aristotle to maintain the thesis that contemplation is at least part of our function? I think not. For suppose we could overcome our human limitations and engage in precisely that kind of contemplation which Aristotle's god enjoys. Even though that would be a better kind of contemplation, it could no longer be even part of our function to engage in it, because it would no longer be peculiar to us. So, Aristotle would have to counsel us not to participate in this improved form of contemplation, in spite of its superiority to the form we currently can enjoy. I find this position paradoxical, and I am reluctant to believe that Aristotle is committed to it. (1979, 473)

I share Kraut's reluctance to believe that Aristotle is committed to this position, but that is because Aristotle himself says that scenarios like the one that Kraut envisions amount to imagining oneself away (*NE* 8.7, 1159ª5–12, 9.4, 1166ª19–22).[49] Kraut invites us to imagine that we could engage in the prime mover's sort of contemplation, which Kraut is granting for purposes of this argument is distinct in type from human contemplation. But since the prime mover and its contemplation are strictly identical, the only way to engage in that sort of contemplation is to *be* that sort of contemplation. So, we are invited to imagine that we are not human, but rather the prime mover. Kraut's counterfactual claim that if we were the

---

[48] Müller (2020) offers a helpful discussion of the merely analogous relationship between human and animal traits that concentrates especially on the difference in type between vices attributed to each.

[49] Thorsrud (2015, 358), Walker (2018, 96), and Whiting (1988, 47 n. 19) remark and explain the incoherence of wishing that oneself or one's friend were divine.

prime mover then the human function would not be applicable to us is obviously correct, since its antecedent and consequent are both necessarily false, and my argument contains nothing that would contravene it.

The second of Kraut's arguments, again quoted in full, is this:

> If Aristotle thinks that contemplation is peculiar to us because human and divine contemplation differ in kind, then he opens himself to this objection: 'In the function argument you have set up a test to determine which good or goods happiness consists in. Doesn't ethically virtuous activity pass that test with higher marks than your own candidate, contemplation? After all, you are looking for what sets human beings off from all other things, and the ethical virtues do this to a greater extent than contemplation. When a human being is just or generous or temperate, he is more unlike anything else than when he contemplates. For the gods, properly conceived, are totally devoid of ethical qualities. And though some animals have traits akin to virtue and vice, these qualities differ radically from their human counterparts; a person's virtues derive in part from reason, a faculty animals lack. How much closer, then, are human and divine contemplation, since both are activities of the same kind of faculty, reason. Though the function argument and your defense of contemplation are mutually consistent, your search for the peculiarly human ought to have led you to make ethical activity the topmost good.' (1979, 473)

The problem with this second argument is that Kraut simply assumes that human and divine contemplation are manifestations of a faculty that they share. But as I have argued, whereas human contemplation is a manifestation of theoretical wisdom, divine contemplation could not be a manifestation of any such thing. The prime mover could not share either the sort of *nous* or the sort of *epistêmê* that theoretical wisdom involves, and so could not have theoretical wisdom of the same type that human beings can possess. As for celestial objects, even if they have rational souls at all and we insist with no textual grounding on describing their thought as theoretical rather than practical, they still would not share with humans the sort of *nous* or *epistêmê* required for theoretical wisdom. In short, Kraut's argument does not take account of the reason for saying that human and divine contemplation are type-distinct, which, as I have argued, is that whereas human contemplation is a manifestation of theoretical wisdom, divine contemplation cannot be.

4.6 Conclusion

I began by introducing the Divinity Thesis, namely that contemplation is not proper to human beings, for divine beings engage in it, too, which is encapsulated in the Argument from Divine Contemplation, as an impediment to solving the Conjunctive Problem of Happiness. Section 2 surveyed existing responses to the Argument from Divine Contemplation, all of which assume that human and divine contemplation are type-identical, and argued that another solution would be preferable to these. Section 3 contended that the principal apparent textual evidence for the type-identity of human and divine contemplation is inconclusive and is interpreted more conservatively as suggesting that human and divine contemplation are merely similar. Section 4 argued that the divine beings recognized by Aristotle, namely the prime mover and celestial objects, cannot engage in the same type of contemplation as human beings can. That is because human contemplation is a manifestation of theoretical wisdom, a virtue that includes *epistêmê* and *nous* (of a particular kind), but Aristotle's divine beings cannot possess or manifest theoretical wisdom because they cannot possess or manifest *epistêmê* or *nous* of the relevant kind. The Argument from Divine Contemplation is invalid because it equivocates on two different uses of 'contemplation,' one designating a human activity, the other a divine activity. Section 5 showed that such a response to the Argument from Divine Contemplation closely parallels a response that Aristotle gives to a similar argument from animals' practically wise and ethically virtuous activities: such activities are proper to human beings because the activities ascribed to animals are not of the same type, but rather are called practically wise and ethically virtuous by analogy to human activities. The upshot is that we can take Aristotle at his word: contemplation, at least of the type that is a manifestation of theoretical wisdom, is proper to human beings. With the Divinity Thesis, like the Divergence Thesis and the Duality Thesis, out of the way, our path is now clear for a solution to the Conjunctive Problem of Happiness, which I will develop in the next chapter.

CHAPTER 5

Solving the Conjunctive Problem of Happiness

5.1   Results of Previous Chapters

Let us take stock of some of the results of previous chapters. Chapter 1 distinguished the following two problems:

Dilemmatic Problem of Happiness
   We must determine which of the following incompatible propositions about happiness Aristotle believes and explain away the apparent evidence that he believes the other:

A)   Happiness (the activity) is virtuous activity, a composite that includes not only contemplative activity, but also ethically virtuous activities as parts.
B)   Happiness (the activity) is contemplative activity, which does not include ethically virtuous activities as parts.

Conjunctive Problem of Happiness
   We must explain how Aristotle can consistently believe both of the following propositions about the same kind of happiness:
   Pluralist Constraint
      Happiness (the activity) is virtuous activity, a composite that includes not only contemplative activity, but also ethically virtuous activities as parts.
   Monist Constraint
      Happiness (the activity) is contemplative activity, which does not include ethically virtuous activities as parts.

I argued that although the Dilemmatic Problem has been the focus of the literature, the Conjunctive Problem is the one that we need to be trying to solve.

Chapters 2–4 addressed three theses, each common among monists, pluralists, and relativists, that thwart solving the Conjunctive Problem. Most interpreters believe at least two of these and many believe all three.

Divergence Thesis

Aristotle thinks that it is possible to possess theoretical wisdom and reliably manifest it in contemplation without possessing practical wisdom and reliably manifesting it in ethically virtuous activities.

Duality Thesis

Aristotle thinks that there are two kinds of happiness, one corresponding to theoretical contemplation and the other corresponding to ethically virtuous activities, and the former kind is superior to the latter.

Divinity Thesis

According to Aristotle, contemplation is not proper to human beings, for divine beings engage in it, too.

As we saw in Chapter 2, the Divergence Thesis makes it impossible to solve the Conjunctive Problem because if one affirms Divergence then one must either deny that happiness is contemplation (the manifestation of theoretical wisdom) in any straightforward sense (the Monist Constraint), or deny that happiness has ethically virtuous activities as parts (the Pluralist Constraint). Here is why. Suppose that the Divergence Thesis is true. If happiness is contemplation, as the Monist Constraint requires, but contemplation can occur without ethically virtuous activities, then happiness can occur without ethically virtuous activities. If happiness can occur without ethically virtuous activities, then ethically virtuous activities are not necessary parts of happiness. Therefore, on the supposition that the Divergence Thesis is true, ethically virtuous activities are not necessary parts of happiness, contra the Pluralist Constraint. (The Pluralist Constraint requires that ethically virtuous activities be necessary parts of happiness because it says that happiness *is* a composite that includes ethically virtuous activities as parts. If pluralists thought that ethically virtuous activities were not necessary parts of happiness then they would, contrary to fact, not raise the immoralist objection against monists that I mentioned in 1.3.2.) From the other direction: If ethically virtuous activities are necessary parts of happiness, as the Pluralist Constraint requires, but contemplation can occur without them, then contemplation can occur without happiness. If contemplation can occur without happiness, then it could not be true that happiness is contemplation except in a contingent predicative sense of 'is' that would be incommensurate with the aspiration to conceptual analysis on display in the Monist Constraint. Therefore, on the supposition that the Divergence Thesis is true, the Monist Constraint cannot be met while meeting the Pluralist Constraint. So, for one who believes the Divergence Thesis, that is, the claim that, for Aristotle, it is possible to possess theoretical wisdom and reliably manifest it in contemplation without possessing practical wisdom and reliably manifesting it in ethically virtuous activities, the Conjunctive Problem is unsolvable.

Fortunately, as I argued in Chapter 2, the Divergence Thesis is false. The passage about Anaxagoras and Thales in *NE* 6.7 that is commonly deployed in defense of this idea is better understood as reporting common, but partially mistaken, opinions that Aristotle's own account regiments and explains. I maintained instead that Aristotle believes that one has and reliably manifests theoretical wisdom in contemplation only if one has and reliably manifests practical wisdom in ethically virtuous activities. The examination of the evidence against the Divergence Thesis also revealed that one reliably manifests practical wisdom in ethically virtuous activities only if one reliably manifests theoretical wisdom in contemplation.

Chapter 3 addressed the Duality Thesis, which is motivated by the standard way of translating the first sentence of *NE* 10.8. This thesis thwarts solving the Conjunctive Problem because every way of spelling out what the virtuous activities involved in the two alleged kinds of happiness would be is either completely ungrounded in the text, pushes the Conjunctive Problem back a step, makes it impossible for the second alleged kind of happiness to fulfill the human *ergon* or meet the finality and self-sufficiency criteria, or directly violates the Pluralist Constraint. The Duality Thesis is also widely regarded as discordant with the rest of the *Nicomachean Ethics* (and with the *Protrepticus*, *Eudemian Ethics*, and *Politics*), or at least thoroughly unexpected. Among the specific questions about coherence that the Duality Thesis raises is this: Why would Aristotle on the next Bekker page (10.8, 1179^{a}29–30, which I discussed in Chapter 2) affirm a biconditional relationship between theoretical wisdom and ethical virtue if he thinks that each is characteristic of a different kind of happiness?

I argued that the support for the Duality Thesis that the first sentence of 10.8 appears to provide is a mere artifact of standard ways of translating it. These assume that 'happy' or 'happiest' (or an equivalent in another language) is the elided predicate. I contended that Aristotle's local argument, as well as the overall argument of the *NE*, makes better sense if we understand '⟨proper⟩ to a human being' as the elided predicate. The distinction that he draws in *NE* 10.7–8, then, is not a shocking one between two kinds of happiness, but rather one for which readers have been prepared by preceding chapters of the *NE*: a distinction between two ways in which attributes can be proper (*oikeion, idion*) to the same subject.

But according to the Divinity Thesis, which I addressed in Chapter 4, contemplation is not proper to human subjects at all since divine beings contemplate, too. This thesis makes it impossible to affirm the Monist Constraint, according to which happiness is a single activity, theoretical contemplation, while adhering to Aristotle's basic commitment that our *ergon*, and therefore our happiness, is proper to us.

I contended that the argument in support of the Divinity Thesis, the argument from divine contemplation, rests on the assumption that human and divine contemplation are type-identical, but Aristotle regards this assumption as false. On his view, contemplation as a manifestation of theoretical wisdom is indeed proper to humans, as are ethically virtuous activities.

The results of these chapters remove the impediments to solving the Conjunctive Problem. But they also contribute helpful materials for a positive solution to the Conjunctive Problem.[1] In this chapter, I will first show *that* this is the case. I will then offer a speculative reconstruction of an explanation that Aristotle could give for *why* the Conjunctive Problem is solvable in this way.

5.2   Solving the Conjunctive Problem

5.2.1   *Formal Elements of a Solution to the Conjunctive Problem*

The Conjunctive Problem is that of showing how Aristotle's theory could meet the Pluralist Constraint, namely that happiness is virtuous activity, a composite that includes not only contemplative activity, but also ethically virtuous activities as parts, and the Monist Constraint, namely that happiness is contemplative activity, which does not include ethically virtuous activities as parts. This will have been done if we can show that Aristotle would endorse the following claims that would make the Pluralist Constraint and Monist Constraint compatible. (Explaining *why* he would endorse them is another task, one that I undertake in the next section.)

---

[1] Rejection of the Divergence Thesis, Duality Thesis, and Divinity Thesis is necessary for solving the Conjunctive Problem, but not sufficient. One could, for example, reject all three theses but suppose happiness to have a structure that violates the Monist Constraint. Thanks to Gabriel Richardson Lear for discussion of this point.

First, all and only those who are happy contemplate, and all and only those who are happy engage in ethically virtuous activities (Chapter 2). Indeed, it is because contemplation and ethically virtuous activities are proper to human happiness that life in accordance with intellectual virtue and life in accordance with ethical virtue are proper to humans (Chapters 3–4). But there are two different ways of being proper (Chapter 3). Contemplation is proper to happiness in a primary way, just as life in accordance with theoretical intellect is proper to humans in a primary way. If contemplation is proper to happiness in a primary way, it is appropriate for Aristotle to say that happiness is contemplative activity, which is the Monist Constraint. (The Monist Constraint, since it answers to the requirement that the human *ergon* be proper, that is, peculiar, to humans, entails that contemplative activity must be proper to happiness in some way.) Ethically virtuous activity is proper to that same kind of happiness (the one and only kind) in a secondary way, just as life in accordance with ethical virtue is proper to humans in a secondary way. Ethically virtuous activities are proper to happiness if they are necessary, characteristic parts of happiness, as they are according to the Pluralist Constraint. This is a coherent story according to which, for Aristotle, the Pluralist Constraint and Monist Constraint are both true of the same kind of happiness. The gist of the solution to the Conjunctive Problem, then, is that ethically virtuous activities are proper to happiness as parts, whereas contemplation, though it is also a part of happiness, is proper to happiness in a different, primary way, a way that is compatible with saying that happiness is contemplative activity. To say that happiness is contemplative activity is not to exclude ethically virtuous activities from being parts of that same happiness, but rather to assign contemplation a priority over ethically virtuous activities that a distinction between a primary and secondary way of being proper tracks. This, in outline, is the solution to the Conjunctive Problem. I will first test it against the constraints that I discussed in Chapter 1. After that, I will offer a speculative account of *why* Aristotle might have believed the aforementioned claims that together show *that* he has a solution to the Conjunctive Problem.

5.2.2 Addressing the Reasons for the Pluralist Constraint and the Monist Constraint

Recall from Chapter 1 that the Conjunctive Problem is that of how to affirm the conjunction of the Pluralist Constraint and the Monist Constraint with respect to one kind of happiness. These constraints have strong

textual and theoretical motivations. I will now argue that the solution to
the Conjunctive Problem that I have just outlined is compatible with those
motivations.

As I argued in Chapter 1, the Pluralist Constraint is motivated by Aristotle's claim that happiness has parts, by his indications that there is a
difference in how ethically virtuous activities and external goods are related to happiness, and by a concern to avoid attributing immoralism to
him. These motivations are accommodated as follows.

When Aristotle speaks of the parts of happiness, he appears to mean
virtuous activities (see Chapter 1, Section 3.1.1). A straightforward way for
intellectually and ethically virtuous activities to be proper to happiness, as
they are according to the outline sketch that I have just given, is for them
to be necessary, characteristic parts of happiness.

If virtuous activities are proper to happiness as parts of it, then it would
be clear how ethically virtuous activities and external goods are related to
happiness in different ways: external goods are not proper to happiness;
after all, one can possess them without being happy.

The solution that I have outlined also avoids committing Aristotle to
immoralism. Recall the immoralist objection to monism: If, as monists
think, happiness is contemplation and ethically virtuous activities are for
the sake of contemplation, then for any case in which contemplation is
available, it is possible that the agent has sufficient reason to choose it over
any other course of action. According to the solution that I have sketched,
Aristotle says that contemplation is proper to happiness in the primary
way, whereas ethically virtuous activities are proper to the same kind of
happiness in a secondary way. This means that contemplation is prior to
ethically virtuous activities in some way, but it need not be, as monists
think, prior to them by their being for its sake, even though they are for
the sake of *happiness* in the familiar way in which parts can be for the
sake of the whole. In fact, since according to the solution outlined above
happiness always requires practical wisdom and the ethical virtues, failing
to act in accordance with right reason is ruled out. This is why Aristotle
can coherently insist, as he does in the texts that I discussed in Chapter 2,
that the contemplator most of all acts rightly and nobly.[2]

---

[2] This answer to the immoralist objection might initially appear similar to one proposed by Heinaman
(1993), but the differences illustrate the importance of distinguishing the Conjunctive Problem from
the Dilemmatic Problem, as I did in Chapter 1, and of arguing against the Divergence Thesis, which
I did in Chapter 2. Heinaman's response to the immoralist objection is that if one does something
immoral in order to promote contemplation, then one does not achieve happiness by contemplating,
but rather its contrary opposite, *kakodaimonia*. But once we have distinguished the Conjunctive

The solution to the Conjunctive Problem that I outlined, then, harmonizes with the motivations for the Pluralist Constraint. It also harmonizes with the motivation for the Monist Constraint. The Monist Constraint arises from the observation that in *NE* 10.7–8 Aristotle argues that various features that belong uniquely to happiness belong uniquely to contemplation and that this argument culminates in the claim that happiness is contemplative activity. This way of arguing makes good sense if the solution that I have outlined is correct. If contemplation alone among virtuous activities is proper to happiness in the primary way, then it alone among virtuous activities could explain why its having features proper to it would guarantee that happiness also has those features proper to it. These features are being the activity that is highest (10.7, 1177^{a}19–21), most continuous (^{a}21–22), most pleasant (^{a}22–27), most self-sufficient (^{a}27 – ^{b}1), most perfect (^{b}1–4), most leisurely (^{b}4–15), in accordance with what is a human being most of all (1178^{a}2–8), and most divine (10.8, 1178^{b}7–32).

So far in this chapter, I have argued as follows. The results of previous chapters yield two main claims that together form Aristotle's basic solution to the Conjunctive Problem: Happiness belongs to all and only those to whom contemplation and ethically virtuous activities belong, and contemplation is proper to happiness in a primary way, whereas ethically virtuous activities are proper to that same kind of happiness in a secondary way. These claims reconcile the Pluralist Constraint and Monist Constraint and address the specific motivations for each. Since previous chapters have already shown that Aristotle believes these claims, we can see *that* the Conjunctive Problem is solved. But *why* would Aristotle believe these claims? In particular, how might he specify the distinction between primary and secondary ways of being proper so as to clarify *why* it would be appropriate, on his theory of predication, to claim that happiness is contemplative

Problem from the Dilemmatic Problem, we can readily understand why Heinaman's suggestion cannot be accepted by monists or relativists: It immediately puts any straightforward vindication of the Monist Constraint out of reach. That is because if Heinaman is correct, then happiness cannot be contemplation, since on his view contemplation, even reliable, frequent contemplation, would be compatible with happiness's contrary opposite. Still less could it be true that, as Aristotle says in a passage that we have already identified as being of central importance to monists and relativists, "happiness extends as far as contemplation does, and to those to whom it more belongs to contemplate, it more belongs also to be happy, not accidentally, but rather in accordance with the contemplation, for this is valuable in itself" (*NE* 10.8, 1178^{b}28–31). The solution to the immoralist objection that I have proposed, unlike Heinaman's, leverages the result of my Chapter 2, the denial of the Divergence Thesis. Thanks to Anthony Price for discussion of the differences between my view and Heinaman's on these points.

activity? At this point, we must reconstruct the reasons available to Aristotle to give such an explanation. The reconstruction that I now commence will fill in the outline sketch that I gave earlier, resulting in what I will call "the Essentialist Theory of Happiness," or "essentialism" for short. Essentialism, unlike existing theories, solves the Conjunctive Problem of Happiness.

5.3   A Reconstruction of Aristotle's Reasons

5.3.1   Essence and Idia in Aristotle's Theory of Predication

I will begin by noting some features of Aristotle's theory of predication that will be important in what follows. According to him, where some A is predicated of some B, A is proper (*idion*) to B if and only if A and B counterpredicate (*antikatêgoreisthai*) (*Top.* 1.8, 103^{b}6–19). A and B counterpredicate if and only if A belongs to all and only those subjects to which B belongs, or in other words, if and only if A and B are coextensive. This is the broad sense of 'proper' (*idion*) (*Top.* 1.4, 101^{b}17–22).[3] But there are two kinds of predicable that are proper in this broad sense. One is a definition (*horos*), which signifies what it is to be the thing in question. Aristotle refers to what the definition signifies as the "what it is to be"[4] or the "essence" (*ousia*).[5] The other kind of predicable that is proper in the broad sense is an *idion* (plural: *idia*) (*Top.* 1.4, 101^{b}22–23).[6] Aristotle characterizes *idia* negatively:

---

[3] Aristotle sometimes uses '*oikeion*' instead of '*idion*' for this broad sense of 'proper.' See, for example, *Top.* 1.2, 101^{a}37 – ^{b}3 and *Metaph.* 8.4, 1044^{a}18 – ^{b}3, where both terms are used in this sense interchangeably, as well as *APo* 1.12, 77^{a}39, *Phys.* 2.3, 195^{b}3, *Meteor.* 4.2, 379^{b}20, *DA* 2.2, 414^{a}26, *Metaph.* 5.29, 1024^{b}33 and 10.9, 1058^{b}22, and *NE* 1.7, 1098^{a}28, 6.1, 1139^{a}17 (where he speaks of a thing's *ergon* being *oikeion*, having spoken of it in 1.7, 1097^{b}34 as *idion*), and 10.2, 1173^{a}32. Throughout this book I have translated both as 'proper.'

[4] τὸ τί ἦν εἶναι

[5] Some instances of '*ousia*,' but not the ones discussed in this chapter, are appropriately translated as 'substance' rather than 'essence.' Aristotle distinguishes between these two uses of '*ousia*' in *Metaph.* 5.8.

[6] '*Idion*' (plural: '*idia*') in either its broad or its narrow sense can be an adjective or a noun. I use 'proper' for the adjectival form of the broad sense and '*idion*' (plural: '*idia*') for the adjectival form of the narrow sense and the noun form of the narrow sense. In contexts where it is necessary to discuss the noun form of the narrow and broad senses, I use '*idion*$_N$' (plural: '*idia*$_N$') and '*idion*$_B$' (plural: '*idia*$_B$'), respectively. Standard translations of the noun form of '*idion*' are 'property' and 'unique property.' Such translations are fine if one remembers that they counterpredicate with that of which they are predicated. I retain the transliterated Greek '*idion*' to minimize confusion about this, since 'property' in current English lacks this sense. Also, 'property' nowadays tends to be associated primarily with the categories of quality and quantity, whereas for Aristotle items in other non-substance categories can be '*idia*.'

An *idion* is what does not reveal what something is, but belongs to it alone and counterpredicates with it. For example, an *idion* of human beings is to be capable of becoming literate. For if one is a human being then he is capable of becoming literate, and if he is capable of becoming literate then he is a human being. (*Top.* 1.5, 102ª18–22)

Similarly negative is *Top.* 1.8, 103ᵇ11–12, where Aristotle says that "this is what an *idion* is, namely, what counterpredicates but does not signify what something is."[7] He gives roughly the same description of the intriguingly named "*per se* accident,"[8] which is standardly regarded either as an, or as one kind of, *idion*:[9]

> 'Accident' (*sumbebêkos*) is said in another way, namely as designating what belongs to each thing *per se* but without being in that thing's essence (*ousia*), as for example having angles summing to two rights in the case of a triangle. (*Metaph.* 5.30, 1025ª30–32)

Having interior angles summing to two rights is not a *mere* accident of triangles, for it belongs to all and only triangles. However, it is not their essence, or even part of their essence, but a *per se* accident, or *idion*, of triangles.[10]

It is clear enough that both essence and *idia* are coextensive with that of which they are the essence and *idia*, and that no *idion* can be the essence.[11] But why is the latter true? Aristotle thinks that *idia* are demonstrable from definitions, which signify the essence, but not vice versa.[12] The fact that the essence belongs to something explains why each of that thing's *idia* belongs to it, whereas none of the *idia* explains why all of the other *idia* belong to that thing. I will refer to this as "the explanatory asymmetry" between

---

7 τοῦτο γὰρ ἦν ἴδιον, τὸ ἀντικατηγορούμενον μὲν μὴ σημαῖνον δὲ τὸ τί ἦν εἶναι
8 καθ᾽ αὑτὰ συμβεβηκός
9 Barnes (1970, 139–140) departs from the standard view, arguing that *per se* accidents are not included among *idia*. He acknowledges, though, that his interpretation renders Aristotle's theory of predication incoherent.
10 The predicables, including *horoi* and *idia*, are (at least) linguistic items that signify things. A *horos* signifies something's essence and *idia* signify something's features or components that are *idia*. Translating '*idia*' as 'properties' or 'unique properties' obscures this. Even if *horoi* and *idia* were purely linguistic items, and only they, rather than what they signify, were properly (uniquely) predicated of things, the things signified by those linguistic items, namely, the essence and *idia*, would be proper to things in the sense that the predicables that signify the essence and *idia* are properly predicable of those things. For this reason, I speak of the essence and *idia* of things as proper to those things.
11 Again, when I use '*idia*' unmodified, I mean it in the narrow sense rather than the broad sense, as mentioned previously (p. 116 n. 6).
12 *APo* 1.7, 75ª39 – ᵇ2, 1.33, 89ª16–19, 2.3, 90ᵇ24–27, 2.13, 96ᵇ21–25.

essence and *idia*. We see Aristotle proposing to investigate something's essence and *idia*, as well as identifying the explanatory asymmetry between them, in *DA* 1.1:[13]

DA 1.1, 402ª7–10

We seek to think about and to know the nature and the essence of the soul, as well as its accidents, of which some seem to be *idia*[14] of the soul and others seem to belong because of the soul to living things.

ἐπιζητοῦμεν δὲ θεωρῆσαι καὶ γνῶ-ναι τήν τε φύσιν αὐτῆς καὶ τὴν οὐ-σίαν, εἶθ' ὅσα συμβέβηκε περὶ αὐ-τήν· ὧν τὰ μὲν ἴδια πάθη τῆς ψυ-χῆς εἶναι δοκεῖ, τὰ δὲ δι' ἐκείνην καὶ τοῖς ζώοις ὑπάρχειν.

DA 1.1, 402ᵇ16 – 403ª2

It seems that not only is knowing what something is useful for thinking about the causes of the accidents associated with essences (as in mathematics know-ing what straight and curved are, or what line and plane are, is useful for observing how many right angles the angles of a tri-angle equal), but also, conversely, know-ing the accidents contributes in large part to knowing what something is.[15] For whenever we are able to give an ac-count of the accidents, either of all of them or of the majority, in accordance with what appears so, then we also will

ἔοικε δ' οὐ μόνον τὸ τί ἐστι γνῶ-ναι χρήσιμον εἶναι πρὸς τὸ θεωρῆ-σαι τὰς αἰτίας τῶν συμβεβηκότων ταῖς οὐσίαις[16] (ὥσπερ ἐν τοῖς μα-θήμασι τί τὸ εὐθὺ καὶ τὸ καμπύλον, ἢ τί γραμμὴ καὶ ἐπίπεδον, πρὸς τὸ κατιδεῖν πόσαις ὀρθαῖς αἱ τοῦ τρι-γώνου γωνίαι ἴσαι), ἀλλὰ καὶ ἀνά-παλιν τὰ συμβεβηκότα συμβάλλε-ται μέγα μέρος πρὸς τὸ εἰδέναι τὸ τί ἐστιν· ἐπειδὰν γὰρ ἔχωμεν ἀπο-διδόναι κατὰ τὴν φαντασίαν περὶ τῶν συμβεβηκότων, ἢ πάντων ἢ τῶν πλείστων, τότε καὶ περὶ τῆς

---

[13] In appealing to *DA* 1.1 to get a better grasp on Aristotle's guidance about how to distinguish the essence from *idia*, I follow Irwin (1980, 38) and (1988, 62) and Shields (2015b, 248–249).

[14] One might take 'ἴδια πάθη τῆς ψυχῆς' to mean "affections/passions peculiar to the soul itself," anticipating *DA* 1.1, 403ª3 – ᵇ19, but outside of *DA* 1.1 Aristotle invariably uses 'ἴδια πάθη' to mean simply ἴδια (*APo* 2.13, 96ᵇ15–21, *Metaph.* 4.2, 1004ᵇ10–17, 13.3, 1078ª5–8). He also uses 'πάθη καθ' αὐτά' in this way (*APo* 1.7, 75ᵇ1–2, 1.9, 76ª13, 1.10, 76ᵇ6–7). Hicks (1907, 178) prefers the interpretation that I have adopted.

[15] The accidents of which Aristotle speaks in this passage are *per se* accidents, as argued by Hicks (1907, 177–178). First, he introduced these as *idia* earlier in the chapter (*DA* 1.1, 402ª7–10). Second, in this passage Aristotle seems to suggest that the accidents that he has in mind can be demonstrated to belong to the *definiendum*. But he thinks that it is not possible, strictly speaking, to demonstrate accidents that are not *per se* accidents (*APo* 1.6, 75ª18). He sometimes uses 'accidents' unmodified or 'per se' unmodified to refer to *per se* accidents (*Top.* 2.3, 110ᵇ22–23, *PA* 1.3, 643ª30–31).

[16] In this passage 'ousiai' is sometimes translated as 'substances.' I prefer 'essences' for three reasons: First, the mathematical example that Aristotle gives to illustrate his point is not about substances.

be able to speak best about the essence. For the starting-point of every demonstration is what something is, so that those definitions that do not result in our knowing the accidents, or at least easily forming conjectures about them, clearly have all been stated in a dialectical and vacuous way.

οὐσίας ἕξομεν λέγειν κάλλιστα· πάσης γὰρ ἀποδείξεως ἀρχὴ τὸ τί ἐστιν, ὥστε καθ' ὅσους τῶν ὁρισμῶν μὴ συμβαίνει τὰ συμβεβηκότα γνωρίζειν, ἀλλὰ μηδ' εἰκάσαι περὶ αὐτῶν εὐμαρές, δῆλον ὅτι διαλεκτικῶς εἴρηνται καὶ κενῶς ἅπαντες.

Aristotle here tells us that for scientific inquiry in general, it is important to have a grasp on the *idia* of what is being investigated. That is because a definition, which reveals the essence, ought also to reveal the reason why each of the *idia* belongs to the thing in question. If a putative definition cannot do this, then it is not a good definition because it has not revealed the genuine essence. This requirement does not hold of *idia*. They must merely be shown to belong to all and only the things in question, for none of the *idia* explains why all other *idia* belong to the things in question. Put another way, all *idia* can be deduced from the definition that reveals the essence, but they cannot all be deduced from each other. Otherwise, definitions would not be required for demonstrative science. *Idia* contribute to knowing what something is in the sense that we check a putative definition to see whether or not those properties are deducible from it.

It is clear, then, that Aristotle's theory of predication features two ways of being proper: as essence and as *idia*. Something's essence, which is signified by a real definition of it, has an explanatory status that the *idia* lack. For this reason, we may say that something's essence is proper to it in a primary way, whereas its *idia* are proper to it in a secondary way.

Second, he has just explicitly flagged that we will need to determine *whether* the soul is a substance or something else (*DA* 1.1, 402ᵃ23–25), and so it would be inappropriate to prejudge that issue in the very description of the methodology to be employed for settling it. Third, he seems to be here resuming the programmatic discussion of 402ᵃ7–10, where '*ousia*' is synonymous with 'nature' – a use of 'nature' spelled out in *Metaph.* 5.4, 1014ᵇ36 and common throughout Aristotle's works, as Hicks (1907, 176) notes – after listing a series of specific problems to be addressed. He uses the same verbs (*theōrēsai, gnōnai*) and speaks both of accidents and *ousia* without having given in the intervening lines any further clarification of the sense in which he means these terms to apply. Hicks (1907, 190–191) interprets 'τῶν συμβεβηκότων ταῖς οὐσίαις' as "of the essential properties which follow from it [the essence]."

5.3.2   *Essence and* Idia *of Happiness*

An Essence-Specifying Definition of Happiness

As I have previously argued, Aristotle's discussion of happiness in the *NE* is committed to a distinction between primary and secondary ways of being proper. Since, as we have just seen, Aristotle's theory of predication features primary and secondary ways of being proper, namely as essence and *idia*, respectively, the distinction between essence and *idia* is *prima facie* relevant for inclusion in a reconstruction of why Aristotle indicates in the *NE* that contemplation and ethically virtuous activities, which are biconditionally related, are proper to happiness in a primary and secondary way, respectively.[17] But is there a direct reason to believe that he intends to apply the theory of predication in which the distinction between essence and *idia* has its home, as it appears in such texts as *APo, Top., DA*, and *Metaph.*, in the *NE*? There is such a reason if Aristotle in the *NE* attempts to give essence-specifying definitions of ethical kinds (e.g., happiness, virtue in general, specific kinds of virtue, voluntariness, friendship). (Notice that it can be true that Aristotle does this without it being true that this is his primary project in the *NE*, or even a direct aim of ethical science as such.) A growing chorus of voices affirms that Aristotle indeed attempts to give such definitions of ethical kinds in the *NE*.[18] For example, Aristotle claims to have given "the essence and the account of what it is to be" (2.6, 1107ᵃ6–7)[19] for virtue, having first specified its genus, state (*hexis*), in 2.5.

This is what Aristotle does in the case of happiness, too. He announces in *NE* 1.2 that the aim of the treatise is to say what happiness is. He says in 1.4 that there is disagreement about what it is. In 1.5 he lists several popular views of what it is that he will reject and foreshadows his later argument that happiness is contemplative activity. At the beginning of 1.7 he repeats his notice that he is going to say what happiness is. He indicates

---

[17] Shields (2015b, 243–249) offers helpful remarks about the distinction between essence and *idia* as that distinction pertains to the *ergon* argument in 1.7. I agree with him that this distinction is important for understanding Aristotle's ethics, and in particular his discussion of happiness. Shields (2015b) does not propose my Essentialist Theory of Happiness, or any overall interpretation of Aristotle's theory of happiness, since his purpose is the more limited one of motivating a particular account of the relationship between Aristotle's theoretical and practical science. However, he does criticize certain interpretations of Aristotle's *ergon* argument, notably Whiting's (1988), that I will discuss in what follows.

[18] For example, Charles (2015), Karbowski (2019), Natali (2007b, 2010), Nielsen (2015), and Salmieri (2009) argue that at various points in the *NE* Aristotle follows the procedure described in *APo* 2 for arriving at real definitions. Karbowski (2019, 199) thinks that Aristotle seeks such definitions for "practically all of the topics in the treatise [*NE*]."

[19] τὴν οὐσίαν καὶ τὸν λόγον τὸν τὸ τί ἦν εἶναι

its genus, activity. But what sort of activity is it? Among those who argue that Aristotle aims to give essence-specifying definitions of ethical kinds, the tendency is to see the definition of happiness as coming in 1.7, the conclusion of the *ergon* argument:[20]

ERGON

The human good turns out to be activity of the soul in accordance with virtue, and if there are multiple virtues, then in accordance with the best (*aristên*) and most perfect (*teleiotatên*). (1098ᵃ16–18)

But if ERGON were an essence-specifying definition of happiness, it would be mysterious why Aristotle would revisit the issue in book 10 and there propose what appears to be a different essence-specifying definition of happiness: "a kind of contemplative activity" (10.8, 1178ᵇ7–8).[21] ERGON, then, seems less likely to be an essence-specifying definition than it is to be what Aristotle says that it is: an outline sketch to be completed later (1098ᵃ20–22), in book 10. In what sense is ERGON an outline sketch? I propose that ERGON is what I will call "an *idia*ᵦ claim."[22] Since something's essence and its *idia*ɴ both fall under its *idia*ᵦ, an *idia*ᵦ claim does not specify the essence. An essence-specifying definition must isolate the essence from among the *idia*. This is why ERGON is an outline sketch rather than an essence-specifying definition. Such a definition comes in book 10. But identifying the *idia*ᵦ of happiness, as Aristotle does in ERGON, sets the agenda for the rest of the *NE* and prepares the way for the essence-specifying definition in book 10.[23]

---

[20] See, for example, Karbowski (2019, 200), Natali (2007b, 379) and (2010, 311), and Nielsen (2015, 36). Gabriel Richardson Lear has suggested in conversation that in speaking of ERGON as a definition of happiness one at best speaks loosely, since what should be said about ERGON is that it is a claim about the human good that, only by taking account of Aristotle's argument previously in *NE* 1 that the human good is happiness, permits the substitution of 'happiness' for 'the human good,' and that it cannot achieve the status of a real definition until Aristotle clarifies the conditional that it contains. Natali (2007b, 379–380) thinks that ERGON is a real definition of happiness, but that its unclarity about the referents of 'soul' and 'virtue' is a "defect" of it that Aristotle later addresses by distinguishing the parts of soul and kinds of virtue. Scott (2015, 149, 169–174) believes that nearly all of the *NE* is dedicated to direct or indirect ways of making the definition of 'happiness' sufficiently definite by clarifying terms like 'soul' and 'virtue' as they occur in ERGON.

[21] θεωρητικὴ τις ἐστὶν ἐνέργεια

[22] Recall that I use the 'B' and 'N' subscripts to distinguish between *idia* in the broad and narrow senses, respectively.

[23] Charles (2015, 75) gives a different and subtle account of the sense in which ERGON counts as an outline sketch. He thinks that the first part of that conclusion "points to the type of definition of the human good which Aristotle is developing," whereas the second part of it "indicates the type of unity it possesses." According to Charles, Aristotle defines the human good as excellent rational activity, but it is not until book 10 that we are shown that contemplation is the "paradigm case" of such activity. It is in reference to this paradigm case, Charles thinks, that practically virtuous

For Aristotle, then, it is true to say, as he does in ERGON, that happiness is virtuous activity, but this is neither the 'is' of identity nor the 'is' of essential predication (definition). Rather, it is the 'is' of *idia*-predication, a species of the 'is' of predication, like the claim that the triangle is a plane figure with interior angles summing to two rights. (Strictly speaking, the claim about triangles is an *idia*$_N$-predication, whereas that about happiness in ERGON is an *idia*$_B$-predication.) This claim about the triangle is not a definition, for it does not specify its essence (three-sided plane figure). But being a plane figure with interior angles summing to two rights belongs to all and only triangles. Likewise, virtuous activity in general, which includes contemplation and practically virtuous activities, belongs to all and only those things that count as happiness, an activity extended over the course of a complete life. In other words, all and only cases of this extended activity, happiness, are cases of virtuous activity in general, having both contemplation and practically virtuous activities as parts.

As I have just indicated, Aristotle thinks, as he says in the sequel of ERGON, that a case of happiness is an activity extended over the course of a complete life:

> Furthermore, in a complete life. For one swallow does not make a spring, nor does one day. Nor, similarly, does one day or a short time make one blessed and happy. (1.7, 1098ª18–20)

One might raise questions about how long a complete life is, but it is clear enough that Aristotle would not regard an afternoon of contemplation as a case of happiness. Happiness is an activity that is so spread out as to characterize a life and therefore temporally encompasses numerous activities and periods of rest.[24] There is one case of happiness per case of

---

activities count as "instances" of the human good that is referenced in ERGON. I do not think of contemplation and practically virtuous activities as instances of happiness, but rather as parts of it. Charles explicitly distinguishes between instances and parts and expresses a decided preference for the former, apparently because he thinks that pluralists have evidence only that the happy *life* has parts (79). I presented evidence in Chapter 1 that happiness (the activity) has parts. I want now to add that the more specific view, which I endorse, that happiness (a virtuous activity) has various virtuous activities as proper parts and contemplative activity is predicated essentially of it, gains some support from ancient sources. Doxography C (ap. Stobaeus, *Anth.* 2.7.20.7–13), commonly (though not uncontroversially) dated to the first century BC, reports as orthodox Peripatetic doctrine that one sort of virtuous activity can be predicated essentially or as *idion*$_N$ of another virtuous activity. The doxographer speaks in terms of being *idion* and κατὰ συμβεβηκός, but since he is clear that the activities in question necessarily counterpredicate, and that the activity's *idion* is what gives it its form, he must mean that all of these are *idia*$_B$, which class divides into essence and *idia*$_N$ (καθ' αὐτὰ συμβεβηκότα).

[24] Kraut (1989, 71–73 and 171) and Lear (2015) offer especially focused treatments of this issue.

happy life per case of happy person; there are not, for example, as many cases of happiness as there are afternoons of contemplation. The happy person and his happy life are made happy by happiness, the extended activity. So, when I say that all and only cases of this extended activity, happiness, are cases of virtuous activity in general (covering contemplation and practically virtuous activity), I do not mean that a particular generous act that takes place over the course of an afternoon is a case of happiness. Generous activity is part of happiness, the extended activity. So is contemplation. But it is false that all and only cases of happiness are cases of particular, continuous episodes of generous activity or particular, continuous episodes of contemplative activity. So, there is no pressure to say that particular, continuous episodes of generous activity *are* particular, continuous episodes of contemplative activity in some way, and no need to attempt to explain how that might be so.[25] Rather, contemplative activity, practically virtuous activity, happiness, and the happy life belong to all and only the same subjects, happy people, and facts about the times at which they are appropriately attributed to happy people are complicated in the way that we have just seen.[26]

One might at first balk at the proposition that an intermittent activity can make a continuous whole of which it is a part the kind of whole that it is. But most interpretations require the truth of such a proposition. Monists who think that happiness is continuous rather than intermittent, but that contemplation is intermittent, must explain how happiness, which they claim to be contemplation, can occur when contemplation does not occur. Monists (or others) who instead believe that happiness, too, is intermittent, but who also think that happiness makes the happy life as a whole happy, and that the happy life as a whole is not intermittent, are already committed to the claim that an intermittent activity can make a continuous whole of which it is a part the kind of whole that it is. Those pluralists who think that happiness has a composite essence of which contemplation is a part and that happiness is continuous and contemplation is intermittent must explain how happiness can occur when part of its essence does not occur. Anyone who instead regards contemplation as only a contingent part of happiness violates the Monist Constraint and thereby immediately renders the Conjunctive Problem unsolvable. Relativists inherit the aforementioned explanatory demands insofar as they agree with monists about

---

[25] Recall that Lear (2004, 194–196) argues that ethically virtuous activities are "contemplation of a sort."

[26] Thanks to Gabriel Richardson Lear for discussion of this issue.

one kind of happiness and with pluralists about another. In short, most interpretations already require it to be true that in some cases an intermittent activity can make a continuous whole of which it is a part the kind of whole that it is. We should expect the explanatory relations between parts and wholes in the domain of activities, especially activities that are as spread out as Aristotle takes happiness to be, to differ in certain respects from the explanatory relations between parts and wholes in the domain of substances.[27]

The distinction between essential predication and *idia*-predication allows us to fill in the outline sketch that I gave earlier, resulting in the Essentialist Theory of Happiness (essentialism). According to that sketch, practically virtuous activities are proper to happiness in a secondary way, namely as necessary, characteristic parts, whereas contemplation, in addition to being a part of happiness, is proper to happiness in a different, primary way, a way that is compatible with saying that happiness is contemplative activity (and compatible with saying that contemplation is a part of happiness). According to essentialism, the Pluralist Constraint – happiness is virtuous activity, a composite that includes not only contemplative activity, but also ethically virtuous activities as parts – features the 'is' of $idia_B$-predication, whereas the Monist Constraint – happiness is contemplative activity, which does not include ethically virtuous activities as parts – features the 'is' of essential predication.

The conclusion of the *ergon* argument is not the only *idia*-predication of happiness in the *NE*. Some *idia*-predications are used on the way to that conclusion:

1. Happiness is the highest human good achievable in action.
2. Happiness is the most perfect activity.
3. Happiness is the most self-sufficient activity.

These set the target for Aristotle's inquiry. Whatever the definition of happiness turns out to be, it must show how these *idia*-predications are true. (1)–(3) do not do much to provide content for a theory of happiness. He says that (1) in particular might seem somewhat uncontroversial. The *ergon* argument is meant to show, at least in outline, how (1) is true. Happiness will be the highest human good achievable in action if it is itself the highest good activity that human beings characteristically perform. ERGON supplies the genus of good characteristic human activities, namely,

[27] For more on this point see Reece (2019).

rational activity in accordance with virtue, and it gestures at the possibility that there is a *highest* activity, which (1) concerns, but it does not yet specify what kind of activity that is. So, ERGON only partially explains the truth of (1). Furthermore, Aristotle does not say that ERGON reveals why (2) and (3) are true. We discover in 10.7 that only the definition of happiness as contemplative activity provides the explanation of the truth of (2) and (3). As he says there, contemplative activity is the most perfect and most self-sufficient activity. Since ERGON does not specify that happiness is contemplative activity, ERGON does not show why (2) and (3) are true. However, ERGON opens the door for that specification by at least partially explaining the truth of (1), and so has a special status among the various *idia*-predications about happiness.

Aristotle offers further *idia*-predications in 1.8. (4)–(6) correspond to *endoxa* that his eventual definition will at least partially vindicate. The parts in parentheses are those that Aristotle thinks must be added in order to make the *endoxa* acceptable:

4. Happiness is that (activity) in virtue of which the happy person lives well and does well.
5. Happiness is (activity in accordance with) practical wisdom.
6. Happiness is (activity in accordance with) theoretical wisdom.
7. Happiness is the activity that is best, finest, and most pleasant.

Among those who argue that Aristotle gives essence-specifying definitions of ethical kinds in the *NE*, it is sometimes held that the truth of ERGON explains the truth of (4)–(7), and that its ability to explain their truth vindicates its status as the essence-specifying definition of happiness. I disagree. For one thing, ERGON does not *explain* the truth of any of these until it is suitably unpacked, or in other words, until it is given content through Aristotle's development of his theory of virtue. ERGON simply does not give enough information about what is involved in virtue, what kinds of virtues there are, or how these virtues are related to each other. An unpacked version of ERGON comprises (5) and (6) and shows how (4) is true by revealing that activity in accordance with virtue entails precisely those things that are thought to be involved with living and doing well, such as friendship, pleasure, and correct use of external goods. This is a reason, in addition to that given previously, why ERGON has a privileged status among *idia*-predications about happiness: ERGON can be unpacked in a way that reveals the truth of various other *idia*-predications. However, even an unpacked version of ERGON cannot explain why (7) is true. As Aristotle tells us in 10.7–8, only contemplative activity is best, finest, and most pleasant. Since ERGON does not reveal happiness to be contemplative activity, it does not explain the truth of (7).

In 10.7–8, Aristotle argues that defining happiness as contemplative activity shows that various *idia* of happiness that he has discussed, as well as some new ones, do indeed belong to it. Whereas ERGON only partially explained the truth of (1) because it did not identify the *highest* virtuous activity, Aristotle accomplishes this at 10.7, 1177^{a}19–21. His definition of happiness as contemplative activity also explains the truth of (2) (^{b}1–4), (3) (^{a}27–^{b}1), and (7) (^{a}22–27, 10.8, 1178^{b}7–32). It explains the truth of (6) simply enough: The activity of theoretical wisdom is contemplation. It explains the truth of (5) since, for Aristotle, contemplative activity requires activity in accordance with practical wisdom in the way that I expounded in Chapter 2. In light of this, since activity in accordance with practical wisdom explains the truth of (4), Aristotle's definition of happiness as contemplative activity does, too. His definition also explains the truth of other *idia*-predications, such as that happiness is the activity that is most continuous (^{a}21–22), most pleasant (^{a}22–27), most leisurely (^{b}4–15), in accordance with what is a human being most of all (1178^{a}2–8), and most divine (10.8, 1178^{b}7–32).

In this section I have been arguing that Aristotle's distinction between essential predication (definition) and *idia*-predication is helpful for understanding his distinction between the ways in which contemplation and practically virtuous activities are proper to happiness. Something's essence and its *idia* are proper to it, but in different ways. There is an explanatory asymmetry between the essence and *idia*, so it would be correct to say that something's essence is explanatorily prior to its *idia*, and thus that the essence is proper in a primary way, the *idia* in a secondary way. According to Aristotle, something's *idia* can be demonstrated from its essence-specifying definition, but not vice versa. This is the procedure that he follows in his inquiry into the essence of happiness. Essentialism solves the Conjunctive Problem of Happiness by distinguishing between essential predication and *idia*-predication and associating these with the Monist Constraint and the Pluralist Constraint, respectively.

This is not, however, the end of the story. Aristotle has reasons for looking in the direction of contemplative activity as the essence-specifying definition of happiness that explains why its *idia* belong to it. These reasons are important to discuss at least because other interpretations of their status frequently have been deployed in arguments for alternative accounts of his theory of happiness.

Subject and Attribute

Aristotle's project of providing an essence-specifying definition of human happiness is complicated by the fact that human happiness is itself an attribute of a human subject. On his view, specifying the essence of the attribute will involve us in a discussion of the essence of the underlying subject (*APo* 2.2, 2.8, *Metaph.* 8.4, 1044^{b}8–20). So, an Aristotelian account of the essence of happiness involves an account of the essence of human beings. Even if Aristotle never furnishes a clear-cut essence-specifying definition of human beings (Kietzmann, 2019), he appears in *NE* 10.7–8 to rely on assumptions about the human essence that have invited various kinds of speculative reconstruction. In particular, he appears to claim that theoretical intellect is what a human being is most of all (*malista*, 10.8, 1178^{a}6–7). This claim and its place in the overall argumentative context have been interpreted in various ways, which I discussed in Chapters 1 and 4. I now want to zero in on my preferred interpretation.

Aristotle begins 10.7 as follows:

T1 (10.7, 1177^{a}12–18)

But if happiness is activity in accordance with virtue, it is reasonable that it should be in accordance with the highest one, and this will be the virtue of the best part. Whether, then, this part is intellect or something else that seems naturally to rule, lead, and understand what is noble and divine, whether by being itself something divine or by being the most divine part in us, this part's activity in accordance with its proper virtue will be perfect happiness. We have already said that it is contemplative activity.

Εἰ δ' ἐστὶν ἡ εὐδαιμονία κατ' ἀρε- ^{a}12
τὴν ἐνέργεια, εὔλογον κατὰ τὴν
κρατίστην· αὕτη δ' ἂν εἴη τοῦ
ἀρίστου. εἴτε δὴ νοῦς τοῦτο εἴτε
ἄλλο τι, ὃ δὴ κατὰ φύσιν δοκεῖ   15
ἄρχειν καὶ ἡγεῖσθαι καὶ ἔννοιαν
ἔχειν περὶ καλῶν καὶ θείων, εἴτε
θεῖον ὂν καὶ αὐτὸ εἴτε τῶν ἐν
ἡμῖν τὸ θειότατον, ἡ τούτου ἐνέργεια κατὰ τὴν οἰκείαν ἀρετὴν
εἴη ἂν ἡ τελεία εὐδαιμονία. ὅτι
δ' ἐστὶ θεωρητική, εἴρηται.   18

Aristotle here affirms that happiness is the activity of our highest, most divine virtue, which is the virtue of our highest and most divine part. He ends the chapter with the claim that this highest and most divine part in us, and indeed what we are most of all, is theoretical intellect:

T2 (10.7, 1178^{a}2–8)

Each ⟨human being⟩ would in fact seem to be ⟨intellect⟩, since it is the determinative and better ⟨part⟩. So, it would be bizarre if

δόξειε δ' ἂν καὶ εἶναι ἕκαστος ^{a}2
τοῦτο, εἴπερ τὸ κύριον καὶ ἄμει-
νον. ἄτοπον οὖν γίνοιτ' ἄν, εἰ

one did not choose a life characteristic of
oneself, but rather a life characteristic of
something else. What was said previously
applies now, too. For what is proper by nature to each thing is best and most pleasant
to each thing. Indeed, life in accordance
with intellect is proper to a human being,
since ⟨intellect⟩ is a human being most of
all. So, this ⟨life⟩ also is happiest.

μὴ τὸν αὑτοῦ βίον αἱροῖτο ἀλλά
τινος ἄλλου. τὸ λεχθέν τε πρό-
τερον ἁρμόσει καὶ νῦν· τὸ γὰρ   5
οἰκεῖον ἑκάστῳ τῇ φύσει κράτι-
στον καὶ ἥδιστόν ἐστιν ἑκάστῳ·
καὶ τῷ ἀνθρώπῳ δὴ ὁ κατὰ τὸν
νοῦν βίος, εἴπερ τοῦτο μάλιστα
ἄνθρωπος. οὗτος ἄρα καὶ εὐδαιμονέστατος.   8

In T2, 'intellect' more plausibly refers to theoretical intellect than to
practical intellect or to intellect undifferentiated between, or combining,
the two.[28] Otherwise, T2 would not comport with its sequel or with T1.
Aristotle tells us in T1 that our best and highest activity is contemplation,
and that this activity is that of the best and highest part in us. He has led us
to expect that the highest part in us is theoretical intellect, since theoretical
intellect's virtue is theoretical wisdom – we already know by this point that
it is our highest and best virtue since it is the virtue of the best part of the
soul and is concerned with the highest things (6.7, 1141^{a}18–20, 1141^{b}2–3,
6.13, 1145^{a}6–8) – and contemplation is the activity corresponding to that
virtue. His claim in the first sentence of T2 about intellect explicitly depends on intellect being our determinative (*kurion*) and better (*ameinon*)
part. This status is supposed to justify why it is most of all what we are
and why life in accordance with it is happiest, as we see in the penultimate
and ultimate sentences of T2. This justificatory structure mirrors that of
T1, making it most natural to read Aristotle as referring in T2 to the same

---

[28] Cooper (1975, 172–173) believes that although in T2 Aristotle says that we are most of all theoretical
intellect, he says in *NE* 9.4 and 9.8 that we are most of all practical intellect. Other commentators
have been unconvinced by Cooper's interpretation of *NE* 9. Kraut (1989, 128–131, 189–190), for
example, argues that Aristotle does not mean in *NE* 9 that humans are most of all practical intellect,
but rather that the ethically virtuous person chooses to identify himself most of all with activity in
accordance with practical intellect. Reeve (1992, 133–137) argues that *NE* 9, like 10, says that we are
most of all theoretical intellect. Lear (2004, 191 n. 32) finds plausible a position similar to Reeve's,
though her remarks about it are briefer. I think that these commentators are correct in defending
Aristotle against Cooper's charge of inconsistency on this point. One might think that there is
another source of inconsistency, namely *NE* 6.2, 1139^{b}4–5, where Aristotle says that "decision is
either a desiring sort of intellect or an intellectual sort of desire, and a human being is this sort of
starting-point" (ἢ ὀρεκτικὸς νοῦς ἡ προαίρεσις ἢ ὄρεξις διανοητική, καὶ ἡ τοιαύτη ἀρχὴ ἄνθρωπος). Is Aristotle here identifying a human being with practical intellect? I think not. Rather, as I
argued in Reece (2019), I take him to be saying here that a human being is the *per se* efficient-causal
starting-point of his actions not under just any qualification, but rather *qua* desirer of a certain sort.
Put otherwise, practical intellect rather than theoretical intellect is what is explanatorily relevant
to acting. That, rather than a claim about the human essence, is Aristotle's interest in 6.2, 1139^{b}4–5.
Thanks to David Charles for encouraging me to address the passages from 6.2, 9.4, and 9.8.

type of intellect that figures in T1: our highest and best part, the one whose virtue is our highest and best (theoretical wisdom), and whose activity is contemplation. This type of intellect is theoretical intellect. In the sequel of T2, which I discussed in Chapter 3, Aristotle reports that practical activities, which are associated with practical intellect, are proper to humans not in the primary way that he has in view in the antepenultimate and penultimate sentences of T2 (^{a}5–7), but in a secondary way. This is precisely because they are in accordance with the other sort of virtue, practical virtue, which is not virtue of theoretical intellect. We can see, then, that if 'intellect' in T2 referred to anything but theoretical intellect, T2 would fit very poorly in its context.

Part of the context that I have not yet discussed, though, has sometimes been thought to introduce a problem for Aristotle's prioritization of theoretical intellect. Just before T2, Aristotle says this:

10.7, 1177^{b}26 – 1178^{a}2

Such a life would be higher than human. For it is not insofar as one is a human being that he will live this way, but insofar as he has some divine part in him. And the activity of this part differs from activity in accordance with the other kind of virtue to the extent that this part differs from the compound. If indeed intellect is something divine compared to a human being, so also will the life in accordance with intellect be divine compared to human life. We should not follow those who exhort us to 'think human things, since you are human,' or 'think mortal things, since you are mortal,' but instead, as far as possible, cast off mortality, and go to all lengths to live a life in accordance with what is highest in us; for even if this is small in bulk, it far exceeds everything in power and honor.	ὁ δὲ τοιοῦτος ἂν εἴη βίος κρείτ- ^{b}26 των ἢ κατ' ἄνθρωπον· οὐ γὰρ ᾗ ἄνθρωπός ἐστιν οὕτω βιώσεται, ἀλλ' ᾗ θεῖόν τι ἐν αὐτῷ ὑπάρ- χει· ὅσον δὲ διαφέρει τοῦτο τοῦ συνθέτου, τοσοῦτον καὶ ἡ ἐνέρ- γεια τῆς κατὰ τὴν ἄλλην ἀρετήν. εἰ δὴ θεῖον ὁ νοῦς πρὸς τὸν ἄν- 30 θρωπον, καὶ ὁ κατὰ τοῦτον βίος θεῖος πρὸς τὸν ἀνθρώπινον βίον. οὐ χρὴ δὲ κατὰ τοὺς παραινοῦν- τας ἀνθρώπινα φρονεῖν ἄνθρω- πον ὄντα οὐδὲ θνητὰ τὸν θνητόν, ἀλλ' ἐφ' ὅσον ἐνδέχεται ἀθανα- τίζειν καὶ πάντα ποιεῖν πρὸς τὸ ζῆν κατὰ τὸ κράτιστον τῶν ἐν αὐτῷ· εἰ γὰρ καὶ τῷ ὄγκῳ μικρόν ἐστι, δυνάμει καὶ τιμιότητι πολὺ ^{a}1 μᾶλλον πάντων ὑπερέχει.

He is not here denying that intellect is what a human being is most of all. Otherwise, he would contradict himself in the immediately subsequent passage, T2. Neither can he mean that life in accordance with it is a life that a divine being can live and a human being cannot, on pain of contradicting the sentence preceding this passage. So, intellect cannot be something that a divine being has *instead of* something that a human being has. Indeed, the intellect that he now describes cannot be something that any divine being that he standardly recognizes has at all, for, as we saw in Chapter 4, he thinks that our intellect cannot be type-identical with any existing divine intellect. What is he saying, then? In this unusually poetic passage, Aristotle diverges from his typical way of applying 'divine' and 'human,' which he employed just before this passage and immediately resumes in the sequel, because he is going out of his way to invoke the mythopoeic portrayal of humanity's heavenly heritage given in Plato's *Timaeus* 89E – 90D and its contrast with the injunctions found in works by various dramatists and poets to think human and mortal thoughts.[29] The *Timaeus* passage, which has numerous similarities with this one, urges human beings to cultivate the highest of the three parts of their soul rather than focusing their attention on their appetites. This highest part is called divine in virtue of its provenance: It has been given to us by the god. To cultivate it is to think divine and immortal thoughts. Attending disproportionately to the appetites, by contrast, involves one in thinking mortal thoughts. Aristotle invokes this passage because he wants to say something similar: We must prioritize what we are most of all, theoretical intellect, which is concerned with the highest, most divine objects (6.7), in spite of other elements within us, particularly bodily appetites, that clamor for our attention. (This is also how he ends the *Eudemian Ethics*.)[30] This Platonic point is made vividly in *Republic* 9, 588C – 589C with the image of the three parts of the human soul in which the appetites appear as a many-headed beast, spirit as a lion, and reason as a human. Reason is the highest part, and we should cultivate it, though it is small in magnitude compared to the other parts (588D4–5; 4, 442A–C). It is with precisely this point about the contrast between intellect's status and its magnitude that Aristotle ends his passage and reverts to his less mythopoeic habit of expression.[31]

---

[29] Examples of such injunctions appear in works by Antiphanes (fr. 289, Kock 1884), Epicharmus (fr. 263, Kaibel 1899, quoted by Aristotle in *Rhet.* 2.12, 1394^{b}24), Euripides (*Alcestis* 799 and *TGF* 1040, Nauck 1889), Pindar (*Isthmians* 5.16), and Sophocles (*Tereus* fr. 590, Radt 1977). The comparison with Plato's *Timaeus* and/or contrast with the dramatists and poets are mentioned by Aufderheide (2020, 188), Burnet (1900, 463), Frede (2020, 966–967), Gauthier and Jolif (1970, vol. 2, 890), Gerson (2004, 370 n. 81), Irwin (2019, 355), Long (2019, 63–69), Sedley (2017, 325–326), Stewart (1892, vol. 2, 448–449), and Zanatta (1986, vol. 2, 1105).

[30] Stewart (1892, vol. 2, 448) mentions this.

[31] The highly local explanation of Aristotle's shift in usage of 'human' that I have offered is more elegant and plausible than is the claim made by Scott (1999) and Thorsrud (2015) that he has a "bifocal anthropology" or "dichotomous anthropology" according to which human beings have two

The context of T2, then, is not meant to indicate that theoretical intellect transcends what we are. Rather, it most of all is what we are. The claim that intellect is most of all (*malista*) what we are is best parsed as an assertion that theoretical intellect is proper to us in the primary way, or in other words, that it is essential to us.[32] Some commentators have not regarded this position as available to Aristotle because of doubts about theoretical intellect's peculiarity to humans. In Chapter 4 I argued that humans alone are capable of the sort of contemplative activity that Aristotle describes in *NE* 10.7–8. That is because only they are capable of the sort of theoretical wisdom, of which contemplation is the manifestation, that he assigns pride of place among intellectual virtues. This sort of theoretical wisdom is the virtue of the kind of theoretical intellect that all and only humans have, namely, voluntarily active intellect. It is this sort of intellect that, according to Aristotle, a human being is most of all. As I argued in Chapter 2, voluntary activations of theoretical intellect imply applications of practical intellect. So, if theoretical intellect (specifically, voluntarily active intellect)

---

essences. It is also preferable to the transhumanist interpretation, discussed in Chapter 4, Section 2, which attributes to Aristotle the claim that the human good is not the *human* good.

[32] My interpretation of this claim is at variance with those of Charles (1999, 220) and Scott (1999, 231–241), who also interpret '*malista*' as suggesting that theoretical intellect is essential to us but mean different things by 'is essential to us.' Charles thinks that in saying that we are *malista* theoretical intellect, Aristotle means that theoretical intellect "is what is especially distinctive of man, the highest of several features in his essence," and that the other features in the human essence include practical intellect and the emotions. According to Charles, these other features are included in the human essence because of their analogical relationship to theoretical intellect. In other words, theoretical intellect is the part of the human essence that makes the rest of the essence what it is. To me, this sounds like an essence of an essence. I find it easier to believe that for Aristotle, when a feature of something is essential and it asymmetrically explains why other features belong to that thing, those other features are (at most) *idia* rather than parts of the essence. Otherwise, it is very difficult to see what might have led Aristotle to distinguish essence and *idia* in his theory of predication in the first place. Scott, responding to Charles and emphasizing the importance of Aristotle's contrast marked by 'primary' and 'secondary' in T2 and its sequel, contends that in saying that we are *malista* theoretical intellect, Aristotle means that the most accurate, strictest answer to the question "What is the human essence?" is "theoretical intellect," even though Aristotle thinks that this question has a secondary, but still legitimate, answer: what Scott calls "our anthropic element." Scott believes that Aristotle has a "bifocal anthropology" according to which "uniquely in the universe, we are in some sense two kinds of thing at once," or in other words, that we have two essences. Rather than taking a position on essences that nothing in Aristotle's theory of predication leads us to expect, I would prefer to suppose that Aristotle here observes his typical distinction between essence and *idia* and this is why he distinguishes between primary and secondary ways of being proper to humans. Among the important points that emerge from this influential discussion between Charles and Scott is that Aristotle uses '*malista*' in a variety of subtly different ways and care is required in sorting out how its use inflects his position on human nature. I agree: I have cited several passages (*EE* 8.3, 1249^{b}16–21, *NE* 1.8, 1099^{a}13–25, and 10.8, 1179^{a}22–32) in previous chapters in which Aristotle uses '*malista*' in a sense different from the one that it has in T2. I do not think that '*malista*' on its own would have provided a definite answer about the human essence, but it naturally suggests one when used, as it is in T2, to distinguish between a primary and secondary way of being proper to humans. I am grateful to David Charles for discussion of this issue.

is *idion* to humans, then so is practical intellect. This much follows from what has preceded. The remaining question is whether practical intellect is *idion*$_N$ to humans, or in other words, *idion* but not essential. In order to show that it is, I will argue that the sort of theoretical intellect that humans have, namely, voluntarily active intellect, is explanatorily prior to practical intellect, that is, that it asymmetrically explains practical intellect, that is, that it explains practical intellect, but not vice versa. If this asymmetrical explanation holds, when combined with Aristotle's claim that we are most of all theoretical intellect it will be good reason for believing that theoretical intellect of this kind is essential to us and practical intellect is *idion*$_N$ to us.[33]

According to Aristotle, practical intellect is intrinsically concerned with human things, such as what is achievable for us in action. Among the human things with which practical intellect is concerned is the development and manifestation of theoretical intellect's virtue, theoretical wisdom (*NE* 6.13, 1145^{a}6–11), as I discussed in Chapter 2. So, practical intellect is concerned with theoretical intellect because the former is concerned with the latter's perfected state. But theoretical intellect cannot be intrinsically concerned with practical intellect. That is because practical intellect is concerned with human activity, and any human activity is contingent, variable, and achievable in action, but theoretical intellect does not intrinsically concern such things (*DA* 3.9, 432^{b}27–28). Theoretical intellect, as well as its virtue and its activity, is what it is independently of practical intellect, as well as its virtue and its activity, being what it is. Theoretical intellect is concerned with necessary, eternal, invariable things, practical intellect with contingent, variable things (*NE* 6.1, 1139^{a}6–17, 6.3, 1139^{b}23–24). Necessary, eternal, invariable things are explanatorily prior to contingent, variable things (*Metaph.* 9.8, 1050^{b}6 – 1051^{a}3).[34] So, the things with which

---

[33] Broadie (2019, 269) alleges that there is an explanatory asymmetry running the other direction. According to her, it is obvious that practical intellect is essential to humans, but theoretical intellect's status must be established with reference to it. Similarly, she believes that practical wisdom's status as a virtue explains theoretical wisdom's status as a virtue. It will soon become clear why I think that such claims are precisely backward.

[34] Eternal things are explanatory of perishable things in at least the following ways: the sun's eternal motion on an inclined circle (in turn explained by other eternal things) at least partially explains the generation and perishing of terrestrial things (*Phys.* 2.2, 194^{b}13, *GC* 2.10, 336^{a}23 – ^{b}12, *Metaph.* 12.6, 1072^{a}3–18), and the elements mentioned in citing material causes of perishable things have tendencies that are explained by their imitation of eternal, celestial things (*Metaph.* 9.8, 1050^{b}28–29; *GC* 1.3, *Metaph.* 12.5–7). (I do not mean to suggest that such considerations are Aristotle's only, or even primary, points of reference in his argument for the priority of eternal to perishable things in the context of *Metaph.* 9.8 itself; my point is rather that this priority claim involves a commitment to explanatory asymmetry.) Reece (ms.) discusses the connection between explanatory priority and ontological priority.

theoretical intellect is concerned, necessary, eternal, invariable things, are prior to the things with which practical wisdom is concerned. Since the things with which something is concerned are explanatorily prior to those that are concerned with them (*DA* 2.4), theoretical intellect is explanatorily prior to practical intellect.[35]

The explanatory priority of theoretical intellect to practical intellect does not imply that we could have or activate theoretical intellect without practical intellect. But this explanatory asymmetry is sufficient to show that although practical intellect is *idion* to humans, it cannot be essential to them. That is because no feature of a thing is explanatorily prior to what is essential to it. So, practical intellect must be *idion*$_N$ to humans.[36]

In this section I have been discussing what is essential and what is *idion*$_N$ to humans because human happiness is an attribute of humans and specifying the essence of an attribute involves us in a discussion of the essence of the subject. The discussion of the subject has revealed that theoretical intellect is essential to humans and practical intellect is *idion*$_N$. The explanatory asymmetry at the level of the subject between theoretical and practical intellect is mirrored by the explanatory asymmetry at the level of the attribute, happiness, between contemplative activity and practically virtuous activity.

5.4 Conclusion

Every current interpreter of Aristotle's theory of happiness needs to explain why he seems so undisturbed by the problem about whether happiness is contemplation or virtuous activity in general. One explanation that has

---

[35] Various adaptations of this argument are possible. One might think, as does Moss (2017, 138), that theoretical intellect is rational because it "can grasp the eternal truths that explain why all phenomena are as they are" and practical intellect is rational because it "can grasp the goals that explain, as final causes, why we should act the way we should." One might add that eternal, invariable things are explanatorily prior to contingent, variable things and that if the nature of *x* is to grasp things that are prior to those that it is the nature of *y* to grasp, then *x* is explanatorily prior to *y*, concluding that theoretical intellect is explanatorily prior to practical intellect. For another adaptation of the argument, one might suppose, as do Plutarch (*De virtute morali* 443D11 – F2) and Prantl (1852, 10), that according to Aristotle theoretical intellect is concerned with things in themselves, whereas practical intellect is concerned with things under a practical qualification (e.g., *qua* to-be-done). Aristotle thinks that for any *x*, *x* is explanatorily prior to qualifications of *x*. (For example, Socrates is explanatorily prior to Socrates *qua* disenchanted with Anaxagoras's books.) Things in themselves are prior to things under a practical qualification. So, the things with which theoretical intellect is concerned, things in themselves, are prior to the things with which practical wisdom is concerned. Since the things with which something is concerned are explanatorily prior to those that are concerned with them (*DA* 2.4), theoretical intellect is explanatorily prior to practical intellect.

[36] Thanks to David Charles, Gabriel Richardson Lear, and Anthony Price for discussion of issues concerned with the explanatory priority of theoretical intellect to practical intellect.

been given is that there are two different theories of happiness in the *NE* and that is because either these theories are not both written by Aristotle or they are not both intended by Aristotle to be part of the same treatise. This does not explain the various internal cross-references.[37] Another explanation is that he simply did not notice the problem. But neither did many generations of his commentators, whose subtlety, ingenuity, and strong sectarian incentives to problematize Aristotle's theory resulted in the formulation of myriad nuanced problems, but not the one that came to be articulated by Hardie (1965). The interpretation that I have given of Aristotle's theory is unsurprising in the way that it should be if it is to explain his unperturbedness: The key interpretive move is so characteristically Aristotelian that we can readily see why he would have felt comfortable assuming it made, and thus would not be worried about the kinds of problems that might have arisen if his theory had not featured it. Aristotle views his theory of predication as foundational for science and freely assumes concepts and distinctions from it throughout his works. So do his ancient commentators, who take his theory of predication as their point of departure for understanding his philosophical system. The availability of this characteristically Aristotelian interpretive move has been obscured by the allure of the Divergence Thesis, Duality Thesis, and Divinity Thesis, all of which I have argued are false.

My argument in this chapter has been that Aristotle has the resources to solve the Conjunctive Problem and thus to vouchsafe the necessity of ethically virtuous activity while clarifying the kind of priority that contemplation has. His distinction between being proper to happiness in a primary and secondary way can be clarified in terms of his standard way of drawing such a distinction, namely as one between essential predication and *idia*-predication. Various claims and arguments throughout the *NE* make best sense if Aristotle is employing this distinction. Most importantly for our purposes, he can say that contemplative activity is essential to happiness and practically virtuous activity is *idion*$_N$ to happiness. This solves the Conjunctive Problem of Happiness: The Pluralist Constraint – happiness is virtuous activity, a composite that includes not only contemplative activity, but also ethically virtuous activities as parts – features the 'is' of *idia*$_B$-predication, whereas the Monist Constraint – happiness is contemplative activity, which does not include ethically virtuous activities as parts – features the 'is' of essential predication. In his account of the nature of happiness then, as in other accounts of things' natures, Aristotle turns out not to be a monist, pluralist, or relativist, but an essentialist.

---

[37] See my p. 7 n. 15.

Bibliography

Ackrill, John L. 1974. Aristotle on *Eudaimonia*. *Proceedings of the British Academy*, **60**, 339–359.

Adkins, AWH. 1978. Theoria versus Praxis in the *Nicomachean Ethics* and the *Republic*. *Classical Philology*, **73**, 297–313.

Akasoy, Anna A, and Fidora, Alexander (eds). 2005. *The Arabic Version of the Nicomachean Ethics*. Leiden: Brill.

Albertus Magnus. 1891. *Ethica*. Paris: Vives.

Alexander of Aphrodisias. 1892. *Scripta minora reliqua (quaestiones, de fato, de mixtione)*. Supplementum Aristotelicum, vol. 2.2. Berlin: Reimer.

Annas, Julia. 1993. *The Morality of Happiness*. New York: Oxford University Press.

Anonymous. 1892. *Eustratii et Michaelis et Anonyma in ethica Nicomachea commentaria*. Commentaria in Aristotelem Graeca, vol. 20. Berlin: Reimer.

Aquinas, Thomas. 1891. *Prima Secundae Summae Theologiae*. Rome: Commissio Leonina.

Aquinas, Thomas. 1950. *In Duodecim Libros Metaphysicorum Aristotelis Expositio*. Vol. 2. Rome: Marietti.

Aquinas, Thomas. 1969. *Sententia Libri Ethicorum*. Rome: Commissio Leonina.

Aquinas, Thomas. 2010. *Quaestiones Disputatae de Virtutibus*. Turnhout: Brepols.

Aspasius. 1889. *In ethica Nicomachea quae supersunt commentaria*. Commentaria in Aristotelem Graeca, vol. 19.1. Berlin: Reimer.

Aufderheide, Joachim. 2015. The Content of Happiness: A New Case for *Theôria*. Pages 36–59 of: Aufderheide, Joachim, and Bader, Ralf M. (eds), *The Highest Good in Aristotle and Kant*. Oxford: Oxford University Press.

Aufderheide, Joachim. 2020. *Aristotle's Nicomachean Ethics Book X*. Cambridge: Cambridge University Press.

Augustine. 1955. *De Civitate Dei, Libri XI–XXII*. Turnhout: Brepols.

Austin, John L. 1979. Ἀγαθόν and Εὐδαιμονία in the *Ethics* of Aristotle. Pages 1–31 of: Urmson, James O, and Warnock, Geoffrey J (eds), *Philosophical Papers*. Oxford: Oxford University Press.

Averroes. 1953. *Averrois Cordubensis Commentarium Magnum in Aristotelis De Anima Libros*. Cambridge, MA: Mediaeval Academy of America.

Averroes. 1984. *Ibn Rushd's Metaphysics: A Translation with Introduction of Ibn Rushd's Commentary on Aristotle's Metaphysics, Book Lām*. Leiden: Brill.

Averroes. 2018. *Le plaisir, le bonheur, et l'acquisition des Vertus: Édition du Livre X du Commentaire moyen d'Averroès à l'Éthique à Nicomaque d'Aristote*. Leiden: Brill.

Baehr, Jason. 2012. Two Types of Wisdom. *Acta Analytica*, **27**, 81–97.

Baker, Samuel H. 2019. What Is 'The Best and Most Perfect Virtue'? *Analysis*, **79**, 387–393.

Baker, Samuel H. 2021. A Monistic Conclusion to Aristotle's *Ergon* Argument: the Human Good as the Best Achievement of a Human. *Archiv für Geschichte der Philosophie*, **103**, 373–403.

Baracchi, Claudia. 2007. *Aristotle's Ethics as First Philosophy*. Cambridge: Cambridge University Press.

Barnes, Jonathan. 1970. Property in Aristotle's *Topics*. *Archiv für Geschichte der Philosophie*, **52**, 136–155.

Barnes, Jonathan. 1997. Roman Aristotle. Pages 1–69 of: Barnes, Jonathan, and Griffin, Miriam (eds), *Philosophia Togata II: Plato and Aristotle at Rome*. Oxford: Oxford University Press.

Bartlett, Robert C, and Collins, Susan D. 2011. *Aristotle's* Nicomachean Ethics. Chicago: University of Chicago Press.

Beere, Jonathan. 2010. *Thinking Thinking Thinking: On God's Self-thinking in Aristotle's* Metaphysics Λ.9. www.philosophie.hu-berlin.de/en/ancient-philosophy/hpold/downloads/beere-thinking-thinking/view.

Berkowitz, Luci, and Squitier, Karl A. (eds). 1990. *Thesaurus Linguae Graecae Canon of Greek Authors and Works*. Oxford: Oxford University Press.

Blyth, Dougal. 2015. Heavenly Soul in Aristotle. *Apeiron*, **48**, 427–465.

Bodéüs, Richard. 1992. *Aristote et la théologie des vivants immortels*. St-Laurent, Québec: Bellarmin.

Bonitz, Hermann (ed). 1848. *Aristotelis Metaphysica*. Vol. 1. Bonn: A. Marcus.

Bordt, Michael. 2006. *Aristoteles' Metaphysik XII*. Darmstadt: Wissenschaftliche Buchgesellschaft.

Bostock, David. 2000. *Aristotle's Ethics*. Oxford: Oxford University Press.

Broadie, Sarah. 1991. *Ethics with Aristotle*. Oxford: Oxford University Press.

Broadie, Sarah. 1993. Que fait le premier moteur d'Aristote? (Sur la théologie du livre Lambda de la «Métaphysique»). *Revue Philosophique de la France et de l'Étranger*, **183**, 375–411.

Broadie, Sarah. 2003. Aristotelian Piety. *Phronesis*, **48**, 54–70.

Broadie, Sarah. 2012. A Science of First Principles: *Metaphysics A* 2. Pages 43–67 of: Steel, Carlos, and Primavesi, Oliver (eds), *Aristotle's* Metaphysics Alpha: *Symposium Aristotelicum*. Oxford: Oxford University Press.

Broadie, Sarah. 2019. Practical Truth in Aristotle. *Oxford Studies in Ancient Philosophy*, **57**, 249–271.

Broadie, Sarah, and Rowe, Christopher. 2002. *Aristotle:* Nicomachean Ethics. Oxford: Oxford University Press.

Brockmann, Christian. 1993. Zur Überlieferung der Aristotelischen Magna Moralia. Pages 43–80 of: Friederike Berger *et al.* (eds), *Symbolae Berolinenses für Dieter Harlfinger*. Amsterdam: Hakkert.

Brown, Eric. 2006. Wishing for Fortune, Choosing Activity: Aristotle on External Goods and Happiness. *Proceedings of the Boston Area Colloquium in Ancient Philosophy*, **22**, 221–256.

Brown, Eric. 2014. Aristotle on the Choice of Lives: Two Concepts of Self-Sufficiency. Pages 111–133 of: Destrée, Pierre, and Zingano, Marco (eds), *Theoria: Studies on the Status and Meaning of Contemplation in Aristotle's Ethics.* Louvain: Peeters.

Brunschwig, Jacques. 2000. *Metaphysics* Λ 9: A Short-Lived Thought-Experiment? Pages 275–306 of: Frede, Michael, and Charles, David (eds), *Aristotle's Metaphysics Lambda: Symposium Aristotelicum.* Oxford: Oxford University Press.

Burger, Ronna. 2008. *Aristotle's Dialogue with Socrates: On the* Nicomachean Ethics. Chicago: University of Chicago Press.

Burnet, John. 1900. *The Ethics of Aristotle.* London: Methuen.

Burnyeat, Myles F. 2008. *Aristotle's Divine Intellect.* Milwaukee: Marquette University Press.

Bush, Stephen. 2008. Divine and Human Happiness in *Nicomachean Ethics. The Philosophical Review,* **117**, 49–75.

Cagnoli Fiecconi, Elena. 2019. Aristotle's Peculiarly Human Psychology. Pages 60–76 of: Keil, Geert, and Kreft, Nora (eds), *Aristotle's Anthropology.* Cambridge: Cambridge University Press.

Callard, Agnes. 2017. *Enkratês Phronimos. Archiv für Geschichte der Philosophie,* **99**, 31–63.

Caston, Victor. 1999. Aristotle's Two Intellects: A Modest Proposal. *Phronesis,* **44**, 199–227.

Celano, Anthony J. 2016. *Aristotle's Ethics and Medieval Philosophy: Moral Goodness and Practical Wisdom.* Cambridge: Cambridge University Press.

Charles, David. 1999. Aristotle on Well-Being and Intellectual Contemplation. *Proceedings of the Aristotelian Society,* **Supplementary Volume 73**, 205–223.

Charles, David. 2014. *Eudaimonia, Theôria*, and the Choiceworthiness of Practical Wisdom. Pages 89–110 of: Destrée, Pierre, and Zingano, Marco (eds), *Theoria: Studies on the Status and Meaning of Contemplation in Aristotle's Ethics.* Louvain: Peeters.

Charles, David. 2015. Aristotle on the Highest Good: A New Approach. Pages 60–82 of: Aufderheide, Joachim, and Bader, Ralph M. (eds), *The Highest Good in Aristotle and Kant.* Oxford: Oxford University Press.

Charles, David. 2017a. Aristotle on Virtue and Happiness. Pages 105–123 of: Bobonich, Christopher (ed), *The Cambridge Companion to Ancient Ethics.* Cambridge: Cambridge University Press.

Charles, David. 2017b. Aristotle's Nicomachean Function Argument: Some Issues. *Philosophical Inquiry,* **41**, 95–104.

Cleemput, Geert Van. 2006. Aristotle on *Eudaimonia* in *Nicomachean Ethics* 1. *Oxford Studies in Ancient Philosophy,* **30**, 127–157.

Cohoe, Caleb. 2014. *Nous* in Aristotle's *De Anima. Philosophy Compass,* **9**, 594–604.

Cohoe, Caleb. 2016. When and Why Aristotle Needs Phantasmata: A Moderate Interpretation of Aristotle's *De Memoria* and *De Anima* on the Role of Images in Intellectual Activities. *Phronesis*, **61**, 337–372.

Cohoe, Caleb. 2020. Living without a Soul: Why God and the Heavenly Movers Fall Outside of Aristotle's Psychology. *Phronesis*, **65**, 281–323.

Coope, Ursula. 2012. Why Does Aristotle Think That Ethical Virtue Is Required for Practical Wisdom? *Phronesis*, **57**, 142–163.

Cooper, John M. 1975. *Reason and Human Good in Aristotle*. Cambridge, MA: Harvard University Press.

Cooper, John M. 1987. Contemplation and Happiness: A Reconsideration. *Synthese*, **72**, 187–216.

Cooper, John M. 2004. Plato and Aristotle on "Finality" and "(Self-) Sufficiency." Pages 270–308 of: Cooper, John M. (ed), *Knowledge, Nature, and the Good*. Princeton: Princeton University Press.

Cooper, John M. 2013. *Pursuits of Wisdom: Six Ways of Life in Ancient Philosophy from Socrates to Plotinus*. Princeton: Princeton University Press.

Corcilius, Klaus. 2009. How Are Episodes of Thought Initiated According to Aristotle? Pages 1–15 of: van Riel, Gerd, and Destrée, Pierre (eds), *Ancient Perspectives on Aristotle's De Anima*. Leuven: Leuven University Press.

Crisp, Roger. 1994. Aristotle's Inclusivism. *Oxford Studies in Ancient Philosophy*, **12**, 111–136.

Curzer, Howard J. 1990. Criteria for Happiness in *Nicomachean Ethics* I 7 and X 6–8. *Classical Quarterly*, **40**, 421–432.

Curzer, Howard J. 1991. The Supremely Happy Life in Aristotle's *Nicomachean Ethics*. *Apeiron*, **24**, 47–69.

Curzer, Howard J. 2012. *Aristotle and the Virtues*. New York: Oxford University Press.

Dahl, Norman O. 2011. Contemplation and *Eudaimonia* in the *Nicomachean Ethics*. Pages 66–91 of: Miller, Jon (ed), *Aristotle's* Nicomachean Ethics: *A Critical Guide*. New York: Cambridge University Press.

Devereux, Daniel. 1981. Aristotle on the Essence of Happiness. Pages 247–260 of: O'Meara, Dominic J. (ed), *Studies in Aristotle*. Washington, DC: Catholic University of America Press.

Devereux, Daniel. 2014. *Theôria* and *Praxis* in Aristotle's Ethics. Pages 159–205 of: Destrée, Pierre, and Zingano, Marco (eds), *Theoria: Studies on the Status and Meaning of Contemplation in Aristotle's Ethics*. Louvain: Peeters.

Dirlmeier, Franz. 1984. *Aristoteles: Eudemische Ethik*. 4 edn. Berlin: Akademie Verlag.

Dirlmeier, Franz. 2014. *Aristoteles: Nikomachische Ethik*. 10 edn. Berlin: Akademie Verlag.

Engberg-Pederson, Troels. 1983. *Aristotle's Theory of Moral Insight*. Oxford: Clarendon Press.

Euripides. 1984. *Euripidis Fabulae*. Vol. 1. Oxford: Clarendon Press.

Fine, Gail. 1984. Separation. *Oxford Studies in Ancient Philosophy*, **2**, 31–87.

Frede, Dorothea. 2019. On the So-Called Common Books of the *Eudemian* and the *Nicomachean Ethics. Phronesis*, **64**, 84–116.

Frede, Dorothea. 2020. *Aristoteles: Nikomachische Ethik*. Berlin: De Gruyter.

Gadamer, Hans-Georg. 1998. *Aristoteles: Nikomachische Ethik VI*. Frankfurt: Vittorio Klostermann.

Gasser-Wingate, Marc. 2020. Aristotle on Self-Sufficiency, External Goods, and Contemplation. *Archiv für Geschichte der Philosophie*, **102**, 1–28.

Gauthier, René Antoine, and Jolif, Jean Yves. 1970. *L'Éthique à Nicomaque: Introduction, traduction et commentaire*. 2 edn. Vol. 2. Louvain: Publications Universitaires.

Gerson, Lloyd P. 1990. *God and Greek Philosophy: Studies in the Early History of Natural Theology*. London: Routledge.

Gerson, Lloyd P. 2004. Platonism in Aristotle's Ethics. *Oxford Studies in Ancient Philosophy*, **27**, 217–248.

Green, Jerry. 2016. *Humanity and Divinity in Aristotle's Ethics*. PhD thesis, University of Texas at Austin.

Greenwood, LHG. 1909. *Aristotle:* Nicomachean Ethics *Book Six*. Cambridge: Cambridge University Press.

Grosseteste, Robert. 1972. *Ethica Nicomachea*. Vol. 3. Leiden: Brill.

Gurtler, Gary. 2003. The Activity of Happiness in Aristotle's Ethics. *Review of Metaphysics*, **56**, 801–834.

Guthrie, WKC. 1981. *A History of Greek Philosophy*. Vol. 6. Cambridge: Cambridge University Press.

Halper, Edward. 1999. The Unity of the Virtues in Aristotle. *Oxford Studies in Ancient Philosophy*, **17**, 115–143.

Hardie, WFR. 1965. The Final Good in Aristotle's Ethics. *Philosophy*, **40**, 277–295.

Heinaman, Robert. 1988. *Eudaimonia* and Self-sufficiency in the *Nicomachean Ethics. Phronesis*, **33**, 31–53.

Heinaman, Robert. 1993. Rationality, *Eudaimonia* and *Kakodaimonia* in Aristotle. *Phronesis*, **38**, 31–56.

'Heliodorus'. 1889. *In ethica Nicomachea paraphrasis*. Commentaria in Aristotelem Graeca, vol. 19.2. Berlin: Reimer.

Henry, Devin, and Nielsen, Karen Margrethe. 2015. Introduction. Pages 1–25 of: Henry, Devin, and Nielsen, Karen Margrethe (eds), *Bridging the Gap between Aristotle's Science and Ethics*. Cambridge: Cambridge University Press.

Herzberg, Stephan. 2013. *Menschliche und göttliche Kontemplation: Eine Untersuchung zum bios theoretikos bei Aristoteles*. Heidelberg: Universitätsverlag Winter.

Herzberg, Stephan. 2016. God as Pure Thinking. An Interpretation of *Metaphysics* Λ 7, 1072b14–26. Pages 157–180 of: Horn, Christoph (ed), *Aristotle's* Metaphysics Lambda – *New Essays*. Berlin: De Gruyter.

Hicks, RD. 1907. *Aristotle:* De Anima. Cambridge: Cambridge University Press.

Hirji, Sukaina. 2018. Acting Virtuously as an End in Aristotle's *Nicomachean Ethics. British Journal for the History of Philosophy*, **26**, 1006–1026.

Hitz, Zena. 2019. *Lost in Thought: The Hidden Pleasures of an Intellectual Life*. Princeton: Princeton University Press.

Hutchinson, DS, and Johnson, Monte Ransome. 2014. Protreptic Aspects of Aristotle's *Nicomachean Ethics*. Pages 383–409 of: Polansky, Ronald (ed), *The Cambridge Companion to Aristotle's* Nicomachean Ethics. New York: Cambridge University Press.

Iamblichus. 1888. *Protrepticus*. Leipzig: Teubner.

Inwood, Brad. 2014. *Ethics after Aristotle*. Cambridge, MA: Harvard University Press.

Irwin, Terence. 1978. First Principles in Aristotle's Ethics. *Midwest Studies in Philosophy*, **3**, 252–272.

Irwin, Terence. 1980. The Metaphysical and Psychological Basis of Aristotle's Ethics. Pages 35–53 of: Rorty, Amélie Oksenberg (ed), *Essays on Aristotle's Ethics*. Berkeley: University of California Press.

Irwin, Terence. 1985. Permanent Happiness: Aristotle and Solon. *Oxford Studies in Ancient Philosophy*, **3**, 89–124.

Irwin, Terence. 1988. *Aristotle's First Principles*. Oxford: Clarendon Press.

Irwin, Terence. 1991. The Structure of Aristotelian Happiness. *Ethics*, **101**, 382–391.

Irwin, Terence. 2012. Conceptions of Happiness in the *Nicomachean Ethics*. Pages 495–528 of: Shields, Christopher (ed), *The Oxford Handbook of Aristotle*. Oxford: Oxford University Press.

Irwin, Terence. 2019. *Aristotle:* Nicomachean Ethics. 3 edn. Indianapolis: Hackett.

Jagannathan, Dhananjay. 2019. Every Man a Legislator: Aristotle on Political Wisdom. *Apeiron*, **52**, 395–414.

Jimenez, Marta. 2016. Aristotle on Becoming Virtuous by Doing Virtuous Actions. *Phronesis*, **61**, 3–32.

Jirsa, Jakub. 2017. Divine Activity and Human Life. *Rhizomata*, **5**, 210–238.

Joachim, Harold Henry. 1951. *Aristotle, The Nicomachean Ethics: A Commentary*. Oxford: Clarendon Press.

Johnson, Monte Ransome. 2005. *Aristotle on Teleology*. Oxford: Clarendon Press.

Judson, Lindsay. 2015. Aristotle's Astrophysics. *Oxford Studies in Ancient Philosophy*, **49**, 151–192.

Kahn, Charles H. 1981. The Role of *Nous* in the Cognition of First Principles in *Posterior Analytics* II.19. Pages 385–414 of: Berti, Enrico (ed), *Aristotle on Science: The Posterior Analytics*. Padua: Antenore.

Kaibel, Georg (ed). 1899. *Comicorum Graecorum fragmenta*. Vol. 1.1. Berlin: Weidmann.

Karbowski, Joseph. 2019. *Aristotle's Method in Ethics: Philosophy in Practice*. Cambridge: Cambridge University Press.

Kenny, Anthony. 1978. *The Aristotelian Ethics*. Oxford: Oxford University Press.

Kenny, Anthony. 1992. *Aristotle on the Perfect Life*. Oxford: Oxford University Press.

Keyt, David. 1983. Intellectualism in Aristotle. Pages 364–387 of: Anton, John P., and Preus, Anthony (eds), *Essays in Ancient Greek Philosophy*, vol. 2. Albany: State University of New York Press.

Keyt, David. 1989. The Meaning of BIOΣ in Aristotle's *Ethics* and *Politics*. *Ancient Philosophy*, **9**, 15–21.

Kietzmann, Christian. 2019. Aristotle on the Definition of What It Is to Be Human. Pages 25–43 of: Keil, Geert, and Kreft, Nora (eds), *Aristotle's Anthropology*. Cambridge: Cambridge University Press.

Kock, Theodor (ed). 1884. *Comicorum Atticorum fragmenta*. Vol. 2. Leipzig: Teubner.

Kosman, Aryeh. 2000. Metaphysics Λ 9: Divine Thought. Pages 307–326 of: Frede, Michael, and Charles, David (eds), *Aristotle's* Metaphysics Lambda*: Symposium Aristotelicum*. Oxford: Oxford University Press.

Kosman, Aryeh. 2014. Aristotle on the Virtues of Thought. Pages 280–297 of: Kosman, Aryeh (ed), *Virtues of Thought: Essays on Plato and Aristotle*. Cambridge, MA: Harvard University Press.

Kraut, Richard. 1979. The Peculiar Function of Human Beings. *Canadian Journal of Philosophy*, **9**, 467–478.

Kraut, Richard. 1989. *Aristotle on the Human Good*. Princeton: Princeton University Press.

Kraut, Richard. 1993. In Defense of the Grand End. *Ethics*, **103**, 361–374.

Laks, André. 2000. Metaphysics Λ 7. Pages 207–243 of: Frede, Michael, and Charles, David (eds), *Aristotle's* Metaphysics Lambda*: Symposium Aristotelicum*. Oxford: Oxford University Press.

Lawrence, Gavin. 1993. Aristotle on the Ideal Life. *The Philosophical Review*, **102**, 1–34.

Lawrence, Gavin. 2001. The Function of the Function Argument. *Ancient Philosophy*, **21**, 445–475.

Lawrence, Gavin. 2005. Snakes in Paradise: Problems in the Ideal Life. *The Southern Journal of Philosophy*, **48**, 126–165.

Lear, Gabriel Richardson. 2004. *Happy Lives and the Highest Good: An Essay on Aristotle's Nicomachean Ethics*. Princeton: Princeton University Press.

Lear, Gabriel Richardson. 2014. Approximation and Acting for an Ultimate End. Pages 61–87 of: Destrée, Pierre, and Zingano, Marco (eds), *Theoria: Studies on the Status and Meaning of Contemplation in Aristotle's Ethics*. Louvain: Peeters.

Lear, Gabriel Richardson. 2015. Aristotle on Happiness and Long Life. Pages 127–145 of: Rabbås, Øyvind, Emilsson, Eyjólfur K., Fossheim, Hallvard, and Tuominen, Miira (eds), *The Quest for the Good Life: Ancient Philosophers on Happiness*. Oxford: Oxford University Press.

Lear, Jonathan. 1988. *Aristotle: The Desire to Understand*. Cambridge: Cambridge University Press.

Lee, Mi-Kyoung. 2014. Justice and the Laws in Aristotle's Ethics. Pages 104–123 of: Lee, Mi-Kyoung (ed), *Strategies of Argument: Essays in Ancient Ethics, Epistemology, and Logic*. New York: Oxford University Press.

Long, Alex G. 2019. *Death and Immortality in Ancient Philosophy*. Cambridge: Cambridge University Press.

Long, Anthony. 2011. Aristotle on *Eudaimonia, Nous,* and Divinity. Pages 92–113 of: Miller, Jon (ed), *Aristotle's* Nicomachean Ethics: *A Critical Guide*. New York: Cambridge University Press.

McCready-Flora, Ian C. 2019. Speech and the Rational Soul. Pages 44–59 of: Keil, Geert, and Kreft, Nora (eds), *Aristotle's Anthropology*. Cambridge: Cambridge University Press.

Menn, Stephen. 2012. Aristotle's Theology. Pages 422–464 of: Shields, Christopher (ed), *The Oxford Handbook of Aristotle*. Oxford: Oxford University Press.

Meyer, Susan Sauvé. 2011. Living for the Sake of an Ultimate End. Pages 47–65 of: Miller, Jon (ed), *Aristotle's* Nicomachean Ethics: *A Critical Guide*. New York: Cambridge University Press.

Michael of Ephesus. 1892. *Eustratii et Michaelis et Anonyma in ethica Nicomachea commentaria*. Commentaria in Aristotelem Graeca, vol. 20. Berlin: Reimer.

Michael of Ephesus. 1901. *In librum quintum ethicorum Nicomacheorum commentarium*. Commentaria in Aristotelem Graeca, vol. 22.3. Berlin: Reimer.

Müller, Jozef. 2018. Practical and Productive Thinking in Aristotle. *Phronesis*, **63**, 148–175.

Müller, Jozef. 2020. Aristotle and the Origins of Evil. *Phronesis*, **65**, 179–223.

Modrak, Deborah KW. 1991. The *Nous*-Body Problem in Aristotle. *The Review of Metaphysics*, **44**, 755–774.

Moline, Jon. 1983. Contemplation and the Human Good. *Noûs*, **17**, 37–53.

Moore, George Edward. 1903. *Principia Ethica*. Cambridge: Cambridge University Press.

Moss, Jessica. 2017. Aristotle's Ethical Psychology. Pages 124–142 of: Bobonich, Christopher (ed), *The Cambridge Companion to Ancient Ethics*. Cambridge: Cambridge University Press.

Nagel, Thomas. 1972. Aristotle on *Eudaimonia*. *Phronesis*, **17**, 252–259.

Natali, Carlo. 1989. *La saggezza di Aristotele*. Naples: Bibliopolis.

Natali, Carlo. 1999. *Aristotele* Etica Nicomachea: *Traduzione, introduzione e note*. Rome: Laterza.

Natali, Carlo. 2007a. Bonheur et unification des vertus chez Aristote. *Journal of Ancient Philosophy*, **I**, 1–24.

Natali, Carlo. 2007b. Rhetorical and Scientific Aspects of the *Nicomachean Ethics*. *Phronesis*, **52**, 364–381.

Natali, Carlo. 2010. *Posterior Analytics* and the Definition of Happiness in *NE* I. *Phronesis*, **55**, 304–324.

Nauck, Johan August (ed). 1889. *Tragicorum Graecorum fragmenta*. 2 edn. Leipzig: Teubner.

Nielsen, Karen Margrethe. 2015. Aristotle on Principles in Ethics: Political Science as the Science of the Human Good. Pages 29–48 of: Henry, Devin, and Nielsen, Karen Margrethe (eds), *Bridging the Gap between Aristotle's Science and Ethics*. Cambridge: Cambridge University Press.

Nightingale, Andrea Wilson. 2004. *Spectacles of Truth in Classical Greek Phi-losophy: Theoria in Its Cultural Context.* Cambridge: Cambridge University Press.

Norman, Richard. 1969. Aristotle's Philosopher-God. *Phronesis*, **14**, 63–74.

Nussbaum, Martha C. 2001. *The Fragility of Goodness: Luck and Ethics in Greek Tragedy and Philosophy.* Revised edn. New York: Cambridge University Press.

Ogden, Stephen R. 2021. Averroes's Unity Argument Against Multiple Intellects. *Archiv für Geschichte der Philosophie*, **103**, 429–454.

Pachymeres, Georgios. 2022. *Commentary on Aristotle,* Nicomachean Ethics*: Critical Edition with Introduction and Translation.* Commentaria in Aristotelem Graeca et Byzantina, vol. 7. Berlin: De Gruyter.

Pakaluk, Michael. 2005. *Aristotle's* Nicomachean Ethics*: An Introduction.* Cambridge: Cambridge University Press.

Panegyres, Konstantine. 2020. The Text of Aristotle's *Ethica Nicomachea* in Laurentianus 81.18. *Prometheus*, **46**, 3–22.

Pellegrin, Pierre (ed). 2014. *Aristote: Œuvres complètes.* Paris: Flammarion.

Peramatzis, Michail. 2011. *Priority in Aristotle's Metaphysics.* Oxford: Oxford University Press.

Pindar. 1971. *Pindari Carmina cum fragmentis.* 5 edn. Leipzig: Teubner.

Plutarch. 1929. *Moralia.* Vol. 3. Leipzig: Teubner.

Polansky, Ronald. 2017. Aristotle's *Nicomachean Ethics* Is a Work of Practical Science. Pages 277–314 of: Wians, William, and Polansky, Ronald (eds), *Reading Aristotle: Argument and Exposition.* Leiden: Brill.

Prantl, Carl. 1852. *Über die dianoetischen Tugenden in der Nikomachischen Ethik des Aristoteles.* Munich: Christian Kaiser.

Price, Anthony W. 1980. Aristotle's Ethical Holism. *Mind*, **89**, 338–352.

Price, Anthony W. 2011. *Virtue and Reason in Plato and Aristotle.* Oxford: Oxford University Press.

Price, Anthony W. 2014. Eudaimonia and Theôria within the *Nicomachean Ethics.* Pages 61–87 of: Destrée, Pierre, and Zingano, Marco (eds), *Theoria: Studies on the Status and Meaning of Contemplation in Aristotle's Ethics.* Louvain: Peeters.

Prichard, HA. 1935. The Meaning of ἀγαθόν in the *Ethics* of Aristotle. *Philosophy*, **10**, 27–39.

Rackham, Harris. 1947. *Aristotle: The Nicomachean Ethics.* 2 edn. London: Heinemann.

Radt, Stefan Lorenz (ed). 1977. *Tragicorum Graecorum fragmenta.* Vol. 4. Göttingen: Vandenhoeck & Ruprecht.

Ramsauer, Gottfried (ed). 1878. *Ethica Nicomachea.* Leipzig: Teubner.

Rapp, Christof. 2019. The Planetary Nature of Mankind: A Cosmological Perspective on Aristotle's Anthropology. Pages 77–96 of: Keil, Geert, and Kreft, Nora (eds), *Aristotle's Anthropology.* Cambridge: Cambridge University Press.

Rassow, Hermann (ed). 1874. *Forschungen über die Nikomachische Ethik des Aristoteles.* Weimar: Hermann Böhlau.

Reece, Bryan C. 2019. Aristotle's Four Causes of Action. *Australasian Journal of Philosophy*, **97**, 213–227.

Reece, Bryan C. 2020a. Are There Really Two Kinds of Happiness in Aristotle's *Nicomachean Ethics? Classical Philology*, 115, 270–280. doi: 10.1086/707809

Reece, Bryan C. 2020b. Aristotle on Divine and Human Contemplation. *Ergo: An Open Access Journal of Philosophy*, 7, 131–160.

Reece, Bryan C. forthcoming. A Theophrastean Interpretation of Aristotle's *De anima* 3.5. *Proceedings of the Boston Area Colloquium in Ancient Philosophy*.

Reece, Bryan C. ms. *Aristotelian Ontological Priority and Metaphysical Grounding*. Under contract with Cambridge University Press.

Reeve, CDC. 1992. *Practices of Reason: Aristotle's* Nicomachean Ethics. Oxford: Clarendon Press.

Reeve, CDC. 2013. *Aristotle on Practical Wisdom:* Nicomachean Ethics *VI*. Cambridge, MA: Harvard University Press.

Reeve, CDC. 2014. *Aristotle:* Nicomachean Ethics. Indianapolis: Hackett.

Robinson, Richard. 1995. *Aristotle:* Politics *Books III and IV*. Oxford: Clarendon Press.

Roche, Timothy D. 1988a. *Ergon* and *Eudaimonia* in *Nicomachean Ethics* I: Reconsidering the Intellectualist Interpretation. *Journal of the History of Philosophy*, 26, 175–194.

Roche, Timothy D. 1988b. On the Alleged Metaphysical Foundation of Aristotle's *Ethics*. *Ancient Philosophy*, 8, 49–62.

Roche, Timothy D. 2014a. Happiness and the External Goods. Pages 34–63 of: Polansky, Ronald (ed), *The Cambridge Companion to Aristotle's* Nicomachean Ethics. New York: Cambridge University Press.

Roche, Timothy D. 2014b. The Private Moral Life of Aristotle's Philosopher: A Defense of a Non-Intellectualist Interpretation of *Nicomachean Ethics* 10.7–8. Pages 207–239 of: Destrée, Pierre, and Zingano, Marco (eds), *Theoria: Studies on the Status and Meaning of Contemplation in Aristotle's Ethics*. Louvain: Peeters.

Roche, Timothy D. 2019. The Practical Life, the Contemplative Life, and the Perfect *Eudaimonia* in Aristotle's *Nicomachean Ethics* 10.7–8. *Logos & Episteme*, 10, 31–49.

Roochnik, David. 2009. What Is *Theoria? Nicomachean Ethics* Book 10.7–8. *Classical Philology*, 104, 69–82.

Rose, Valentin. 1871. Über die Griechischen commentare zur Ethik des Aristoteles. *Hermes*, 5, 61–113.

Ross, WD. 1924. *Aristotle's* Metaphysics: *A Revised Text with Introduction and Commentary*. Oxford: Clarendon Press.

Sachs, Joe. 2002. *Aristotle:* Nicomachean Ethics. Newburyport, MA: Focus.

Salmieri, Gregory. 2009. Aristotle's Non-'Dialectical' Methodology in the *Nicomachean Ethics*. *Ancient Philosophy*, 29, 311–335.

Schütrumpf, Eckart. 1989. Magnanimity, Μεγαλοψυχία, and the System of Aristotle's *Nicomachean Ethics*. *Archiv für Geschichte der Philosophie*, 71, 10–22.

Schwitzgebel, Eric, Rust, Joshua, Huang, Linus Ta-Lun, Moore, Alan T, and Coates, D. Justin. 2012. Ethicists' Courtesy at Philosophy Conferences. *Philosophical Psychology*, 25, 331–340.

Scott, Dominic. 1999. Primary and Secondary *Eudaimonia. Proceedings of the Aristotelian Society*, **Supplementary Volume 73**, 225–242.

Scott, Dominic. 2015. *Levels of Argument: A Comparative Study of Plato's* Republic *and Aristotle's* Nicomachean Ethics. Oxford: Oxford University Press.

Sedley, David. 2017. Becoming Godlike. Pages 319–337 of: Bobonich, Christopher (ed), *The Cambridge Companion to Ancient Ethics*. Cambridge: Cambridge University Press.

Segev, Mor. 2017. *Aristotle on Religion*. Cambridge: Cambridge University Press.

Shields, Christopher. 1999. *Order in Multiplicity: Homonymy in the Philosophy of Aristotle*. Oxford: Clarendon Press.

Shields, Christopher. 2015a. The *Summum Bonum* in Aristotle's Ethics: Fractured Goodness. Pages 83–111 of: Aufderheide, Joachim, and Bader, Ralph M. (eds), *The Highest Good in Aristotle and Kant*. Oxford: Oxford University Press.

Shields, Christopher. 2015b. The Science of Soul in Aristotle's *Ethics*. Pages 232–253 of: Henry, Devin, and Nielsen, Karen Margrethe (eds), *Bridging the Gap between Aristotle's Science and Ethics*. Cambridge: Cambridge University Press.

Silverman, Allan. 2010. Contemplating Divine Mind. Pages 75–96 of: Sedley, David, and Nightingale, Andrea Wilson (eds), *Ancient Models of Mind: Studies in Human and Divine Rationality*. Cambridge: Cambridge University Press.

Sim, May. 2018. The Phronimos and the Sage. Pages 190–202 of: Snow, Nancy E. (ed), *The Oxford Handbook of Virtue*. New York: Oxford University Press.

Simplicius. 1894. *In Aristotelis de caelo commentaria*. Commentaria in Aristotelem Graeca, vol. 7. Berlin: Reimer.

Stewart, JA. 1892. *Notes on the* Nicomachean Ethics *of Aristotle*. Oxford: Clarendon Press.

Stobaeus, Joannes. 1884. *Anthologium*. Vol. 2. Berlin: Weidmann.

Susemihl, Franz (ed). 1887. *Aristotelis Ethica Nicomachea*. Leipzig: Teubner.

Thorsrud, Harald. 2015. Aristotle's Dichotomous Anthropology: What Is Most Human in the *Nicomachean Ethics? Apeiron*, **48**, 346–367.

Tricot, Jules. 2007. *Éthique à Nicomaque*. Edition révisée edn. Paris: Vrin.

Tuozzo, Thomas M. 1995. Contemplation, the Noble, and the Mean: The Standard of Moral Virtue in Aristotle's Ethics. *Apeiron*, **28**, 129–154.

Urmson, JO. 1988. *Aristotle's Ethics*. Oxford: Blackwell.

Vuillemin-Diem, Gudrun, and Rashed, Marwan. 1997. Burgundio de Pise et ses manuscrits Grecs d'Aristote: Laur. 87.7 et Laur. 81.18. *Recherches de Théologie et Philosophie Médiévales*, **64**, 136–198.

Walker, Matthew D. 2011. Aristotle on Activity 'According to the Best and Most Final' Virtue. *Apeiron*, **44**, 91–110.

Walker, Matthew D. 2017. How Narrow Is Aristotle's Contemplative Ideal? *Philosophy and Phenomenological Research*, **94**, 558–583.

Walker, Matthew D. 2018. *Aristotle on the Uses of Contemplation*. Cambridge: Cambridge University Press.

Wedin, Michael V. 1988. *Mind and Imagination in Aristotle.* New Haven: Yale University Press.

White, Stephen A. 1992. *Sovereign Virtue: Aristotle on the Relation between Happiness and Prosperity.* Stanford: Stanford University Press.

Whiting, Jennifer. 1986. Human Nature and Intellectualism in Aristotle. *Archiv für Geschichte der Philosophie,* **68**, 70–95.

Whiting, Jennifer. 1988. Aristotle's Function Argument: A Defense. *Ancient Philosophy,* **8**, 33–48.

Whiting, Jennifer. 2002. *Eudaimonia,* External Results, and Choosing Virtuous Actions for Themselves. *Philosophy and Phenomenological Research,* **65**, 270–290.

Wilkes, Kathleen V. 1978. The Good Man and the Good for Man in Aristotle's Ethics. *Mind,* **87**, 553–571.

William of Moerbeke. 1973. *Ethica Nicomachea.* Vol. 4. Leiden: Brill.

Witt, Charlotte. 2015. 'As if by Convention Alone': The Unstable Ontology of Aristotle's *Ethics.* Pages 276–292 of: Henry, Devin, and Nielsen, Karen Margrethe (eds), *Bridging the Gap between Aristotle's Science and Ethics.* Cambridge: Cambridge University Press.

Wolfson, Harry Austryn. 1973. The Problem of the Souls of the Spheres from the Byzantine Commentaries on Aristotle through the Arabs and St. Thomas to Kepler. Pages 22–59 of: Twersky, Isadore, and Williams, George H. (eds), *Studies in the History of Philosophy and Religion,* vol. 1. Cambridge, MA: Harvard University Press.

Wood, James L. 2011. Contemplating the Beautiful: The Practical Importance of Theoretical Excellence in Aristotle's *Ethics. Journal of the History of Philosophy,* **49**, 391–412.

Woods, Michael. 1986. Intuition and Perception in Aristotle's Ethics. *Oxford Studies in Ancient Philosophy,* **4**, 145–166.

Zagzebski, Linda Trinkaus. 1996. *Virtues of the Mind: An Inquiry into the Nature of Virtue and the Ethical Foundations of Knowledge.* Cambridge: Cambridge University Press.

Zanatta, Marcello. 1986. *Aristotele Etica Nicomachea: Introduzione, traduzione e commento.* Milan: Biblioteca Universale Rizzoli.

Zeller, Eduard. 1879. *Die Philosophie der Griechen in ihrer geschichtlichen Entwicklung.* 3 edn. Leipzig: Reisland.

Zingano, Marco. 2014. *Eudaimonia* and Contemplation in Aristotle's Ethics. Pages 135–158 of: Destrée, Pierre, and Zingano, Marco (eds), *Theoria: Studies on the Status and Meaning of Contemplation in Aristotle's Ethics.* Louvain: Peeters.

Glossary

endoxon	an existing opinion worth taking seriously, but often not entirely correct.
epistêmê	the developed capacity to give scientific demonstrations.
ergon	something's characteristic activity, function, or work.
eudaimonia	happiness (the activity).
idia	see p. 116 n. 6.
nous	the developed capacity to grasp principles intuitively.
phantasia	imagination.

Index of Passages

Index of Authors

Index of Terms

activity, contemplative, 3, 4, 11, 12, 21, 30, 31, 64, 71, 78, 80, 109, 112, 113, 115, 116, 120–127, 131, 133, 134

activity, ethically virtuous, 3–6, 9, 11, 12, 14–22, 29–32, 42, 44, 62–65, 69–72, 78, 82, 84, 85, 88, 89, 96, 105–115, 120, 123, 124, 134

activity, fine, 5, 34, 35, 42, 44, 45, 55, 56, 61

activity, intellectually virtuous, 2, 4, 5, 53, 70, 84

activity, voluntary, x, 35, 44, 53–56, 61, 131

amusement, 21, 22

Anaxagoras, 3, 25, 26, 31, 33, 35–41, 52, 56, 61, 111, 133

animals, 24, 29, 70, 80, 82, 85, 87–89, 93, 103, 105–108

apparent good, 99, 101

appetite, 23, 49, 51, 55, 87, 99, 130

celestial objects, 92, 94, 96, 98, 100–104, 107, 108

cleverness, 34, 46, 48–52, 55, 56

completeness, *see* perfection

composite essence, 4, 25, 26, 84–86, 123

Conjunctive Problem of Happiness, xi, xii, 2, 3, 12, 13, 30–33, 49, 61–64, 66, 69, 77–79, 81, 82, 84, 85, 108–116, 123, 126, 134

contemplation, x, 2–7, 11, 14, 15, 17, 19–33, 35, 42, 44–56, 59, 61–65, 69, 70, 78, 80–92, 94–98, 102, 103, 106–108, 110–115, 120–124, 126, 128, 129, 131, 134

counterpredication, 116, 117, 122

courage, 2, 19, 23, 25, 34, 45, 48, 50, 67, 86, 106

decision, 34, 54, 55, 128

definition, 116, 117, 119–122, 124–127

deliberation, 28, 34–36, 51

demonstration, 33, 35, 53, 94–98, 102, 118, 119

desire, 39, 40, 99–103, 128

Dilemmatic Problem of Happiness, 1–3, 6, 8–12, 14, 15, 17, 20, 30, 109, 114, 115

Divergence Thesis, 30–33, 35, 37–41, 47, 48, 50, 53, 57, 58, 60, 61, 64, 81, 108, 110–112, 114, 115

Divinity Thesis, 30, 81, 82, 95, 107, 108, 110, 112

dominant end, 2

Doxography C, 16, 122

dualism, *see* relativism

Duality Thesis, 30, 62–64, 66, 68, 79, 81, 108, 110–112

enkrateia, 48–52, 55, 56

epistêmê, 33, 35, 43, 53, 54, 94–97, 102, 107, 108

ergon, 7, 9, 10, 13, 14, 26, 39, 47, 63, 72, 73, 80–86, 103, 111–113, 116, 120, 121, 124

essence, 4, 25, 26, 40, 83–86, 90, 94, 100, 105, 116–122, 125–128, 131, 133

essentialism, 116, 120, 124, 126, 134

euboulia, 34

Eudoxus, 101

eusunesia, 34

external goods, 9–11, 16–18, 20, 67, 114, 125

finality, *see* perfection

Form of the Good, 40, 59, 60

friendship, 2, 106, 120, 125

function, *see* ergon

generosity, 2, 23, 25, 34, 45, 49, 87, 107, 123

gods, 23, 24, 41, 48, 69, 86–89, 96, 107

health, 11, 47, 48

heavenly bodies, *see* celestial objects

honor, 2, 4, 64, 65, 129

idion, 80, 83, 86, 112, 116–122, 124–126, 131–134

imagination, 98, 102, 103

immoralism, 11, 19, 32, 60, 110, 114, 115

inclusive end, 2

inclusivism, *see* pluralism

intellect, practical, 26, 53–56, 61, 84, 128, 129, 131–133

intellect, theoretical, 8, 21, 22, 24–26, 44, 53, 54, 64, 72, 79, 84, 113, 127–133

157

Printed in the USA
CPSIA information can be obtained
at www.ICGtesting.com
LVHW020724021123
762637LV00008B/239

9 781108 486736